DIRECTLY ELECTED MAYORS IN URBAN GOVERNANCE

Edited by David Sweeting

D1610356

P

First published in Great Britain in 2018 by

Policy Press
University of Bristol
1-9 Old Park Hill
Bristol
BS2 8BB
UK
t: +44 (0)117 954 5940
pp-info@bristol.ac.uk
www.policypress.co.uk

North America office:
Policy Press
c/o The University of Chicago Press
1427 East 60th Street
Chicago, IL 60637, USA
t: +1 773 702 7700
f: +1 773-702-9756
sales@press.uchicago.edu
www.press.uchicago.edu

© Policy Press 2018

British Library Cataloguing in Publication Data
A catalogue record for this book is available from the British Library

Library of Congress Cataloging-in-Publication Data
A catalog record for this book has been requested

ISBN 978-1-4473-2702-8 paperback
ISBN 978-1-4473-2701-1 hardcover
ISBN 978-1-4473-2705-9 ePub
ISBN 978-1-4473-2706-6 Mobi
ISBN 978-1-4473-2704-2 ePdf

Cover design by Hayes Design
Front cover image: www.dreamstime.com
Printed and bound in Great Britain by by CPI Group (UK) Ltd, Croydon, CR0 4YY
Policy Press uses environmentally responsible print partners

To M.A.C.D,

M.A.S.C. and

D.D.J.S.C.

Contents

List of tables and figures

Tables

Figures

Notes on contributors

Alasdair Blair is Jean Monnet Professor of International Relations and Head of the Department of Politics and Public Policy at De Montfort University, Leicester, UK. He is also Director of the Jean Monnet Centre of European Governance. His main areas of research and teaching are European Union politics, British foreign policy and student learning in higher education.

Paul Burton is Professor of Urban Management and Planning and Director of the Cities Research Centre at Griffith University, Australia. He is a founding member of Regional Development Australia, Gold Coast, and a member of the National Education Committee of the Planning Institute of Australia. In 2002–03 he chaired the Bristol Democracy Commission, which recommended the introduction of a directly elected mayor for the city of Bristol.

Christine Cheyne is an Associate Professor and leads the Resource and Environmental Planning programme at Massey University, New Zealand. She has carried out research on various aspects of local government including representation, participation, funding, political leadership, reorganisation, metropolitan governance and electoral systems. In 2006–07 she was a member of the NZ government-appointed Local Government Rates Inquiry.

Colin Copus is Professor of Local Politics and Director of the Local Governance Research Unit in the Department of Politics and Public Policy, De Montfort University, Leicester, UK. His academic interests are central–local relationships, local party politics, local political leadership and the changing role of the councillor. He has worked closely with policymakers and practitioners and has been an adviser to parliamentary select committees. He has published widely in academic journals.

Michael Dadd was a PhD student in the Department of Politics and Public Policy, De Montfort University, Leicester, UK. His PhD focused on local political leadership and he spent over a year working closely with Leicester City Council as the new office of elected mayor developed in the city. Michael sadly passed away in 2015.

Björn Egner is Senior Researcher at the Institute for Political Science at Technische Universität Darmstadt, Germany. Björn chairs the research group 'Methodology and Philosophy of Science' at the institute. His research interests include local politics, quantitative methodology, and policy analysis.

Howard Elcock was Lecturer/Senior Lecturer in Politics, University of Hull and Head of the School of Government at Newcastle Polytechnic (now Northumbria University), UK. He also taught at Fredonia State College, New York, USA. He wrote a textbook on *Local Government* and has published widely in the field.

Adam Gendźwiłł is Assistant Professor of Political Sociology at the University of Warsaw, Poland. He works at the Faculty of Geography and Regional Studies, Department of Local Development and Policy. His research interests include local politics, electoral studies, political representation and party organisations.

Robin Hambleton is Emeritus Professor of City Leadership at the University of the West of England, Bristol, UK, and Director of Urban Answers. He was the Dean of the College of Urban Planning and Public Affairs at the University of Illinois at Chicago (2002–07). His latest book is *Leading the Inclusive City: Place-based Innovation for a Bounded Planet* (Policy Press, 2015).

Nicola Headlam is an interdisciplinary urbanista whose work is on the governance, management and leadership of cities. She has followed concerns about implementation of policy in the subnational UK from working as a local government officer through a PhD within the Centre for Urban Policy Studies (CUPS) at the University of Manchester; then post-doctorally at the Heseltine Institute for Public Policy and Practice at the University of Liverpool. Since 2015 she has been a knowledge exchange fellow working within the Government Office for Science and the Urban Transformations portfolio at the University of Oxford.

Paul Hepburn is a post-doctoral researcher in the Heseltine Institute for Policy and Practice at the University of Liverpool, UK. His research interests centre on how we can shape our emerging digital society to enhance the governance, democracy and resilience of our localities. An experienced researcher Paul works with local civic actors and other academics to explore how Liverpool might exploit the 'smart' city and 'big data' policy agendas to improve the quality of life in the urban environment.

Nasrul Ismail is a Visiting Research Fellow at the University of Bristol, UK. His research interest lies in the fields of Policy and Politics, Law, and Public Health. Nasrul is also a guest lecturer at the School of Social and Community Medicine, Bristol, for the Health Commissioning and Priorities Setting module.

Petr Jüptner is the Director of the Institute of Political Studies of the Faculty of Social Sciences, Charles University in Prague, Czech Republic. He has broad research interests in local politics. Petr was the principal investigator in two projects of the Czech Science Foundation focused on reforming the local level and the amalgamations of municipalities.

Thom Oliver is a Research and Business Development Manager at University of the West of England, Bristol, UK and a Visiting Fellow at Oxford Brookes Business School, UK. Thom received his PhD in 2011 from INLOGOV at the University of Birmingham. He is convenor of the Liberals and Liberalism Specialist Group and a founding member of the Qualitative Research Specialist Group of the Political Studies Association.

James H. Svara is Visiting Professor in the School of Government, University of North Carolina at Chapel Hill, USA. He specialises in local government politics, management, and ethics. He is an honorary member of the International City/County Management Association and a fellow of the National Academy of Public Administration.

David Sweeting is Senior Lecturer in the School for Policy Studies at the University of Bristol, UK. He has a longstanding interest in local government studies, urban politics and city leadership. He has published in various academic journals, and this is his third edited book in the field of comparative local government and politics.

Paweł Swianiewicz is Professor of Economics at University of Warsaw, Chair of the Department of Local Development and Policy, Faculty of Geography and Regional Studies. His teaching and research concentrates on local government finance, local politics, decentralisation and territorial reforms in Poland and other countries of Central and Eastern Europe.

Katarzyna Szmigiel-Rawska is Assistant Professor in the Department of Local Development and Policy, at the Faculty of Geography and Regional Studies at the University of Warsaw, Poland. She specialises in local government studies, internationalisation and inter-organisational collaboration, and is author of numerous articles, chapters and books, as well as participant and coordinator of several research projects.

Acknowledgements

Many people have helped directly and indirectly in the production of this book. Sarahs Ayres and Brown indulged me by agreeing to three panels on directly elected mayors at the 2014 *Policy & Politics* conference, where this volume started to take shape. Many thanks to them and all the participants in those panels. Other colleagues in the School for Policy Studies at the University of Bristol have also been very supportive, particularly those in the Centre for Urban and Public Policy Research, who have patiently sat through various presentations of mine on directly elected mayors, and my attempts to link disparate strands of academic thought to them. Many MSc Public Policy students have also witnessed the same. Outside the University, Robin Hambleton has over many years proven time and again to be a supportive colleague and friend. Robin offered me my first job in academia in 1998, on a project on local political leadership in Bristol. It proved to be a good move. Our work then on leadership in Bristol and in other places formed the platform for much of my work since. This book has also benefitted from exchanges at various times and in different places with Gary Bridge, Stephen Cope, George Jones, Alex Marsh and Murray Stewart. Thanks also to the ever supportive people at Policy Press, particularly Emily Watt who originally commissioned the book, and to Laura Vickers who patiently helped to move it along. Miguel also helped with the figures. Thanks of course go to all the chapter authors, some of whom I still haven't met.

But most of all, I'd like to thank all the mayors and other city leaders around the world, who are simply trying to make their towns and cities better places to live.

ONE

Introduction: directly elected mayors in urban governance

David Sweeting, University of Bristol, UK

This book is about directly elected mayors – political leaders who head multi-functional municipal authorities and are voted into power directly by citizens in those municipalities. In many countries, such as the US, Canada and Japan, directly elected mayors are a typical or traditional feature of local political systems. In many others, they have been taken up as a reform to a system of local, urban or metropolitan government, and have been introduced more recently in many countries including Italy, Germany, Poland, Hungary and England (Hambleton and Sweeting, 2014). Supporters of the model of electing city leaders directly by popular vote tend to argue that it has both democratic process and functional efficiency advantages. Directly elected mayors are portrayed as being more visible, more accountable, more legitimate and more powerful than other sorts of city leader. As a result, it is asserted that directly elected mayors are therefore better equipped with greater capacity to govern than other sorts of political actor.

Marsh (2012) noted that directly elected mayors have enduring and widespread appeal to policymakers, and this book taps in to that interest. For example, In the UK, directly elected mayors are not only seen as a way of improving urban governance (Sims, 2011), they are also a key part of the city-regional agenda (Harrison, 2015), and the government has passed the Cities and Local Government Devolution Act 2016 to pave the way for 'metro-mayors', with responsibilities across city regions across England. In Australasia, a debate continues about the ways that directly elected mayors can play a stronger role in governance there (Sansom, 2012). A fairly typical policy-related rationale comes from the Plain English Guide to the Localism Act, from the UK Government (DCLG, 2011). As part of a programme designed to encourage the creation of directly elected mayors in cities in England outside London, the government argued:

Many major cities in the world outside of the UK have a strong and powerful executive mayor. The Government believes that elected mayors can provide democratically accountable strong leadership which is able to instigate real change for the benefit of our largest cities. Mayors will be clearly identifiable as the leader of the city and will have a unique mandate to govern as they will be directly elected by all local electors. People will know who is responsible for a decision and where the buck stops. Elected mayors would help strengthen the governance of the city. With a four year term of office, and a direct mandate to lead, the mayor would be able to focus on long-term strategic decisions – such as bringing together different agencies to make public services work better, and attracting jobs and investment to the city (DCLG, 2011: 6)

Much rests on the institution of the mayor, who is seen to personify principles of democracy and accountability through profile and direct election. Moreover, as strong leaders, empowered by the electoral process that gives them a legitimacy and stability denied other sorts of actor, they are able to push through decisions and projects that others are unable to, and are even better placed to secure economic prosperity.

There is of course a much more nuanced reality of the powers, functions and activities of directly elected mayors, which is expanded upon in the pages of this book. The image of the all-powerful city mayor can mislead; to borrow a phrase from Granovetter (1973), there is much to be said for the strength of 'weak' mayors. It has long been recognised that directly elected mayors who might lack many formal resources of decision making powers can facilitate rather than direct (see Svara, Chapter Seven of this volume; and Greasley and Stoker, 2008). Moreover, the essence of urban political leadership can entail harnessing the contributions of different actors, shaping longer-term visions, and brokering cross-sectoral agreement in order to progress towards them (Stone, 1989; John and Cole, 1999).

The elected mayor is an institutional and political figure. As an institutional figure the mayor is endowed to a greater or lesser extent with formal powers related to the city bureaucracy. The formal resources usually include powers relating to budgets, policy proposals and appointments (Sweeting, 2003). Informally, the 'soft powers' include influence and persuasion (Sims, 2011) and also those that rely on networks of support, most commonly political parties (independent mayors aside). Playing a leading party role or not, a directly elected mayor's political role expectations include both to exercise political leadership and to ensure quality services (Copus, 2006). City leadership involves a mix of formal and informal powers, institutional resources, persuasion, deal-making, brokering, facilitation, profile, charisma, and vision to achieve goals and satisfy followers (Greasley and Stoker, 2008; Leach and Wilson, 2000; John and Cole, 1999; Svara, 1994; Kotter and Lawrence, 1974). There can be something of an assumption that directly elected mayors are only really suitable for big cities, as suggested in the quotation above. Think mayoral leadership, think Rudy Giuliani (New York), Boris Johnson (London) or Richard Daley (Chicago). Yet directly elected mayors can and do exist in many smaller towns and cities, and may be regarded as the essence of representative democracy. In many countries (to draw examples from this volume), including in Poland, the US, New Zealand, and Germany, directly elected mayors exist across the spectrum of local and urban authorities. The focus of this book is about mayors in urban governance, and it is very much about big *and* small urban areas, and many arguments may apply in rural areas too.

Identifying the core of the directly elected mayor model of political leadership

While there are various types of political leadership in local government, and different typologies that describe them, there is no one directly elected mayor model of local political leadership. Several contributions have included discussion of mayoral governance within them. One is the contribution from Mouritzen and Svara (2002) that puts forward a typology of four forms of government: the strong mayor form, the committee leader form, the collective form, and the council manager form. Another is from Heinelt and Hlepas (2006). It divides different executive arrangements, and the countries in which they are based, into categories of political, executive, collegiate or ceremonial mayors. Svara (Chapter Seven in this volume; 1990) developed and used a distinction between council manager forms of government, and mayor council forms of government, and Sweeting (2003) explored the distinction between 'strong' and 'weak' mayoral systems.

The comparative literature on local government systems is however not helpful in identifying the essential features of directly elected mayoral models of government. There is only a variety of hybrid forms of the directly elected mayoral model across different countries, as the contributions in this volume demonstrate. Indeed, often within countries, there is variation. Moreover, the directly elected mayor model does not fit neatly or exclusively into any one of the above categories. For example, while many directly elected mayors have much in common with the 'strong mayor' forms of government from Mouritzen and Svara (2002) and Sweeting (2003), they need not have the formal powers associated with those types. Indirectly elected mayors can also be strong mayors, as the case of Spain shows (Navarro and Sweeting, 2015), and there are also directly elected mayors in both mayor council and council manager forms of government. Directly elected mayors also fit into both political and executive forms offered by Heinelt and Hlepas (2006), and there are forms outside these typologies that include directly elected mayors, such as in the commission form of government. Consequently, it is not possible to list a set of institutional powers or characteristics that are common to directly elected mayors from a reading of the comparative literature on local government.

What it is possible to do is deduce, from the common feature of the model – that of direct election – and the consequences of that feature, some core aspects that are present whatever the formal institutional characteristics of different directly elected mayoral systems. First, and most obviously, mayors are elected directly by the people that reside in the area in which they stand for election. There may be different ways of deciding the winning candidate, for example including systems of first and second preference voting, but the winning candidate is chosen directly by voters, and not, for example, through some subsequent election involving councillors or party members. Second, the result of the election produces a clearly identifiable, individual political leader. The leader may be attached to a party, or be an independent candidate, but that person takes up a formal position of political leadership in municipal government. Informally as a result of that direct election, and in addition in many cases formally as a result of institutional design, there is a concentration of power and influence in that leader. Third, direct election creates a secure term of office until the next election, or at least until the activation of a recall procedure that would enable their removal from office. It is difficult to remove a directly elected mayor from office between elections, for example, as a result of losing support from councillors, without the consent of the electorate. These features promote what Mouritzen and Svara (2002) have referred to as the organising principle of political leadership, in preference to lay or professional influence over and involvement in decision making. They also underlie the vexed and nuanced debate around the advantages and disadvantages of directly elected mayors.

Whether the directly elected mayor form of government is the most suitable in which to exercise city leadership is debatable and contested, and the advantages and disadvantages of this form are discussed in several chapters of this book. Much of this debate returns to value judgements around the nature of essentially contested concepts such as leadership, accountability, and democracy. It is also infused with perceptions of the motives of political parties, and is of course context specific, taking place within different historical trajectories. Despite inevitable simplifications and overlaps, these arguments are summarised in Table 1.1.

Table 1.1: Advantages and disadvantages of directly elected mayors

Feature of system	Advantages	Disadvantages
Direct election of political leader by citizens	• Direct link between leaders and electors • Increased public interest in elections • Increased visibility for leader • Underpins leadership of place • Draws in candidates from outside established parties	• Focus on personality • Media driven, populist politics • Potential election of unsuitable candidates • Draws attention away from more fundamental matters
Creates individual, identifiable leader	• Concentrates power and authority • Facilitates construction of 'vision' • Focus for accountability	• Overloads individual actor • Little space for different or opposing voices • Accountability to other actors blunted
Secure term of office	• Long term outlook • Clear process for replacement	• Indifference to electorate between elections • Can be difficult or impossible to remove mayor

The direct election of the political leader creates a direct link between electors and the political executive, unmediated by, say, a group of councillors who might otherwise select a municipal head. Hence it can be argued that it is a more democratic form of selecting those who exercise authority on behalf of the citizenry. Moreover, this link creates public interest in elections as voters have a direct say in the identity of the office holder, giving mayors visibility denied to other sorts of politician. Such a link can also lead to the office holder feeling loyalty to the place that elected them, over and above the party that they represent, or the organisation that happens to be located in municipal offices. There is a city-wide mandate given to the mayor. Whereas individual councillors in ward based systems might only have a fraction of the electorate on which to base their mandate, the mayor is elected across the city, orienting the office holder towards the place that elected them. Such 'place based leadership' (see Hambleton, Chapter Fourteen in this volume) is therefore likely to attract a variety of candidates from outside the political class or bubble, connecting local politics to local people in a real and tangible sense.

Critics counter these sorts of arguments in various ways (see Copus, 2006; Jones, 2016; Orr, 2004). Mayoral contests can become personality driven. Instead of focusing on different policy options and alternative manifestos, mayoral contests instead become detached from community concerns and party labels, and instead focus on the personal characteristics of individual candidates. Given the role of the media in such contests, candidates who are media friendly are likely to prevail. Hence those opposed to directly elected mayors can argue that, rather than somehow energising local politics with new ideas, what can emerge is a superficial and artificial form of politics that is conducted through traditional and social media, unconnected with the day-to-day concerns of voters, or with the need to keep the support of a local party. In such a situation, directly elected mayors, far from having an intimate connection with the places that put them into power, are not embedded in parties that represent public interests in society, or the organisations that produce the services upon which voters rely. Hence the process of direct election can produce candidates that are unsuitable for the very office that they are being elected to. This is in addition to and separate from the potential for the election of 'joke' or celebrity candidates who might be able to take advantage of their status in order to win mayoral elections, as they may not need to go through a party based selection process.

Supporters of the mayoral model argue that the creation of an individual, identifiable leader supports a more effective and accountable decision making structure. As a result of direct election, often augmented by formal institutional processes and resources, power resides in the office of the mayor. The vision and clarity provided by individual leaders can be pursued and implemented as a result of this concentration of power. This is particularly apposite in networks of governance, where 'informal influence, based on popular mandate, rather than position within a hierarchy, allows mayors to engage in light touch coordination beyond the council offices, right across the wider network of service providers' (Sims, 2012: 60). As power is concentrated, and the mayor is directly elected, it is easy for the mayor to be held to account at election time.

Yet critics argue the concentration of power is itself one of the weaknesses of mayoral systems. It overloads an individual decision maker, who may be tempted to share power with unelected officers or advisers, rather than other elected actors (Jones, 2016). It might create 'bottlenecks' in decision making, slowing down the progress of policy initiatives (Hambleton and Sweeting, 2015). The assumption that individualised leadership is somehow more efficient or effective can also be questioned. As Jones (2016) points out, the lack of pressure to test ideas informally with some sort of formal committee, such as a cabinet, or informally in a party forum, may lead to poorly thought out policies becoming adopted. The representation of alternative views – important in multi-ethic, diverse urban environments – is likely to be hampered as an individual is not capable of reflecting distinct and disparate perspectives. Moreover, while accountability to the electorate might be increased in terms of holding the office holder to account, accountability is in other ways decreased. Accountability is about more than standing for re-election every few years; it entails democratic, constitutional and learning elements (Bovens et al, 2008) implying a long term process of interaction, and cannot therefore be reduced to a 'one-shot' process of re-election, Moreover, if a mayor decides that their current term will be their last, the electorate has no obvious way of holding them to account.

Supporters of the model point to the stability it offers. Mayors are in post for the term of their mandate. Such stability therefore supports and underpins long term, strategic decision making. Where there is a process of recall in order to replace a mayor, it offers a clear route to publicly substitute a mayor, rather than a replacement emerging through behind the scenes negotiations or party coups. Yet criticisms can again be levelled at this aspect of mayoral governance. Recall mechanisms may be difficult to activate, or in some cases non-existent, so there may be limited ways to get rid of a mayor who is acting improperly – the recently deceased former Mayor of Toronto, Rob Ford, being a case in point. As mayors are secure in post for a number of years, they may act in a manner that is indifferent to, or opposed to, public opinion.

A number of these sorts of criticism apply to systems where the mayor is not directly elected, and there are ways round these criticisms. For example, mayors can choose to involve cabinet members or councillors in different ways, and there can be many sorts of arrangements introduced to enhance accountability between elections and invite scrutiny of mayoral performance.

More broadly, there is the issue that the debate over the form of leadership might be a distraction from more significant matters, such as the extent of centralisation, the powers of city governments or the nature of international capitalism, each of which might be more significant than leadership form. This brings consideration of the broader context into view. What is the context within which the debates around mayors take place, and the trends in which they operate? One is suggested by the title of this work – urban governance – and the other is ubiquitous in social science – globalisation. What follows is a brief sketch of how these processes shape the nature of urban political leadership generally, and the academic debates around them, and how they set the context for the possibilities for mayoral leadership in particular.

Urban governance is set to continue to rise in importance as at the global level. Sometime in the last decade or so, the world urban population overtook the world rural population for the first time in human history (UN, 2015). Mega cities are getting larger, and there are more of them, though most urban dwellers live in cities of much smaller size. The concentration of the world's growing urban population is set to expand from about 54% in 2016, to 66% by 2050.

Important though such population trends are, urbanisation has always been about much more than population growth in cities. Political, economic and technological developments are coming together at the urban level in a way that is enhancing the importance of the city within the nation state. Ben Barber's influential book *If Mayors Ruled the World* (2013) argues that a greater role is being played by cities and city leaders, and that they hold the capacity to adapt successfully to change. Faced both with common problems of poverty, climate change, and migration, and also the day-to-day imperatives of running a city, Barber argues that cities are better placed than nation states to attend to society's needs and wants. Supported by active cross-national networks, cities are seen as places that adapt, survive and flourish, and city leaders, unencumbered by questions of national sovereignty and political dogma, simply get on in a pragmatic way to problem solve and to make life better for their citizens.

One example of this is in relation to sustainability and climate change. While it might be that urban areas consume and pollute out of proportion to their population size, the argument goes that they hold the potential to develop a more sustainable future (Bulkeley, 2013). Cities, and the urban authorities within them, will often be in charge of functions that are crucial for sustainability (such as transport, energy and planning). While national governments dither and international agreements fail to deliver, cities are able to draw on knowledge of experimentation and concentrations of expertise within them in order to find local solutions to problems of sustainability. Cities are at the 'sharp end' of sustainable development, and lead the way in matters such as neighbourhood heat networks, mass transit systems and sustainable living.

The phrase 'smart cities' is shorthand that brings together developments in personal communications, infrastructure and 'big data', ostensibly in order to make places more liveable and lives more pleasant (Townsend, 2014). There are heated debates over the questions of the implications of such technology, both at a personal and societal level (Hambleton, 2015). However, the point is that urban governments can play a key role in developing the environment that facilitates and embeds such technology, and also guide the process towards socially useful outcomes, and perhaps away from the more technologically driven agenda.

There is also the longstanding question of the capabilities of cities to lead in terms of economic development and generate wealth. While cities might have initially developed around the existence of a market in order to facilitate trade, by the 1980s, much of the debate was about urban decline in the post-industrial era (Harding and Blokland-Potters, 2014). More recently, however, much literature from global development organisations makes the link between urbanisation, economic growth and wealth creation (Turok and McGranahan, 2013). In this context, cities compete internationally for inward investment, with urban governments often playing a key role in defining a niche for their cities to exploit (Tallon, 2010).

It would be misleading to overplay the importance of urban governance in these contemporary developments. Clearly, national and international actors are still important, and there may be, of course, a hint of academic fashion about the emphasis on the urban. Yet the point is, at a time when more people are living in urban areas, many issues are crystallising at the urban level. Thus urban governance is of increasing importance for societies as a whole. Governance has been described as 'the interplay between state and society and the extent to which collective projects can be achieved through a joint public and private mobilization of resources' (Pierre, 2011: 5). There has been debate over whether there has been a 'shift' from government to governance, or whether governance was there all along anyway (Pierre, 2011); the extent to which government exists alongside or is active within governance (Davies, 2011); and the extent to which governance exists 'in the shadow of hierarchy' (Whitehead, 2003).

Nevertheless, there is agreement that urban governance involves public sector agencies, including elected authorities; private sector entities, large and small; and 'civil society', whether in the guise of third sector or community sector organisations, or individual citizens. There are different theoretical perspectives on the processes, power relations and drivers of collaboration in governance, including the more institutional Anglo-governance school of Lowndes (2009) to the Atlanta-inspired regime theory approaches (Stone, 1989). These cross-sectoral perspectives on the nature of urban governance are joined by those that see urban governance as part of a larger multi-levelled (Bache and Flinders, 2004) system extending above and below the level of the city; upwards to national and international levels, and downwards to district and neighbourhood (Smith et al, 2007). There will of course be cross-national and inter-city variation, but it is helpful to view city government, in the case of a municipal authority, as nested within a broader urban governance web, which is itself part of a broader set of relationships, actors and processes extending from the neighbourhood to the global level.

Urban governance is set against the backdrop of an increasingly globalised world. The accelerating pace of communication, international trade via transnational corporations, new technology and the importance of knowledge drive cities towards particular imperatives, including: to compete with other cities for economic investment; to emphasise their own particular distinctive niche; and to retreat from traditional welfare functions (Kearns and Paddison, 2000). Winners and losers in the globalisation game vary across and within cities (Hambleton and Gross, 2007). Networks of cities also extend globally, acting as forums to collaborate, share ideas, and to act as pressure groups on the global stage (Kern and Bulkeley, 2009). Cities and powerful actors within them are exposed to fashions about how they should act and what policies they could adopt, including being more creative, more entrepreneurial or greener.

What then, do these trends mean for the leadership of cities? One clearly is for the need to be outward facing, beyond the municipal authority, and beyond the local area, locally, nationally and internationally. While it has long been recognised that leadership in local government is about much more than heading a bureaucracy that produces services, or representing the needs of an area to other levels of government (Sweeting, 2002), the governance environment and the processes of globalisation place particular demands on leaders related to economic growth, competitiveness, and profile on the international stage (Beal and Pinson, 2013; Martins et al, 2007). The broader contours of international capitalism, coupled with multi-levelled and multi-sectoral nature of governance mean that city leaders on the one hand contend with an external environment of both national and international commerce and trade, and higher tier governance actors and levels; and on the other an urban environment of other public sector agencies, local, national and international capital, and a civil society of organised and less organised citizens and community groups. Thus, not only do municipal leaders look 'up' to national and international levels and 'down' to community and neighbourhoods in their own cities, they also look 'all around' as various interests and issues enter, and move up and circulate on the agenda of the city. The agenda of the city is, as the discussion on urbanisation above indicates, at the same time becoming more crowded, as issues and attention focuses on the urban level, from migration, to economic development to sustainability. It is in this context, in order to cope with a more demanding governance environment that calls for stronger urban political leadership are made (Borraz and John, 2004), perhaps involving (where they do not already exist) the creation of directly elected mayors.

Outline of the book

This book draws on examples of directly elected mayors from within and beyond the UK in practice to examine the ways in which they work, and explores the debates around their introduction and impacts of this sort of leadership in urban governance. Following this introductory chapter there are three parts to the book. Part I focuses on the introduction of mayors in England; Part II has country-specific chapters covering the US, Australia, New Zealand, Germany, Poland and the Czech Republic; and Part III has two comparative contributions.

Part I (Chapters Two to Six) contains five chapters on England, where there has been considerable debate over the introduction of mayors, including latterly the introduction of mayors in city regions. In Chapter Two Robin Hambleton and I consider the introduction of a directly elected mayor in Bristol. This chapter draws on an evaluation of the introduction of the mayoral system in the city. The analysis, drawing on empirical research, shows how different sectors respond in different ways to the reform, and also highlights how responses vary according to different evaluation criteria. Thom Oliver's discussion in Chapter Three also examines governance change in Bristol. Oliver's concern is to analyse the ways in which the Bristol experience illustrates whether the institution of mayoral governance can deliver change, and the barriers to such change. In a detailed narrative exploration, Oliver gives an intimate feel for the interactions of formal institutions of governance and individuals who operate within them. Chapter Four, by Howard Elcock, draws on interviews with a number of English mayors. Using a framework called the 'political leadership matrix', Elcock tracks the activities and attitudes of mayors in relation to their government, governance and allegiance roles, and discusses matters such as mayoral relationships with other actors, their personal styles and their own assessments of their impacts. Nicola Headlam and Paul Hepburn consider the case of Liverpool in Chapter Five. Drawing on surveys, interview data and diary analysis, Headlam and Hepburn paint a vivid picture of the activities of the Mayor of Liverpool, and connect it to broader questions of governance, arguing that to an extent the model can 'suck the oxygen' from consideration of more fundamental questions about the public sector – an example of the way that mayoral governance can be a distraction from more fundamental debates, as suggested above. Nasrul Ismail's contribution in Chapter Six uses the notion of social responsibility through leadership to explore the first terms of the mayors of Bristol and Liverpool. Analysing and comparing on dimensions of 'paving the way', 'inspiring a shared vision' and 'challenging the process', Ismail describes how each mayor has pursued objectives relating to social responsibility.

Part II of the book (Chapters Seven to Twelve) starts with James Svara's exploration of debates in the US around the questions of institutional setting of leadership of, on the one hand, the council manager form of government and, on the other, the mayor council form of government. In these 'executive' or 'facilitative' forms, different roles and functions are associated with the office of elected mayor. Svara then draws together arguments used in referendum campaigns regarding change in the form of government used in cities across the US to explore the advantages and disadvantages of those forms, and the exercise of mayoral leadership within them. In Chapter Eight, Paul Burton reviews of the arrangements for local political management in Australia, where directly elected mayors have been in existence in some parts of the country for over 100 years. Burton then offers insights on the practice of political leadership of two directly elected mayors. In doing so, he illustrates how mayors in Australia can use the office as springboard to higher office, the ways in which mayors can act beyond their formal powers, and the importance of a supporting administrative office around the position of mayor. Christine Cheyne's contribution on New Zealand (Chapter Nine) looks at the broader influences within which mayors operate. Cheyne presents a framework of individual, informal and formal/institutional influences on local political leadership, and focuses on the latter to explore the development of the New Zealand model of mayoral leadership.

A perspective on German mayors comes in Chapter Ten, from Björn Egner. Egner's interest is in testing whether different formal competences of directly elected mayors in Germany lead to different perceptions about how powerful mayors are among actors in local governance. Egner constructs a detailed index of mayoral power and applies it to survey data collected from a large sample of mayors in Germany. He demonstrates the variability of the formal powers of mayors, and demonstrates that, in the German case at least, it is not possible to conclude that mayoral potency is directly associated with the acquisition of formal powers. Continuing the international perspective, Adam Gendźwiłł and Paweł Swianiewicz consider Polish mayors in Chapter Eleven. Direct election for mayors was introduced there in 2002, and the authors explore debates around the introduction of mayors, the impact on parties and the effects on inter-governmental relationships using a mix of survey data and statistics on mayoral elections. Chapter Twelve, by Petr Jüptner, concentrates on the debates around whether or not to introduce mayors in the Czech Republic. Unlike many other Easter European states, the Czech Republic does not have directly elected mayors. However, by charting the debates around their introduction, Jüptner reveals the shifting positions of parties on the issue, and the ways in which the issue moves up and down the reform agenda.

Part III contains two comparative chapters. Chapter Thirteen is a comparative piece by Colin Copus, Alasdair Blair, Katarzyna Szmigiel-Rawska and Michael Dadd, considering England and Poland. As with many other chapters they also consider questions of institutional design, and focus on the interplay between central and local priorities in designing and redesigning the decision making structures of and around directly elected mayors. In Chapter Fourteen, Robin Hambleton considers the notion of 'place based leadership' and how it is enacted with reference to cases in England, the US and Germany. Taking issue with writers such as Barber (2013), he argues that place based leadership needs to be more values based, and that overvaluing the pragmatic displaces appreciation of the importance of ideological, politically driven and powerful city leadership.

In the final chapter, I attempt to draw the threads together in the debates about directly elected mayors.

References

Bache, I. and Flinders, M. (2004) *Multi-level Governance*, Oxford: Oxford University Press.

Barber, B. (2013) *If Mayors Ruled the World. Dysfunctional Nations, Rising Cities*, New Haven and London: Yale University Press.

Beal, V. and Pinson, G. (2013) 'When Mayors Go Global: International Strategies, Urban Governance and Leadership', *International Journal of Urban and Regional Research*, 38(1), 302–17.

Borraz, O. and John, P. (2004) 'The transformation of urban political leadership in Western Europe', *International Journal of Urban and Regional Research*, 28(1), 107–20.

Bovens, M., Schillemans, T. and t'Hart, P. (2008) 'Does public accountability work? An assessment tool', *Public Administration*, 86(1), 225–42.

Bulkeley, H. (2013) *Cities and Climate Change*, Abingdon, Oxon: Routledge.

Copus, C. (2006) *Leading the Localities*, Manchester: Manchester University Press.

Davies, J. (2011) *Challenging Governance Theory*, Bristol: Policy Press.

Department for Communities and Local Government (DCLG) (2011) *A plain English Guide to the Localism Act*, DCLG: London.

Granovetter, M. (1973) 'The Strength of Weak Ties', *American Journal of Sociology*, 78(6), 1360–80.

Greasley, S. and Stoker, G. (2008) 'Mayors and Urban Governance: Developing a Facilitative Leadership Style', *Public Administration Review*, 68(4), 722–30.

Hambleton, R. (2015) *Leading the Inclusive City*, Bristol: Policy Press.

Hambleton, R. and Gross, J. (2007) *Governing Cities in a Global Era*, New York: Palgrave Macmillan.

Hambleton, R. and Sweeting, D. (2014) 'Innovation in urban political leadership. Reflections on the introduction of a directly-elected mayor in Bristol, UK', *Public Money & Management*, 34(5), 315–22.

Hambleton, R. and Sweeting, D. (2015) *The Impacts of Mayoral Governance in Bristol*, Bristol: School for Policy Studies, University of Bristol.

Harding, A. and Blokland-Potters, T. (2014) *Urban Theory*, Sage: London.

Harrison, B. (2015)' Just how powerful will UK city-region mayors be?', Centre for Cities, www.centreforcities.org/blog/just-how-powerful-will-uk-city-region-mayors-be

Heinelt, H. and Hlepas, N. (2006) 'Typologies of local government systems', in Bäck, H., H. Heinelt and A. Magnier (eds) *The European Mayor: Political Leaders in the Changing Context of Local Democracy*, Wiesbaden, Germany: VS Verlag, pp 21–42.

John, P. and Cole, A. (1999) 'Political leadership in the new urban governance: Britain and France compared', *Local Government Studies*, 25(4), 98–115.

Jones, G. (2016) 'The case against directly elected mayors', LSE British politics and policy blog, http://blogs.lse.ac.uk/politicsandpolicy/the-case-against-directly-elected-executive-mayors

Kearns, A. and Paddison, R. (2000) 'New Challenges for Urban Governance', *Urban Studies*, 37(5–6), 845–50.

Kern, K. and Bulkeley, H. (2009) 'Cities, Europeanization and Multilevel Governance: Governing Climate Change through Transnational Municipal Networks', *JCMS: Journal of Common Market Studies*, 47, 309–32.

Kotter, J. and Lawrence, P. (1974) *Mayors in Action*. New York: Wiley.

Leach, S. and Wilson, D. (2000) *Local Political Leadership*, Bristol, UK: Policy Press.

Lowndes, V. (2009) 'New institutionalism and urban politics', in J. Davies and D. Imbroscio (eds) *Theories of Urban Politics*. London: Sage, pp 91–105.

Marsh, A. (2012) 'Is it time to put the dream of elected mayors to bed?', *Policy & Politics*, 40(4): 607–11.

Martins, L. and Rodríguez Álvarez, J. (2007) 'Towards glocal leadership: taking up the challenge of new local governance in Europe?', *Environment and Planning C: Government and Policy*, 25(3), 391–409.

Mouritzen, P, and Svara, J. (2002) *Leadership at the Apex*, Pittsburgh: University of Pittsburgh Press.

Navarro, C. and Sweeting, D. (2015) 'La elección directa de alcaldes. Caracterísitcas, experiencias comparadas, y el singular caso de los alcaldes quasi-directamente elegidos españoles', *Anuario de Derecho Municipal*, UAM: Madrid, pp 105–26.

Orr, K. (2004) 'If Mayors are the Answer then What was the Question?', *Local Government Studies*, 30(3), 331–44.

Pierre, J. (2011) *The Politics of Urban Governance*, Basingstoke: Palgrave Macmillan.

Sansom. G. (2012) *Australian Mayors: What Can and Should They Do?* Sydney: Centre for Local Government, University of Technology.

Sims, S. (2011) *Making the Most of Mayors*, London: Institute for Government.

Sims, S. (2012) 'Joining the dots: mayors and the coordination of public services', in Gash, T. and S. Sims (eds) *What can Elected Mayors do for our Cities?* London: Institute for Government.

Smith, I., Lepine, L. and Taylor, M. (eds) (2007) *Disadvantaged by Where You Live? Neighbourhood Governance in Contemporary Urban Policy*, Bristol: Policy Press.

Stone, C. (1989) *Regime Politics*, Lawrence, Kansas: University Press of Kansas.

Svara, J. (1990) *Official Leadership in the City: Patterns of Conflict and Cooperation*, Oxford: Oxford University Press.

Svara J. H. (ed) (1994) *Facilitative Leadership in Local Government*, San Francisco: Jossey Bass.

Sweeting, D (2002) 'Leadership in Urban Governance: The Mayor of London', *Local Government Studies,* 28(1), 3–28.

Sweeting, D. (2003) 'How strong is the Mayor of London?', *Policy & Politics*, 31(4), 465–78.

Tallon, A. (2010) *Urban Regeneration in the UK*, London: Routledge.

Townsend, A. (2014) *Smart Cities*, New York: W. W. Norton & Company.

Turok, I. and McGranahan, G. (2013) 'Urbanization and economic growth: the arguments and evidence for Africa and Asia', *Environment and Urbanization*, 25(2), 465–82.

United Nations (UN) (2015) 'World Urbanisation Prospects, 2014 Revision', http://esa.un.org/unpd/wup/Publications/Files/WUP2014-Report.pdf

Whitehead, M. (2003) '"In the shadow of hierarchy': meta-governance, policy reform and urban regeneration in the West Midlands', *Area*, 35(1), 6–14.

Part I
UK perspectives

TWO

Mayoral governance in Bristol: has it made a difference?

David Sweeting, University of Bristol, UK, and
Robin Hambleton, University of the West of England,
Bristol, UK

Introduction

Bristol introduced a directly elected mayor model of governance in November 2012. This radical reform replaced the former system whereby the leader of the council was selected from among the 70 elected councillors in the city. This chapter situates the Bristol reforms in context, introduces a new conceptual framework for understanding urban leadership, analyses the impact of the new system as recorded in before and after surveys of the views of citizens and civic leaders, and identifies themes emerging from the research on Bristol that could be of relevance to the wider international debate about how to improve the leadership of urban governance. The chapter draws on ongoing action research on urban governance in Bristol and the Bristol city region. However, the authors are also long-time residents of the city and have been active in debates about local democracy in the city for many years. The narrative is informed by this tacit knowledge of governance and community politics in the city as well as the hard data generated by systematic research on the mayoral model of governance.

A directly elected mayor for Bristol – the local context

The UK Conservative and Liberal Democrat coalition government, elected in 2010, moved swiftly to pass the Localism Act 2011. This measure was intended to spur English cities to introduce directly elected mayors: it required the 12 largest cities in England to hold referendums on whether or not to adopt a directly elected mayor model of governance (Fenwick and Elcock 2014). In the event, ten referendums were held in May 2012 as two cities – Liverpool and Salford – opted to introduce mayoral governance using existing legislation. In nine cities local citizens rejected the mayoral form of governance. Bristol was the only city to vote 'yes' and the fact that the city chose a distinctive path generated national media interest. Citizens voted for the directly elected mayor model of governance by a margin of around 5,100 votes. On a turnout of 24%, 41,032 people voted for the mayoral model, while 35,880 voted against. The subsequent election, held in November 2012, attracted 15 mayoral candidates, more than in any other mayoral election in England. Some 90,273 votes were cast – a voter turnout of 28% – and an independent candidate, George Ferguson, won the contest, beating the Labour candidate, Marvin Rees, into second place. Ferguson, an architect and urbanist, who gained more first and second preferences than Rees, was able to use his long experience of bringing about successful regeneration in the city to his electoral advantage.

Bristol bucked the national trend in opting for a mayoral system of governance but the reform movement did not come out of the blue. There have long been local calls for change in the form of governance. For example, the authors' earlier study of leadership in Bristol, covering 1990–2000, found that leadership was, at best, implied and fragmented:

> The arrangements for partnership working, which are complicated and bureaucratic, soak up the enthusiasm of local leaders. Personal style counts for little, and managers and brokers struggle to achieve consensus in a situation of fragmented multi-organisational bargaining. (Sweeting et al, 2004, pp 362–3)

Other studies also suggested that all was not well with Bristol's city governance. For example, in 2001 the *Bristol Democracy Commission*, following a consultation process, advocated adopting a new system of governance in the city, including the introduction of a directly elected mayor (Burton 2001).[1] The Commission's advice fell on deaf ears.

While the election in 2012 of an independent politician as executive mayor was something of a surprise, it was not hugely so – other mayoral elections in England have yielded successful independents (Fenwick and Elcock, 2014). How, then, do we explain why the citizens of Bristol opted for radical change in the governmental arrangements for their city? It seems clear that many Bristol voters felt that 'party politics', or, more specifically, the perceived short-termism of political parties acting in their own interests rather than the wider interests of the city, was holding Bristol back. In the debate prior to the referendum on the introduction of the mayoral system, much was made of the number of leaders and the frequency of leadership change at the city council. In the 15 years or so prior to 2012, the council moved from one with a comfortable Labour Party majority, and a stable Labour leadership, to one where the balance of power shifted into periods of no overall control, with different coalitions or minority administrations led by the Labour or Liberal Democrat parties, or with the Liberal Democrats holding an overall majority. Consequently, in this period the control of the council, and the position of the leader within it, appeared unstable, with several politicians gracing the leadership stage and departing in quick succession, with some to re-emerge with the shifting politics of the city.

There is something in the argument that this instability was detrimental to the running of the city, but it would be easy to overplay the fragility of governing control at the council. In the period up to the introduction of the mayoral system, the Liberal Democrat Party maintained an influential profile, eventually with an outright majority of seats on the council. Yet the accusation of instability stuck, and critics used it as part of a broader narrative about Bristol 'not punching its weight', with matters such as poor public transport, traffic congestion and the poor reputation of schools being used as examples. It is also the case that the 'Vote Yes' campaign was remarkably well organised – a lively group of civic activists, which included several creative small business leaders, was very effective in advocating the case for reform and getting its message out. Its cause was, to some extent, advanced by the support of prominent national figures visiting the city to endorse the mayoral model (including Prime Minister David Cameron and Boris Johnson, Mayor of London), by the enthusiasm for the idea of mayoral leadership shown by the local press (*Bristol Post*) and by the relative ineffectiveness of the 'Vote No' campaign. In the referendum campaign, the local Conservative Party was in favour, the local Labour Party split and did not campaign either way, and the Liberal Democrat Party officially backed the directly elected mayor model but, because of internal divisions, was not that visible in the debate.

Locating the Bristol reforms in a wider context

Alongside, and entwined with, the city leadership debate in Bristol is an ongoing debate about the governance of the city region of Bristol and the surrounding area. The sub-region, or city region, is most commonly thought of in terms of the four unitary authorities of Bristol (population 442,000), Bath and North East Somerset (182,000), North

Somerset (208,000), and South Gloucestershire (272,000). Partnership arrangements linking these local authorities have existed for many years, notably the West of England Partnership and, latterly, the West of England Local Enterprise Partnership (LEP). Other regional efforts at collaboration, such as a 'Great Western Cities' initiative launched in 2015, cover a wider geographical area. In this case the cities of Bristol, Newport and Cardiff have indicated that they intend to improve co-operation, particularly in relation to economic development and environmental strategy. Yet it is the penumbra formed by the defunct Avon County Council, which comprised the area containing Bristol plus the current three unitary authorities adjacent to the city, which continues to shade and colour inter-authority relationships in the city region. Despite its short existence – it was created in 1974 and abolished in 1996 – and that it is now 20 years since its abolition, calls for a recreation of some form of governance for CUBA (the County that Used to Be Avon) continue to circulate. Functional imperatives tend to drive this debate, most obviously around transport, and also in relation to matters such as housing, inward investment and external representation. Such calls tend to be resisted most sharply by the three authorities outside Bristol in the sub-region.

However, the importance of improving city region governance has been given fresh impetus by the Conservative government's efforts to promote devolution in England. Elected in May 2015, the UK central government is actively encouraging local authorities across the country to form alliances in order to benefit from 'devolution deals'. The Cities and Local Government Devolution Act 2016 provides the legislative framework to enable groups of authorities to form 'combined authorities' that can bid for enhanced powers. Ministers have, in their speeches and in their discussions with groups of local authorities, made it clear that they would prefer the new combined authorities to be headed by directly elected mayors. Indeed, they have indicated that only areas that agree to introduce directly elected city region mayors can expect to win significant additional powers from Whitehall (Cooper 2015).

In the period from May 2015 to June 2016 Chancellor George Osborne and Communities and Local Government Secretary of State Greg Clark were particularly enthusiastic about the potential of devolution deals to deliver directly elected mayors for city regions. When, in the UK Referendum held on 23 June 2016, voters decided to leave the European Union the country entered a period of political turmoil. Theresa May emerged as the new Prime Minister. She dismissed George Osborne and appointed Philip Hammond as

Chancellor, and she moved Greg Clark to a new position as Secretary of State for Business, Energy and Industrial Strategy. Some wondered if the enthusiasm for so-called metro mayors would dissipate. However, after a period of uncertainty the Prime Minister confirmed that that she favoured the introduction of directly elected mayors for city regions. In all likelihood seven metro mayors for various city regions in England will be elected in May 2017. This will include a directly elected mayor for the Bristol city region. The area included in the West of England Combined Authority (WECA) Order 2016 covers the local government areas of Bath and North East Somerset, Bristol City and South Gloucestershire. North Somerset, lying to the south west of Bristol, decided not to join this new combined authority.

At the same time the government is strongly committed to a programme of massive year-on-year cuts to local government spending. In the period 2010–15 the Conservative and Liberal Democrat coalition government cut local government financial support to all local authorities. The reduction in financial support to Bristol City Council in this five-year period was 35% (from £201 million in 2010/11 to £131 million in 2014/15). These unprecedented reductions were executed under the rubric of a need for 'austerity' in the nation's public finances. The current Conservative government proposes, in the 2015–20 period, a further 65% cut in financial support to Bristol City Council (from £131 million in 2014/15 to £45 million in 2019/20) (Hambleton, 2016). These cutbacks are unprecedented in the history of UK local government and many local government services will suffer; indeed, some will be erased altogether.

This extraordinary collapse in fiscal support for local government is important for our analysis of mayoral leadership in Bristol. The extreme centralisation of power within England means that locally elected authorities, whether they have directly elected mayors or not, have no choice other than to implement drastic cuts in local government services. A mayor can do little about the environment of 'austerity urbanism' (Meegan et al, 2014). It can be argued that the UK central government is introducing 'devolution deals' in order to ensure that it is local leaders, rather than ministers, who will be blamed for the decimation of local government services that will take place. It is clear that the public spending cutbacks are having a major impact on communities in Bristol. For example, there are plans to close a significant number of libraries in the city. Understandably, but quite wrongly, some local citizens blame the directly elected mayor of Bristol for spending cuts that are not of his making. It is essential to be aware of this wider national context when assessing the impact of mayoral governance in Bristol.

Understanding the dynamics of urban leadership

The evidence underpinning the findings presented in this chapter stem from an ongoing evaluation of the performance of the mayoral model of governance in Bristol – the Bristol Civic Leadership Project. This study is a form of 'engaged scholarship' in that it both analyses the changes taking place in public affairs, and attempts to engage with stakeholders in working out practical and appropriate policy responses (Flinders, 2013). Launched in September 2012, the project addresses two important questions: 'What difference does a directly elected mayor make?' And, second, 'What steps can be taken to ensure that the introduction of a directly elected mayor brings about benefits and avoids potential disadvantages?' It is a collaborative project led by Bristol's two universities, involving Bristol City Council, and the city's business and third sectors.[2]

In previous research on place-based leadership, one of the authors has distinguished three different realms of civic leadership (Hambleton, 2009). Civic leaders operate at many geographical levels – from the street block to an entire sub-region and beyond. The suggestion made here is that it is helpful to distinguish three realms of place-based leadership reflecting different sources of legitimacy (see Figure 2.1), and these realms of leadership form an important part of the Bristol study:

- *Political leadership* – referring to the work of those people elected to leadership positions by the citizenry. These are, by definition, political leaders. Thus, directly elected mayors, all elected local councillors and MPs are political leaders. Having said that we should acknowledge that different politicians carry different roles and responsibilities and will view their political roles in different ways.
- *Public managerial/professional leadership* – referring to the work of public servants appointed by local authorities, other public sector agencies, and central government to plan and manage public services, and promote community wellbeing. These officers bring professional and managerial expertise to the tasks of local governance.
- *Community and business leadership* – referring to the work of the many civic-minded people who give their time and energy to local leadership activities in a wide variety of ways. These may be community activists, business leaders, social entrepreneurs, trade union leaders, voluntary sector leaders, religious leaders, higher education leaders and so on.

Figure 2.1: Realms of civic leadership

Potential innovation zones

Parallel international research on urban leadership shows that leaders from all these 'realms of civic leadership' can, if collaboration across the realms is orchestrated effectively, play a critical role in the leadership of a city (Hambleton, 2015).[3] Those elected or appointed to senior positions in a city are certainly expected to exercise civic leadership, but leadership capacity is much more widely dispersed. The mayoral model provides an opportunity for the senior political leader to relate to all three realms of civic leadership in different ways to the traditional UK model of urban governance. The three overlapping realms of leadership are all important in the civic leadership of a city.

The Bristol Civic Leadership Project

The Bristol Civic Leadership Project uses the framework set out in Figure 2.1 to guide information gathering and analysis. The model draws attention to the variety of interests that contribute to urban governance. Thus, the surveys of civic leaders, reported on below, were designed to elicit the views of respondents drawn from these three realms of civic leadership. In addition, the various workshops the authors have organised, as well as the interviews and focus groups, have sought the views of actors from all three realms.

The question 'What difference does a directly elected mayor make?' points to the need for a 'before' and 'after' assessment of the impact of the mayoral model, specifically an evaluation study (Palfrey et al, 2012). As a way of framing this evaluation the project has drawn on a policy document published by central government when the idea of considering new forms of local leadership was first mooted in the UK (HM Government, 1993). The central government policy document suggests six criteria for evaluation. These criteria signal the importance not just of assessing the impact of governance change on leadership, but also the need to consider the impacts of the introduction of the elected mayor on different aspects of city governance processes. The criteria are:

- leadership in the community
- effective representation of the citizen
- legitimacy and accountability
- effectiveness in decision making and implementation
- effective scrutiny of policy and performance
- responsiveness to local people.

Versions of these criteria were used by Hambleton in his study of local political management arrangements in the US, New Zealand and Norway (Hambleton, 1998), and by Sweeting (2012) in his study of local government in Spain. Use of these criteria enables us to generate specific insights that are relevant to what Palfrey et al (2012) call the 'real world' of decision making. Using these six criteria a number of statements were developed in order to assess the perceptions of different groups in Bristol regarding the changing arrangements for city leadership and urban governance.

The research in Bristol included questionnaires that were sent to members of the public in Bristol, and to civic leaders across the realms of leadership. This chapter reports on the findings emerging from the surveys of both these groups and, in each case, we have before and after data. The same questions were repeated in the surveys to enable us to track change in the views of the residents of Bristol as well as the views of Bristol's civic leaders. The questionnaire of Bristol residents was administered as part of the Bristol Citizens' Panel Survey, which uses a stratified sample of Bristol residents representative of the adult population in the city. The first survey was sent in September 2012 to 1,863 people, and returned 658 responses, a response rate of about 35%. The second survey was sent in January 2014 to 2,104 people, and returned 1,013 responses, a response rate of 48%. For the survey of civic leaders, we surveyed all 70 Bristol City Council councillors, and 35 from each of Bristol City Council officers, other public sector officers outside the council in the city, the private sector and the third sector. This gave a total of 210 respondents and covered perspectives in equal measure from inside and outside the city council, and accessed the views of those involved across different sectors of governance. For the first survey of civic leaders, there were 123 responses, or 59%; for the second survey, there were 103 responses (49%). The figures reported in Table 2.1 are the sum of agree and strongly agree to each question, and the change between before and after the introduction of the mayor has been subject to testing for statistical significance.

Evaluating the performance of mayoral governance

The set of statements in Table 2.1 asked for agreement to a number of propositions around the six evaluation criteria, broken down according to views of the public, and by views of civic leaders.[4] In the opinion of our survey respondents, leadership of the city of Bristol has improved both in terms of visibility, and in terms of having a vision for the city, both for members of the public and for civic leaders. The figures relating to these aspects of the evaluation criteria are striking, with more than two thirds of the public in Bristol agreeing that the city of Bristol has visible leadership after the introduction of the mayor compared with less than one quarter before – a remarkable rise of 45.5%. For civic leaders, this rise is even more staggering, up nearly 55%, with over 90% of civic leaders agreeing that the mayoral model is delivering visible leadership. There are also less marked rises in agreement over perceptions of the leadership of the council having a vision for the city. Clearly, the change has bought about significant improvements to the leadership of the city.

For effective representation of the citizen, the evidence offered by the surveys is not so positive. For members of the public, there are small, albeit statistically significant, increases for statements on involvement in decision making, and in the representation of citywide views by the council. However, while the direction of change is positive, in absolute terms, the percentages that agree with those statements (33% and 24%) are still lower than one would want in a developed democratic system of decision making. The views of civic leaders on representation of the citizen are more troubling. While the overall agreement for these two statements is, at 39% and 31%, higher than for those of the public, the 2014 results are lower than the 2012 results. In other words, following the introduction of the mayoral model of governance, civic leaders are less likely to believe that the system of governance provides adequate opportunities for citizen views to be represented. The picture on representation that emerges from the surveys is, at best, mixed.

A more positive picture for legitimacy and accountability emerges from the survey evidence. For the statements on clarity regarding who is making decisions at the council, and on trust in the council to make good decisions, there are rises for both statements for citizens and civic leaders. There is a particularly notable rise of over 20% for

Table 2.1: Before and after the election of a mayor, views of citizens and civic leaders (% agree)

Criteria	Statement	Bristol citizens			Civic leaders		
		2012	2014	% change	2012	2014	% change
Leadership in the community	The city of Bristol has visible leadership	24.1	68.6	+44.5**	35.6	90.2	+54.6
	The leadership of the Council has a vision for the city	25.2	56.3	+31.1**	50.0	69.6	+19.6
Effective representation of the citizen	There are many opportunities to get involved in decision making in important affairs in the city	27.4	33.0	+5.6*	50.0	39.2	-10.8
	City wide views are well represented by the Council	18.3	23.7	+5.4*	39.8	30.7	-9.1
Legitimacy and accountability	It is clear who is responsible for making decisions at the Council	17.5	38.2	+20.7**	36.8	46.5	+9.7
	I trust the Council to make good decisions	18.5	22.7	+4.2*	28.2	29.6	+1.4
	Decisions are made in a timely way by the Council	13.1	15.5	+2.4	23.9	19.2	-4.7
Effectiveness in decision making and implementation	The leadership of the council can influence... central government	12.5	19.3	+6.8*	19.5	32.3	+12.8
	other local public service providers	38.8	45.7	+6.9**	39.5	52.1	+22.6
	neighbouring authorities	26.2	31.0	+4.8*	28.9	24.7	-4.2
	business interests	35.8	44.3	+8.5**	20.2	45.4	+25.2
	the voluntary sector	39.7	48.3	+9.0**	49.1	53.6	+4.5
Effective scrutiny of policy and performance	It is clear who people should approach if they are not happy with local issues	36.3	34.1	-2.1	48.7	42.4	-6.3
	Ward councillors provide an effective check on Council leadership	20.6	19.6	-1.0	30.8	30.6	-0.2
	The leadership of the Council ensures that Council services are responsive to local people's needs	17.9	24.4	+6.5**	38.5	31.6	-6.9
Responsiveness to local people	The needs of my community are well represented in decision making in the city	16.2	22.5	+6.3**	39.8	26.5	-13.3

Notes: **Significant at 1% level; *significant at 5%, level using Pearson chi square score.

the statement on responsibility for making decisions among citizens. However, agreement with each of the statements is still lower than half of all respondents in all cases in 2014.

In relation to the criterion of effectiveness in decision making and implementation, few agreed that decisions were made in a timely manner in 2012, and perception of performance on this criterion had changed little by 2014. Furthermore, the percentage agreement for timeliness is the lowest of all across all statements for both citizens and civic leaders. Yet there are clear increases in those agreeing with statements around the ability of the city's leadership to influence others in governance. For members of the public, one might argue that they are not in a good position to judge this sort of aspect of government. However, one could also argue that the perception of influence is important to gauge. For civic leaders, who might well be in a better position to assess this matter, there are increases of 23% and 25% in relation to other local public service providers and the business sector respectively, perhaps reflecting the mayor's profile and background in the city. For the ability to influence national government, there is also a 13% increase. Interestingly, and pertinent to the discussion on relationships between the four local authorities in and around Bristol, the perception of civic leaders on the ability of the leadership of the council to influence neighbouring authorities has fallen from a lowly 29% to a lower 25%.

For effective scrutiny of policy and performance, there are, for citizens, only marginal (and statistically insignificant) decreases in agreement for both statements – that is, on whom to approach in the case of dissatisfaction, and on the ability of councillors to act as a check on council leadership. The levels of agreement stay at around one third and one fifth of respondents respectively. For civic leaders, there is a similar picture of little change and, although the levels of agreement are a few percentage points higher, they still remain well below half of the respondents. These findings on effective scrutiny are significant. They suggest that most people appear to feel that they have little ability to hold the directly elected mayor to account.

For responsiveness to local people, the responses bear a considerable resemblance to those for representation. From a low level of agreement in 2012, there is some improvement in public views, though not much; civic leaders overall appear to think that services have become less responsive, and that representation of community voices has lessened.

As with any survey data there are, of course, ambiguities, and results can be interpreted in different ways. However, it is clear that, in relation to providing high profile leadership with a sense of direction, the change in governance to a mayoral model has been very successful in the views of both civic leaders and Bristol citizens. For 14 of the 16 statements in Table 2.1, citizens appear more positive about leadership in the city in 2014 than 2012. This is particularly the case for clarity of decision making. For many of the other statements, this change is only marginal, though the results for citizens do indicate across the board improvement. It is however also important to record that, for the 2014 results for Bristol citizens, levels of agreement for all statements not related to exercising leadership are below 50%, and considerably so for some variables. Civic leaders' views, on the one hand, tend not to differ dramatically from those of citizens when comparing the overall levels of agreement between the two surveys conducted in 2014. However, it is striking that, for 15 of the 16 statements in the survey in 2014, there is more agreement among civic leaders than the citizens of Bristol. Sometimes this is by only a few percentage points, but it does suggest that those who are active in the networks of governance in the city are more comfortable with the new system as compared with the public at large. What is also interesting to note, however, is that while citizens tend on the whole to have more positive attitudes in 2014 as compared with 2012, for civic leaders there are both positive and negative changes between these two years. For the 16 statements presented here, in eight they become more positive, and for eight they become more negative. Overall, then, the results from the civic leader surveys present a more enthusiastic, and yet more ambivalent, response to the mayoral model of governance when compared to the responses of the public.

In his first 18 months in office, the new mayor introduced several policies that were clearly associated with his personal priorities, such as reducing the speed limit in large parts of the city to 20 mph, and rolling out plans for restricting residential, on-street parking for parts of the city. He has also created an advisory cabinet of senior councillors, drawn from the council, with all four parties represented on it. This, in itself, is a radical departure from established practice in UK local government as the party with the most councillors normally fills the cabinet with politicians from their party.

Reflections and conclusions

A key challenge for those wishing to evaluate changes in forms of democratic urban governance is establishing cause and effect, and our research on Bristol is no exception. Not surprisingly, we have found it difficult to isolate the impact of the new model – that is, the introduction of new mayoral governance institutional arrangements – from other factors that are also shaping changing public perceptions relating to the quality of governance in the city. We have, for example, already referred to the ruthless cuts in local government spending impacting on Bristol. Imposed by ministers in UK central government these cuts are happening to English local authorities whether or not they have a mayoral form of governance. But the citizens of Bristol may not always be entirely clear about the respective roles of central and local government in the making of public spending decisions.

In addition, the personal qualities of the person elected as mayor shape attitudes to the mayoral model of governance – for good or ill. A third complicating factor is that, in the Bristol case, citizens elected an independent candidate. Mayor Ferguson does not belong to an established political party and this, in itself, is an unusual situation for a major English city. Moreover, it is also the case that it is early days. The mayoral model of governance is still fairly new to Bristol and it will, inevitably, take time for the new arrangements to bed down. While acknowledging the existence of these various complicating factors we are able to highlight several findings from the Bristol Civic Leadership Project.

First, it is clear that the mayoral model of governance has made a difference to the governance of the city – in some respects a big difference. On the plus side the model has provided a platform for highly visible, outgoing civic leadership. This is important in two respects: those that are external to the city and those that are internal to the city. In the modern era, an era in which cities are forced to compete in an international marketplace for inward investment and to attract talented people, it is important for cities to develop a distinctive and appealing vision of where they see themselves going in the future. The existence of mayoral governance in Bristol enabled Mayor Ferguson, and his team, to project a forward-looking and ambitious vision for the city to a variety of audiences. Led by the mayor, the external-facing activities of the city council have helped to bring about a dramatic rise in the profile of the city in national and international circles. The reputation of the city as an innovative, eco-friendly city has received a significant boost. While the groundwork enabling Bristol to win recognition as European Green Capital in 2015 was carried out before Mayor Ferguson was elected, he added his own personal commitment to this initiative. During 2015 some 74 international delegations visited the city, around ten times the number in preceding years. In addition, the city was successful in its application to join the network of 100 Resilient Cities, run by the Rockefeller Foundation in the US, and is now an active member. In 2014 Bristol was the only city from Europe to win a Guangzhou International Award for Urban Innovation. The national and international profile of the city was much lower in the period before 2012.

Turning to the changing perceptions of leadership within the city, our research shows that Bristol citizens take the view that the visibility of city leadership soared after the introduction of the mayoral model. Leaders from across our realms of civic leadership agree with this change. The hope here is that, because civic leadership is more visible and policy options relating to the future of the city have become more discernible, levels of citizen involvement in public policymaking will rise. Perhaps the model will result in an increase in voter participation in local elections. The increase in voter turnout in the May 2016 local elections from 28% in 2012 to 45% in 2016 lends support to the view that mayoral governance can strengthen citizen interest and voter turnout in local elections.

On the downside, our research suggests that mayoral governance is not a panacea for urban democracy. Perhaps it is too early to judge, but our 'before' (2012) and 'after' (2014) data suggest that public perceptions of trust in and timeliness of decision making have improved only very slightly and are still low. Concerns have been expressed to us that the way the mayoral model is working in Bristol is too centralised. The argument here is that, if too much power is concentrated in the hands of one individual, councillors and other stakeholders can come to feel excluded from the local policymaking process. This, in turn, may weaken the legitimacy of the decisions taken by the mayor and diminish support for important initiatives. Moreover, highly centralised decision making does not make good use of the leadership talents available, particularly the skills and experience of senior councillors. Clearly a balance needs to be struck between, on the one hand, appropriate centralisation of power around the strategic objectives set by the directly elected mayor and, on the other, delegation of authority by the mayor to other players to act on his or her behalf.

In May 2016 the citizens of Bristol elected a new mayor. Marvin Rees, a young and charismatic candidate, delivered an emphatic victory for the Labour Party. Rees polled 68,750 votes (63%), 29,000 more votes than the incumbent, George Ferguson, with 39,577 votes (37%). Mayor Rees has a very different style of leadership to Mayor Ferguson. He favours delegating power and responsibilities to members of his Cabinet of senior councillors. Interestingly he has retained Mayor Ferguson's innovation of having all four parties in the City Council Cabinet. Ferguson and Rees provided the electorate with different visions for the future of the city, and the emphasis Rees put on needing to tackle growing inequality in the city proved to be a vote winner. The two leaders are passionate about the city and fought a hard campaign, but they respect each other. Mayor Rees has invited Ferguson to be an international ambassador for the city and he has accepted this role.

This chapter has presented a case study of governance change in one particular city covering a relatively short period of time. It would be unwise to generalise too freely on the basis of just one example. Nevertheless, the evidence presented does suggest that introducing a directly mayor model of governance can make a major difference to the way a city is perceived and is governed. We hope that the methods we have used to assess the performance of the mayoral model will be of interest to researchers studying changing approaches to city leadership in different countries and contexts.

Notes

[1] The Bristol Democracy Commission was chaired by Paul Burton, author of Chapter Eight in this volume.

[2] The Bristol Civic Leadership Project involves the University of Bristol and the University of the West of England, Bristol in collaboration with city leaders and citizens in Bristol. The authors wish to acknowledge the financial support provided for this work by the Economic and Social Research Council's Impact Acceleration Scheme, and Bristol City Council. For more information visit: http://bristolcivicleadership.net

[3] Hambleton has developed this idea of 'realms of civic leadership' and a more refined version of the model has five realms of leadership, rather than three (Hambleton 2015). This five-realm conceptual framework is outlined in Chapter Fourteen. In the Bristol Civic Leadership Project we have retained the three-realm model as we wish to compare before and after data on civic leaders views of mayoral governance (and our 2012 data uses the three-realm framework).

[4] These figures can be disaggregated according to various characteristics. A fuller analysis is provided in a research report – see Hambleton and Sweeting (2015).

References

Burton, P. (2001) *Local Democracy in Bristol: Final Report of the Bristol Democracy Commission*, Bristol: Bristol City Council.

Cooper, K. (2015) 'How ministers' beloved mayors rarely win the love of councillors', *Local Government Chronicle*, 8 October, pp 10–13.

Fenwick, J. and Elcock, H. (2014) 'Elected Mayors: Leading Locally?', *Local Government Studies*, 40(4), 581–99.

Flinders, M. (2013) 'The politics of engaged scholarship: impact, relevance and imagination', *Policy & Politics*, 41(4), 621–42.

HM Government (1993) *Community Leadership and Representation: Unlocking the Potential*, The report of the Working Party on the Internal Management of Local Authorities in England, July. London: HMSO.

Hambleton, R. (1998) *Local Government Political Management Arrangements – An International Perspective*, Edinburgh: The Scottish Office.

Hambleton, R. (2009) 'Civic leadership for Auckland: An international perspective', in *Royal Commission on Auckland Governance*, 4, Part 11, pp 515–52.

Hambleton, R. (2015) *Leading the Inclusive City. Place-based Innovation for a Bounded Planet*, Bristol: Policy Press.

Hambleton, R. (2016) 'Mayors: Strong leadership or unchecked power', The Bristol Cable, https://thebristolcable.org/2016/04/mayor-unchecked-power/

Hambleton, R. and Sweeting, D. (2015) *The Impacts of Mayoral Governance in Bristol*, Report of the Bristol Civic Leadership Project, September. Bristol: School for Policy Studies, University of Bristol.

Meegan, R., Kennett P., Jones J. and Croft, J. (2014) 'Global economic crisis, austerity and neoliberal urban governance in England', *Cambridge Journal of Regions, Economy and Society*, 7, 137–53.

Palfrey, C., Thomas P. and Phillips C. (2012) *Evaluation for the real world*, Bristol: The Policy Press.

Sweeting, D. (2012) 'Analysing local political management in Spain', *Local Government Studies*, 38(2), 231–47.

Sweeting, D., Hambleton, R., Huxham C., Stewart, M. and Vangen S. (2004) 'Leadership and Partnership in Urban Governance: Evidence from London, Bristol and Glasgow', in Boddy, M. and Parkinson, M. (eds) *City Matters. Competitiveness, Cohesion and Urban Governance*, Bristol: Policy Press, pp 349–66.

THREE

Can the directly elected mayoral model deliver? Innovation, limitation and adaptation: lessons from the City of Bristol

Thom Oliver, University of the West of England, Bristol, UK

Introduction

When Bristol's first directly elected mayor independent George Ferguson was elected early on the morning of 16 November 2012 he asserted "I believe today we have voted for a new way of doing things" (Ferguson, 2012). This chapter seeks to explore the capacity of the role to enable things to be done differently.

Beyond legalistic conceptions, the role of directly elected mayors is itself contested. The constitutional vagueness of the role, coupled with the variable geometry of City Deals negotiated before and after the mayoral election, posed challenges as well as opportunities for the incumbent mayor. There were significant opportunities for innovation available to the mayor following a City Deal that gave scope to leverage growth in business rates, exert greater control over a wide property portfolio of over £1 billion worth of assets and utilise a new growth hub at the Temple Quarter Enterprise Zone to draw in investment and incubate growth (Cabinet Office, 2011). The position of elected mayor also enabled the incumbent to deliver change on the basis of an electoral proposition from a direct mandate from the citizens of Bristol. As such, the mayoral model also conferred a different type of legitimacy. Conversely the capacity to do things differently is naturally bound by a pre-existing institutional system where the roles, functions and procedures are historically informed and institutionally engrained and often slow to adapt to change. The chapter explores a series of individual challenges met by the first directly elected mayor of Bristol during his first term of office and the challenges faced by his successor Marvin Rees. By addressing them in turn it assesses the capacity of the role and direct mandate of an elected mayor to innovate, adapt and overcome the temporal, structural and institutional barriers to achieve change. The data for this chapter comes from a series of interviews across three years with councillors including former council leaders and cabinet members and council officers from a larger project contrasting councillor perceptions of leadership roles in local government. The project was funded by a Central Research Grant from Oxford Brookes University. Assessment also derives from a situated appraisal by the author as an academic, community activist and resident of the City of Bristol.

Collective action problems and lobbying from above

As residents of ten large English cities voted in referendums on introducing elected mayors there was hope for a reinvigoration of local democracy and a redefinition of relationships between local government and the centre. The referendums were preceded by significant announcements from then Prime Minister David Cameron and Cities Minister Greg Clark that laid out a series of benefits of a 'yes' vote. The strongest incentive came with the proposals for mayors to be 'leading citizens' who would meet bi-annually within a 'Cabinet of Mayors' under the chairmanship of the Prime Minister. The much vaulted Cabinet of Mayors posed a magnificent opportunity for cities to have a hotline to the heart of Whitehall and the autonomy to choose their own solutions to achieve the growth which the government hoped devolution could deliver. As the returning officers announced the results of all ten referendums it was clear that only Bristol had opted for a directly elected mayor and the new incumbent of the role faced a significant collective action problem. While George Ferguson was given a clear mandate on a turnout of 27.9% and the advantage of high visibility and prominence as an independent candidate, he faced a significant barrier to achieving the lobbying power of the leaders of other English cities. Although the government had a vested interest in delivering for the only city that had chosen its flagship policy in adopting a mayor, and despite access to government ministers over the course of his first term the mayor came back from Whitehall with little more than had previously been offered by the pre-existing City Deal. Lacking the administrative machinery and networks of comparative city leaders from the main political parties, the newly elected mayor faced an uphill struggle to lobby for, and deliver, financial resources and new powers alongside others with more established clout in Whitehall.

Ferguson moved quickly to position himself as an integral part of the Core Cities group taking the lead on low carbon and energy. An architect by background, he came into power after Bristol had secured European Green Capital Status for 2015 so was well placed to adopt this portfolio. The mayor also looked to build new networks and draw in resource and expertise from international sources, with a great deal of success. In 2013 Bristol was one of 33 cities selected by the Rockefeller Foundation Resilient Cities Centennial Challenge for funding. The funding award provided resources to employ a Chief Resilience Officer to develop a resilience strategy as well as access to experts and services to assist in the implementation of such a strategy. Bristol also took a formative role in the nascent Global Parliament of Mayors founded by Ben Barber. Barber is a strong advocate of the power of mayors as a collective solution to the intractable problems of urban governance (Barber, 2013).

With the position of elected mayor delivering few if any additional formal powers, the mayor looked to maximise 'soft power' in the form of positioning Bristol as an exemplar in doing things differently. Italian Prime Minister Matteo Renzi when Mayor of Florence posited that "This city doesn't need a mayor; it needs a marketing expert". In some respects so did Bristol, which was lagging behind cities such as Manchester, Cardiff and local neighbour Bath as a cultural and tourist destination. In an interview with the *Guardian*, George Ferguson outlined his priority as "making Bristol known across the world so we don't have to say it's a port somewhere near Bath, which I have found myself saying in China, America and India" (*Guardian*, 2013). To address the perceived shortfall Ferguson smartly leveraged Bristol's position as European Green Capital to give it a platform on the international stage, in particular at the 2015 United Nations Climate Change Conference in Paris (COP21). In moving Bristol onto a more international footing the mayor sought to lobby from above as well as below. While the tangible benefits of this international approach are yet to be fully realised, the autonomy of the mayor and the mandate which gave him a platform to speak for the city was utilised to its maximum potential to position Bristol on the international stage.

Institutional roadblocks

Another significant challenge for the incoming mayor came in the form of a series of significant clashes between systems and individuals competing within the formal governance framework of the city. When considering competing models of governance in English local government, Lowndes and Leach (2004) stressed that changes to governance systems are conditioned by well engrained local norms and practices. This assertion was seemingly manifested by the conflicted and contested environment which arose during the early days under mayoral governance in Bristol.

An election campaign that targeted party politicians as the short-termist, self-interested groupings that held Bristol back resulted in there being little love lost between the independent mayor and the formerly dominant Labour and Liberal Democrat groupings on the council. Following the campaign which depicted the Labour candidate Marvin Rees as the puppet of the Labour Party in London, the decision of the local Labour Party to turn down invitations to join a multi-party cabinet (*Bristol Post*, 2012) went some way in defining relationships between many local councillors and the newly elected mayor for his first year of office. As the mayor began his time in office suddenly councillors found that many elements of their traditional role were taken away or lost. The first political hurdle for the elected mayor would come when seeking to put through the first budget of his term of office. At the full council meeting the elected councillors were unwilling and the procedural systems ill equipped to let go of old ways of working. In line with a requirement to make upwards of £35 million worth of cuts handed down from central government the task of the mayor to deliver a successful budget was unenviable.

The governance arrangements of the mayoral model required the mayor to set a budget which could only be overturned by a two thirds majority and if overturned could result in an intractable legal stalemate. This led to a complex interplay of suggested amendments from the main political parties. The Liberal Democrats in particular, as the outgoing administration, were well placed to know where the budget could be adjusted and reserves utilised in order to offset elements of the cuts. What played out was a succession of 'claim making' actions from the mayor and councillor groups whereby each took credit for reversing or altering cuts. The mayor came away with an agreed budget settlement having given a number of concessions from his original outlined plans. Over the next two years the mayor successfully managed to avoid the breadth of concessions on his budget by reasserting the notion of his mandate and using his platform as figurehead to significantly broaden the extent and focus of the budget consultation. In adopting a more direct engagement process, the mayor managed to circumvent councillors and be able to take credit for concessions delivered before the budget vote and thus prevent his mandate being undermined within the public full council meeting. During the 2014/15 Budget

Consultation over 3,900 people responded to the budget survey, there were approximately 10,000 views of the consultation website and over 1,300 people attended public meetings. This represented a significant upturn on previous years and allowed the mayor to both amend his proposals on the basis of responses before the decisions came to full council and also gave him a platform to suggest his proposals carried public opinion, evoking direct democracy and a different form of accountability and legitimacy to his predecessors.

Catching up with scrutiny

The strongest criticism of the mayoral model from its detractors is that far from dispersing democracy it concentrates too much power in the office of mayor and too much power in the hands of one individual, running the risk that mayors try to rule in 'Napoleonic fashion without being held to account' (Kenny and Lodge, 2008). An inquiry day held at Bristol City Council in advance of the mayoral election considered the potential role of overview and scrutiny under mayoral governance and identified and outlined clear risks (Bristol City Council, 2012). First, the new mayor could ignore or sideline scrutiny activities, leaving councillors significantly weakened in their capacity to call the mayor, his policies and council officers to account. The other risk was that the relationship between the new mayor and the council could become increasingly conflict ridden with scrutiny moving further from scrutinising policy and more about internal infighting.

In the case of Bristol, the movement to the mayoral model drew power away from local councillors and neighbourhoods and the procedural mechanisms of council meetings and formal scrutiny process were initially ill equipped to cope with the new model of governance. While needing a significant boost in light of the changes, elements of scrutiny were downgraded, notably and most visibly being a reduction in number, attendance and length of scrutiny meetings according to the majority of interviewees. With potentially contentious decisions being made over the sale of land at the Port of Bristol, Metrobus (a long planned rapid transport route between the south and north of the city) and proposals for a 12,000 capacity arena near Temple Meads railway station, councillors felt forced to 'call in' decisions which they perceived to have been made without "proper consideration by anyone outside of the executive team of mayor and officers" (Liberal Democrat former cabinet member, interview, 22 July 2014). Two of the 'call ins' pertained to issues being removed from individual scrutiny commissions, with councillors feeling they had little control or ownership over the scrutiny work programme, while others related directly to strict confidentiality clauses precluding councillors from accessing and sharing council papers without signing a 'blank exempt status' to access the data. This culminated in an unprecedented joint statement from group leaders and scrutiny chairs which effectively suggested that they had been gagged (*Bristol Post*, 2014). A study of on 'The Impacts of Mayoral Governance in Bristol' also noted councillors felt their 'ability to scrutinise policy and decision making under model was less so than under the previous system' (Hambleton and Sweeting, 2015: 40).

The mayor moved to stem criticism with a reinvigoration of constitutional arrangements with a new constitution being adopted on a 'suck it and see basis' at full council in June 2014. The acceptance of the new constitution was bound up with negotiation over submissions to the Electoral Commission over a maintenance of councillor numbers in the upcoming boundary review (Bristol City Council, 2014). The city council also commissioned the Centre for Public Scrutiny (CfPS) to conduct a Review of Overview and Scrutiny in the city. The CfPS highlighted a number of problem areas. In particular, the report called directly for greater transparency and clarity about the process of how policies are made, agreed and implemented, greater use of pre-decision scrutiny, and the creation of greater capacity for scrutiny to fulfil a policy development role (CfPS, 2015). Overall, while it is widely acknowledged that scrutiny in local government is failing to achieve its potential, the position of elected mayor in Bristol was severely limited in its potential by systems which positioned councillors as external and reactive to policymaking. Forced to retreat into a reactive and rear guard action due to a constitution and organisational system ill-suited to mayoral governance, councillors found themselves far from any tangible form of policy influence, and where influence was possible it could be met by a simple veto.

The issue was exacerbated by the complex dynamics between an independent mayor and councillors of five political parties. The mayoral system left councillor roles diminished and ill-defined. Councillors re-asserted themselves as local ward champions, caseworkers and electoral campaigners but the loss of their creativity in policymaking through robust overview and scrutiny created a significant divide between what one former cabinet member defined as "council's officers and mayor on the one hand and the rest of the council on the other" (former cabinet member, interview, 15 June 2015). To evoke a simple model of the policy process, the system removed scope for councillors in the areas of agenda setting and policy formulation, allowed them to be democratically bypassed at policy legitimation and focused their attention on post hoc, often unconstructive, scrutiny. With both underdeveloped scrutiny mechanisms and party political dynamics it remains no surprise that councillors continue to struggle with the role of mayoral scrutiniser (Copus, 2008).

Lines of accountability

Early evaluations of the directly elected mayoral model in Bristol have shown that the mayor is better known and more visible than previous council leaders, and often a clear focal point for engagement with the electorate. Survey data collected before and after the introduction of the mayoral system in Bristol showed clearly that respondents across three realms – political, public management and professional – and community and business believed the city had improved in terms of the visibility of its leadership (Hambleton and Sweeting, 2015). The independent mayor George Ferguson has adopted a position of 'change agent' (Stoker, 2004) with a clear focus on delivering the city council out of a period of turmoil and a failed system of party politics. To do this Mayor Ferguson sought to create a rainbow cabinet or a 'cabinet of all the talents' as self-defined. Despite early difficulties when during the first six months of his term the local Labour Party refused to allow its members to join the cabinet, the rainbow cabinet has continued and been shuffled according to council composition at each election. Bristol until 2016 had been elected by thirds meaning that a third of councillors were elected every year over a four year cycle (with no elections in the fourth year), a contributing factor to the perceived political instability and stagnation of previous years. The rainbow cabinet embodied Ferguson's new politics and was a significant political innovation in the city; the innovation was further augmented in late 2015 as two Green Party councillors, Fi Hance and Daniella Radice, entered Ferguson's cabinet on a job share basis.

While choosing a broad and experienced cabinet, Mayor Ferguson opted to hold ultimate responsibility for all major policy decisions, while some of this responsibility could have been delegated or shared with assistant mayors. The advisory function of cabinet members' left them as a tenuous institutional bridge between mayor and full council. One former cabinet member highlighted in an interview that meetings between the cabinet allowed everyone

> 'to speak freely, but ultimately the mayor kept his own counsel, we could put markers down on our positions for the record, mainly in line with the stance of our party

groups, but beyond the nuclear option of resignation we
held little to no power'. (Former cabinet member, interview
24 November 2014)

Instead assistant mayors were drawn into managerial aspects of their
individual portfolios, and found striking a balance between this role and
being part answerable to party groupings "complex" and "challenging".
The difficulty was compounded as assistant mayors were tasked with
attending scrutiny on behalf of the executive. Outlining a particular
instance where a scrutiny chair was questioning the motives for a
particular policy, another cabinet member felt unable to offer a full
account for mayoral policy: "I found myself deferring to the officers
time and time again, they were answerable to George and often better
placed to know, all the avenues led to the mayor's door". In practice the
mayor's cabinet was "little more than window dressing" (group leader
interview, 2014) for the majority of councillors interviewed. This led
to many policy decisions being made before then being dissected and
reconstructed in the public arena at council meetings, most notably
on residents parking zones, where the mayor's individual decision on a
blanket roll out of parking zones to combat commuter parking was met
with fierce opposition at full council from all parties. A motion to full
council which called on the mayor to halt the process and take a more
phased approach gained striking cross party support at full council (49
in favour, 2 against, with 9 abstentions) (Bristol City Council, 2013:
8–9). Subsequently the mayor admitted he 'had kicked a hornet's nest'
(*Bristol Post*, 2013) by rolling out his plans too quickly. This example
represents an interesting depiction of Archibald Brown's 'Myth of the
Strong Leader' thesis (2014), that the more power that is concentrated
in one individual's hands, the more likely they will make catastrophic
policy errors.

While it is simple to suggest that political naiveté and a lack of trust
in party politicians came together to create the policy difficulties,
structural factors rendered such an outcome likely. In spite of the
cloudiness pertaining to the mayor's status as an independent among
party politicians, it was an uphill struggle for the mayor to road test his
policy ideas. With an advisory cabinet the mayor lacked the democratic
back room environment where he could try out ideas and have the
rough edges knocked off before they entered the public domain.
The mayor lacked the robust informal pre-decision scrutiny enjoyed
by his predecessors, council leaders who enjoyed a responsive if not
coherent party political group environment, where policy ideas could
be shaped, improved and any perceived failures addressed and avoided.

At the start of Fergusons term the Labour and Liberal Democrat party groupings were composed of a great number of councillors who had held experience in leadership and opposition. This coupled with a formalised and institutionally supported group structure meant that there was a longstanding schedule of group meetings ahead of all full council and scrutiny meetings. This gave councillors the time and intellectual room to air and road test ideas among colleagues from diverse areas of the city and come to collective decisions on votes, debate speakers and where colleagues were allowed to abstain or evade the whip. The mayor did not have this recent institutional knowledge, or the benefits of constructive criticism from colleagues operating under the same political grouping. The collective institutional knowledge also held by the Labour and Liberal Democrat councillors also gave them a clear advantage of knowing what had been tried, and with it the learning and potential pitfalls. The administration churn delivered by elections by thirds also meant predecessors had developed a cohesive rapport and institutional knowledge across party lines. While the previous model of governance is depicted as leading to periods of 'dysfunctional decision making' (Fenwick and Elcock, 2014: 17), the system had engendered a highly developed system of cross party briefing, and soundings through party whips and leads, delivering a coherent rapport through shared experience across party lines. An officer who worked under both governance systems highlighted the efficiency of the previous model in delivering consensus.

> 'It was amazing how quickly things moved, we would leave a meeting with a cabinet member thinking a policy decision would be stuck for a while, and suddenly it would be good to go for a vote at full council, often even ahead of the full council whips meeting, the back channels were really well developed.'

While there are implications in terms of transparency of conducting such business behind closed doors, the mayor was negatively affected by the lack of this resource and was left with the local press as a test bed for ideas. This effect was compounded as, in the more open and visible world of direct election, it was clear that any mistakes were his and his alone, and there were few offers to help. Both in terms of institutional hardware (formal rules and structures) and institutional software (practices taking place around and within the hardware) (Skelcher et al, 2005) the role of mayor was restricted in its capacity to deliver policy change in Bristol.

Shifting sands and someone else's agenda

With the notable amplified focus on the mayor as an individual there was a challenge for the mayor to show both individual leadership and make agendas his own. With the City Deal settlement negotiated by the outgoing Liberal Democrat administration with the leaders of North Somerset, South Gloucestershire, Bath and North East Somerset Councils, and the West of England Local Enterprise Partnership, the mayor had to try to adapt and work with a pre-existing devolution settlement. There was also a significant responsibility to deliver the European Green Capital year in 2015. As the first UK city to receive the award and with the award being secured by work from previous Labour and Liberal Democrat administrations, all eyes were on the mayor to deliver.

With the mayor standing on an electoral platform that put him directly at odds with a key element of the existing City Deal offering to 'strike a new City Deal with Government that includes enhanced rail, tram and bus service alternatives to the flawed BRT bendy bus (Metrobus)' (Bristol 1st, 2012) the task of negotiation with central government was substantial. Ultimately the intractability of the existing settlement from government meant Ferguson succeeded only in re-routing a section of the route away from Bristol's Harbourside. This early interaction with government exposed the depth of challenge the mayor faced in both creating and securing his own agenda. Government money for capital investment beyond the City Deal came into the city via other avenues: £7 million arrived to support Bristol Green Capital following extensive lobbying of Chief Secretary to the Treasury Danny Alexander by Bristol West MP Stephen Williams. Other funding relating to the Bristol Arena project was secured by the Local Enterprise Partnership to purchase a derelict Royal Mail building (£5.4 million) and begin work on an Arena Island Bridge (£11 million) with the respective funds coming from the Department for Communities and Local Government and the Homes and Communities Agency. While the mayor did not have great success in securing government funding directly he did manage to secure funding and other commitments via commercial partners. Taking a hands on and direct approach drawn both from his background as a successful architect and entrepreneur Mayor Ferguson managed to utilise his formal status and the associated perception of that status to assert increased opportunities for investment and influence. With the assistance of then Assistant Mayor Councillor Mark Bradshaw, he negotiated with local bus companies gaining concessions on fares and routes. While it is hard to delineate the relative effect of leadership approach and the status of elected mayor, it is unlikely that council leaders would have been in a strong position to negotiate such concessions. The mayor also enjoyed success in securing an operator for the proposed Bristol Arena near Bristol Temple Meads. The mayor's zeal in leading the city as opposed to the council placed Bristol firmly on an international stage; for instance, launching the Bristol Declaration on Climate Change at COP21 opened up previously underdeveloped opportunities to secure funds through collaborative working.

While the mayor faced a large test to secure a coherent personal policy platform for Bristol he was also hampered by the shifting sands of the changing context of government options for further devolution. Being the sole rider of the first referendum wave that chose to adopt an elected mayor he faced a distinct challenge. He found himself on a restricted and lonely path, constrained by the pre-existing devolution settlement in the form of the City Deal and bound with local government partners each invested in that original deal. The capacity to negotiate a better deal for Bristol from the already Bristol centric settlement would prove too difficult. While scope to deliver greater powers and funds for the Bristol initially diminished, new avenues seemed to open in the light of alternative growth settlements and collaborative governance arrangements. The growth agenda, while remaining focused on functional economic geographies, shifted to alternate models of governance in the form of Combined Authorities. Greater Manchester, Sheffield, Liverpool, West Yorkshire and the North East moved quickly to put the case for bespoke devolution settlements following the Cities and Local Government Devolution Bill 2015, while Bristol seemed stuck with the cards it had played. Following a protracted internal debate Ferguson moved to broaden Bristol's options by submitting a new devolution bid with his existing West of England partners which stopped short of the governments originally preferred devo-mayor, while also entering into a collaborative agreement with Cardiff and Newport in the form of 'South Western Powerhouse', the Great Western Cities scheme.

Delivering democratic change and accelerating policy

While changing contextual and intergovernmental factors restricted the scope to make significant inroads in terms of transformative change, the position of elected mayor opened up local government in the City of Bristol in new ways. In terms of policy the agenda progressed as the mayor advanced existing policy innovations in terms of 20 mph zones, residents parking zones, and the launch of Bristol Energy, an alternative energy provider developed by the city council. European Green Capital helped the mayor to deliver significant environmental policy initiatives, in particular building Filwood Green Business Park in the south of the City, investment in renewables and community energy schemes, and the Warm Up Energy scene which co-funded through Green Deal subsidies targeted insulation and energy saving interventions to those suffering fuel poverty. These initiatives set in train by previous administrations were accelerated under George Ferguson, doing so with an assured mandate as an independent and an individual drive to get things done. The Bristol Arena plan for many also represented an important step forward in the cultural development of the city and its place as a viable competitor in the UK leisure and entertainment industry. To move forward this arena plan marked a significant advance, which again can be attributable to the personal leadership characteristics of the mayor to set and force the agenda coupled with the revenue opportunities emerging from his inherited City Deal.

Unsurprisingly evaluative discussion of the mayoral model centres on around arguments about democracy. The mayor's advisory cabinet, centralised model of decision making and fractious relationships with other elected representatives stand out strongly for critics of the mayoral model. Significant questions were asked about the roles of councillors as they looked to re-assert themselves in this new governance context. Interestingly, however, the mayor has advanced other democratic initiatives during his time in office in alternative ways through sidestepping elements of representative democracy in favour of novel methods of engagement with citizens. The city council and, even more so, the mayor are tangibly more evident and accessible (Hambleton and Sweeting, 2015: 21). The challenge of a significant restructuring of the council's leadership secretariat and a refurbishment and rationalisation of the majority of the council's municipal buildings to bring efficiency savings was successfully delivered. The mayor's approach to a more direct form of engagement also led to a series of other democratic innovations, including Mayor's Question Time town hall meetings across the city, on the radio and online, and an annual State of the City Address. The mayor maximised his use of the platform of elected mayor to position himself as an active and engaged mayor, taking the role out of the council house, and onto social media and the world stage.

The new opportunities for citizen engagement also represented a change from the norm; the depth of consultations particularly around the budget was notable in terms of accessibility. Attention and effort was drawn away from negotiation with councillors and channelled into a more direct discussion with citizens. The creation of an 'Ideas Lab' online crowdsourcing platform also represented a novel innovation even if its potential has yet to be fully realised. Consultative governance was widened further in 2013 with the introduction of five independently chaired Mayoral Commissions. Each commission sought to address key priorities for the city, defined as Education and Skills, Fairness, Homes, Sports, and a Women's Commission. The increased profile of the mayor and his conception of doing things differently have proved to be the catalyst to open up new forms of democratic engagement and a modernisation of consultative processes.

Conclusion

When the government pushed the agenda of directly elected mayors it alluded strongly to the idea that once a city went down the mayoral route, it was more likely to receive extra resources and additional powers. When Bristol was the only city to opt for the deal through a referendum it was set on a singular course and suddenly the rules of the game changed. This chapter has given an illustrative narrative account of how the role of the mayor was limited by history, context and structure. Furthermore, examples have shown how through a capacity to adapt his approach along with being consistent and assertive in the definition of his role and capabilities, Bristol's independent mayor has managed to deliver across a number of dimensions to overcome longstanding barriers to change.

Academic attention on the subject of elected mayors in England has often concentrated on the relative stickiness of the concept (Marsh, 2012) as it remains contested as to whether the role of directly elected mayor is a successful governance innovation to improve policymaking, democratic engagement and a solution to the complex issues and fiscal challenges of local government in England. The case of Bristol contributes to the evidence base to support the positive benefits of elected mayors while giving equal fodder for those who believe the idea should finally be lost. One element which should be appreciated in evaluating the case of Bristol is that as the mayor entered office it represented a single significant change which the institutional hardware, that is the rules and procedures of council, scrutiny and accountability processes are still adapting to. The waters clouded by a simplistic but definitive divide between a strongly independent mayor and a wounded series of political groups resulted in a clash of cultures where the institutional software; the shared practices and understandings of policymaking were also lost or corrupted. The mayor, while benefitting from the perception as someone who was taking hard decisions upfront, subsequently suffered as policy initiatives slowed or stalled distracting from perceptions of the role being able to deliver a new form of governing.

The mayor's choice of an advisory cabinet left lines of accountability unclear. Without formal delegated powers, assistant mayors were asked to be held to account on the basis of a policy platform other than their own and the resultant scrutiny process left councillors more often than not deferring to officers for information on the mayor's plans. The lack of pre-decision scrutiny was marked, even at formal cabinet meetings which were left as little more than a simple rubber stamping exercise. With the fiscal challenges becoming deeper with further reductions in the financial settlement from central government, the mayor was increasingly challenged to look beyond the individual and in order to use all the resources in his armoury, and maximise the lobbying of the council, needed to carry the councillor contingent with him. As advocated by the Institute for Government if the mayoral model is to work to its full potential under an independent mayor, they will need to 'proactively engage with councillors and make use of pre-decision scrutiny' and 'seriously consider the delegation of executive powers to individual cabinet members as a way of attracting talent to their cabinets and sending a signal they are willing to work with the rest of the council' (Institute for Government, 2011: 43).

Criticism of the mayoral model highlights the danger posed by a concentration of power in the hands of one individual. While in terms of the tried and tested mechanisms of representative democracy in Bristol things have remained static, the role of elected mayor has been utilised to significantly drive a more direct form of political interaction. The mayor is the epitome of 'place based leadership' (see Hambleton, Chapter Fourteen in this volume), taking leadership of the City of Bristol, as opposed to leading the council. George Ferguson significantly raised the profile of Bristol on a national and international stage by taking a distinct approach to 'identity leadership' (Verheul and Schapp, 2010), balancing both identity forming and connective aspects of leadership.

The power of a clear and direct mandate in tandem with a sense of individual autonomy derived from his status as an independent allowed George Ferguson to open the black box of elected mayors and unlock some of the promise of what the mayoral role can deliver. The role itself gave scope to innovate and a capacity to do things differently from the norm and, while constrained by circumstance in a number of areas, the mayor has been able to deliver a more direct and interactive form of citizen consultation, leveraged a deal with local bus companies and progressed plans for a significant capital investment in Bristol Arena. In playing to his own strengths, stressing his mandate, building on notions of direct democracy he successfully asserted his locally rooted legitimacy and used soft power to achieve his aims.

Clear democratic questions remain in relation to the representative role of councillors: what is their role in shaping policy? How can they influence or take credit without undermining the mayor? Are councillors left as mere mouthpieces, civil servants and reactive scrutineers? With an advisory cabinet where all roads lead to the mayor's door, who can they trust? Can an independent truly delegate to party political elected members and if not how can they expect to manage and provide adequate oversight to the associated workload? To counter the critique of a power shift upwards solutions could come in two forms, first through an offer of sustainable democratic solutions where democratic engagement is a regular occurrence not simply the chance every four years to deliver a coronation or the boot. By offering a devolution of power and responsibility down to ward level there is also a possibility to re-invigorate the role of local councillors. With a successful outward facing mayor there is plenty of room for councillors to deliver local place based leadership with an equal level of dynamism if assured of both the power and mandate.

Addendum: Marvin Rees, lessons learned and new prospects for mayoral governance in Bristol

Labour's Marvin Rees became Bristol's second directly elected mayor by a decisive margin of 68,750 votes against 39,377 for incumbent George Ferguson following elections on 5 May 2016 on a turnout of 44.87% of registered voters. The turnout was significantly up on the 27.92% of 2012 and came alongside the city's first all-up (all seats contested) elections which also delivered a Labour majority of seats on the council. Despite this dominance Rees continued the pattern of appointing a cross-party cabinet instigated by Ferguson but chose to increase the size of his cabinet to ten including himself. Of the ten members, over half are women and the other parties on the council are represented by one member (one Liberal Democrat, one Conservative and one from the Green Party). While increasing the number of portfolios and voices around the cabinet table, Rees like his predecessor chose to retain ultimate responsibility for all major policy decisions as opposed to delegating or sharing this with cabinet members. In his inaugural speech Rees alluded to a more holistic approach to city leadership as a 'collective endeavour' and laid out plans to set up a City Office to bring together the expertise and priorities of institutions and individuals and ensure that all 'major elements that make up civil society will not just be consulted, but empowered to lead' (Rees. 2016).

Rees's leadership model seems to borrow from Total Place and other partnership approaches, learning drawn from his time as Director of the Bristol Local Strategic Partnership and partnership roles in the National Health Service. Against an increasingly challenging financial climate, where continued cuts need to be made, alongside the responsibility to maintain statutory services, Rees is moving to bring partners and their budgets around the table in a move to increase the effectiveness of investment across local partners. In a recent interview Rees stressed he was striving for a 'whole public spending approach where the police, health, education and Job Centre Plus all work together in the area for wider social justice goals', highlighting that 'we can only really deliver on some of the "wicked problems" if we're coordinated and we agree what the shared priorities are.' (Angell, 2016: IV).

The choice of a party mayor as opposed to an independent also represents a shift away from the previous incumbent who often found himself hampered by the dynamics of a multi-party council without a cohesive collective behind him or his ideas. Rees with both a Labour majority on the council and a potential unbroken four years without elections has greater scope to deliver his policy platform. Yet Rees is confronted with the same challenges that stymied his predecessor including a thinning financial settlement from central government and the challenges of working across local authority boundaries. A new West of England devolution settlement is currently out for consultation between Bristol City, Bath and North East Somerset, and South Gloucestershire Councils (North Somerset initially chose to opt out of the deal). The proposed £1 billion devolution deal could deliver a West of England Combined Authority and potentially a directly elected West of England Mayor as well as further powers, many of which are highly relevant to addressing many of the challenges the City of Bristol faces over the next four years. The proposed Combined Authority will be given powers over transport including the ability to franchise bus services, implement Clean Air Zones and take responsibility for the Key Routes Network of roads, all of which could be tools to address Bristol's main transport challenges. In housing, the Combined Authority will be given stronger strategic planning powers including around compulsory purchasing, powers to set up development corporations to facilitate house building, and powers to determine cross-boundary infrastructure applications which so often in the past have been mired in parochial, logistical and governance complexity. Rees, like Ferguson, has inherited a devolution deal which is not his own, but one which offers more significant opportunities particularly around confronting two of Bristol's most intransigent issues: housing and transport.

For Marvin Rees the challenge is equal to that faced by George Ferguson but with an additional complexity and insecurity following Britain's vote to exit the European Union. However, by taking some of the approaches and lessons learned from the experiences of Bristol's first directly elected mayor alongside a more partnership based approach, Rees may also find that the strongest benefits of mayoral governance come not from the powers of the role but instead the leadership approach taken by the individual.

References

Angell, R. (2016) "It's enjoyable because it's meaningful' Being mayor is about bringing people together Marvin Rees tells Richard Angell', *Progress*, July 2016, p 4.

Barber, B. R. (2013) *If Mayors ruled the World: Dysfunctional Nations, Rising Cities*, New Haven: Yale University Press.

Bristol City Council (2012) 'Overview and Scrutiny in Mayoral Bristol', Report of the Inquiry Day, 14 September.

Bristol City Council (2013) Minutes of Full Council Meeting, CNL 23 June, https://www2.bristol.gov.uk/committee/2013/ta/ta000/0618_mins.pdf

Bristol City Council (2014) 'Stage 1 – Council Size: Submission to the Local Government Boundary Commission for England', 10 June, https://www.lgbce.org.uk/__data/assets/pdf_file/0018/22734/Bristol-Council-Size-Submission-v1-2.pdf

Bristol 1st (2012) Election Communication: 'George Ferguson for Mayor, YOUR Mayor not a PARTY Mayor', https://electionleaflets.org/leaflets/7320/images

Bristol Post (2012) 'Labour in turmoil over decision on mayor's cabinet', 27 November, www.bristolpost.co.uk/Labour-turmoil-decision-mayor-s-cabinet/story-17433731-detail/story.html

Bristol Post (2013) 'Mayor admits he kicked hornets' nest with RPZs', 28 June, www.bristolpost.co.uk/Mayor-admits-kicked-hornets-nest-RPZs/story-19417706-detail/story.html

Bristol Post (2014) 'Three biggest political parties on Bristol City Council claim they are being gagged from talking about arena', 14 November, http://www.bristolpost.co.uk/Cross-party-complaint-arena-report-gagging-order/story-24531970-detail/story.html

Brown, A. (2014) *The Myth of the Strong Leader*, London: Bodley Head.

Cabinet Office (2011) *Unlocking Growth in Cities*, December, p iv.

Centre for Public Scrutiny (CfPS) (2015) 'External Review of Overview and Scrutiny in Bristol', https://democracy.bristol.gov.uk/Data/Overview%20&%20Scrutiny%20Management%20Board/201502261800/Agenda/0226_8.pdf

Copus, C. (2008) 'English Councillors and Mayoral Governance: Developing a New Dynamic for Political Accountability', *The Political Quarterly*, 79(4), 590–604.

Fenwick, J. and Elcock, H. (2014) 'Elected Mayors: Leading Locally?', *Local Government Studies*, 40(4), 581–99.

Ferguson, G. (2012) 'Acceptance Speech: First Elected Mayor of Bristol', Speech at the University of the West of England, Bristol, 16 November.

Guardian (2013) 'Bristol mayor puts party politics aside in pursuit of city revamp', 21 January, www.theguardian.com/uk/2013/jan/21/bristol-mayor-george-ferguson

Hambleton, R. and Sweeting, D. (2015) 'The Impacts of Mayoral Governance in Bristol', The Bristol Civic Leadership Project, University of Bristol and University of the West of England, September, https://bristolcivicleadership.files.wordpress.com/2013/03/impacts-of-mayoral-governance-in-bristol-web-version.pdf

Institute for Government (2011) *Making the Most of Mayors: Lessons learnt from the existing mayoral local authorities*, London: Institute for Government

Kenny, M. and Lodge, G. (2008) 'Mayors rule', *Public Policy Research*, 15(1), 12–21.

Lowndes, V. and Leach, S. (2004) 'Understanding local political leadership: constitutions, contexts and capabilities', *Local Government Studies*, 30(4), 557–75.

Marsh, A. (2012) 'Debate: Is it time to put the dream of elected mayors to bed?', *Policy & Politics*, 40(4), 607–11.

Rees, M. (2016) Swearing-in speech at M-Shed, Bristol, 9 May.

Skelcher, C., Mathur, N. and Smith, M. (2005) 'The public governance of collaborative spaces: Discourse, design and democracy', *Public Administration*, 83(3), 573–96.

Stoker, G. (2004) 'How are mayors measuring up?', Preliminary findings – ELG Evaluation team UK, Office of the Deputy Prime Minister, London.

Verheul, J and Schapp, L. (2010) 'Strong Leaders? The Challenges and Pitfalls in Mayoral Leadership', *Public Administration*, 80(2), 439–54.

FOUR

Do mayors make a difference?
In their own words...

*Howard Elcock, Northumbria University,
Newcastle upon Tyne, UK*

Introduction

This study is based on interviews with 12 elected mayors in eight communities, conducted between 2003 and 2014. The communities were all in the North East of England or the Midlands. They ranged from small towns to a major city. In one town we were able to interview three successive holders of the office. In another case we interviewed two mayors. We were unable to interview other actors in most of the communities involved, carry out observations of the activities of the mayors or assess objectively the impact of their periods in office. However, most mayoral offices have survived: only two of our selected mayoralties were subsequently abolished by referendums. A third survived a referendum proposing abolition of the office. The office survived but the incumbent mayor, an independent, lost the subsequent election to a Labour candidate. All this suggests that the office, once established, has usually won and retained public support, although specific incumbents have lost office.

The advantage of research focused on a series of semi-structured interviews over more extensive single case studies of individual mayors and their communities is that it has enabled us to identify the wide range of mayoral responses to the various issues that confront them (see also Copus, 2006). They included the management of their local authorities, including their relationships with the council and its party groups, their Chief Executive Officers and other senior staff. It also identifies the varying ways in which mayors deal with their relations with outside bodies and other authorities including the local business community and a wide range of other interest and lobby groups, as well as well as with the wider citizenry. The main analysis here, to discuss whether or not elected mayors think they have made a difference within their governmental milieu, will be conducted using the three leadership roles identified in the political leadership matrix (Elcock and Fenwick, 2012). The government role includes leading and managing the local authority of which they are the elected heads; their governance roles – the way they have developed their relations with other governments and organisations, including business, trades unions, the NHS and others, as well as with other local authorities and the central government. Last come their allegiance roles: their approach to maintaining their support in their councils, parties and the public together with their campaigning to secure re-election.

Their professional backgrounds varied widely. One had formerly been a high profile police officer; another had been an accountant, mostly in local government and a third had previously been a head teacher in a deprived area of her borough. Another mayor had previously been a teacher in the town he represented. Several but not all had previously served as councillors. A more unusual background was the mayor who had been the town football team's mascot and had had no previous political experience. His election was unexpected and he admitted that "I upset the apple cart!" By contrast, another mayor had long been a full time politician, having previously served as his council's leader before becoming one of the city's MPs. Most mayors saw their previous careers as having some but not a crucial relevance to their roles as mayor. All of them were in one way or another determined to make a difference and felt that they had indeed done so.

Creating mayors

The circumstances in which mayors were adopted varied widely but often because of a belief that they would make a difference or address widely recognised problems of local government. Certainly the leading politicians of both main parties that have advocated elected mayors, notably Michael Heseltine and Tony Blair, expected that elected executive mayors would make a difference (Fenwick and Elcock, 2014). The interviews indicated three motivations for creating an elected mayor, although these are not exclusive. Anna Randle argued that the early mayoral systems had been established 'in places where there had been a demonstrable lack of community leadership and ambition, a long history of social and economic decline and dissatisfaction with the ability of the previous political administration to articulate a way out of these circumstances' (n.d.:24). Our interviews largely confirmed her findings.

First, some mayors were created as a result of a crisis in the affairs of the council. In one case several leading councillors were jailed for corruption, creating a leadership vacuum that resulted in the rise of a newly elected councillor to the office of elected mayor within three years. He declared that "I valued the public's view that things should be done differently ... Of course the people wanted the council run differently and they opted for the mayor as a part of that". However, "it took a long time for the new system to become embedded". He was a Labour member who survived for two terms but was defeated at his third mayoral election by a minor party candidate who was in his turn defeated by a female Labour nominee. The independent mayor survived for two terms and his office survived an attempt to abolish it by referendum but he too was then defeated. The third mayor also had to cope with a crisis in the council's Children's Services Department which was severely criticised by inspectors after a public scandal. Nevertheless, this mayor managed to convince the Secretary of State to allow the council to retain local control over the service because "we managed to persuade him to let us do it because we know more than they do about our children here".

Second, mayors were created from public and political disillusion with the way the council was being run and a sense that change was needed. Dissatisfaction was frequently reflected in the removal of long established single party regimes in mayoral and council elections following the creation of the mayoral office. In one case a longstanding Labour council that had fallen foul of the central government, including being 'rate-capped' – a process by which the government limits the amount of local tax the council can levy, introduced a mayoral system. The first incumbent, a Conservative, was forced to resign soon after being elected because he was accused of personal misconduct. He was replaced by a female Conservative. Since then the office has oscillated between the Conservative and Labour parties. The Conservative interviewee explained that "support for the elected mayor option for the borough was *the only way to change things*. It has taken the mayoral system to get the council back on track" (interviewee's emphasis). She also claimed that citizens were "turning to the mayor because they were not being heard by the councillors". She claimed that she had made "big differences from before", including quicker decision making and better inter-departmental coordination. Svara and Watson (2010) report similarly that, in the United States, cities that face problems such as urban decline or managerial misconduct tend to adopt the mayor council form.

Third, some mayoral systems were established through the impact of a powerful local personality who wished to see the office adopted and occupy it him or herself. In one case, in a large city a council leader who had been elected to the House of Commons chose to resign and campaign both for the adoption of an elected mayor and then secure election as that city's elected mayor. At interview he declared that by contrast with the House of Commons "It's a real job being mayor: you can make things happen!" In the second case, a locally prominent former police officer campaigned for the mayoral office as an independent candidate and won. This mayor saw his office as being "in contrast to the old system", and wanted to provide the prerequisites for business success and give political direction and leadership because "there had been no such direction of leadership under the old system".

In all these three sets of circumstances mayors were clearly expected to make a difference. Their offices had been created and they had been elected to govern their communities in ways different from an unsatisfactory past. The following sections set out their views on what they have achieved in doing this. There is a last preliminary point to make. Mayors commonly stressed their local origins and careers in business, teaching and other professions. Several firmly declared that they had been born and bred in the communities they govern. Such emphasis on local roots is a finding frequently found abroad (see Elcock, 2009): local roots are important everywhere. The main mayoral roles can now be discussed in turn.

Government

Here we discuss the impact of elected mayors on the local authorities they have been elected to lead. Most mayors claimed to have achieved more or less radical changes to the government and management of their councils: a frequent claim was that they had achieved speedier decision making. Most mayors claimed that decisions were considerably quicker than they had been under the former committee system. One argued that

> 'Only a few decisions go to council – three or four strategic plans and the budget. The rest come via the cabinet, which meets more frequently [than the former committees], so decisions are taken more quickly but the need for consultation delays decisions.'

An independent mayor claimed that "Local decision-making is now much quicker – we took away the old slow local government". Some mayors also claimed to have made the system more open, for example the mayor who declared that "the new [system] is more open and transparent. All cabinet and council meetings are open to the public and they can ask questions". Two respondents stressed that they held cabinet meetings in different parts of their boroughs: one declaring that "I take the cabinet with me, we don't hide behind four walls or in an ivory tower". Many mayors declared that getting out and about, meeting local communities and their area or neighbourhood committees or holding public meetings were vital aspects of their duties.

Another frequent issue was whether elected mayors had managed to improve local government's chronic problem of poor inter-departmental coordination. Here the evidence was more mixed. Many mayors claimed that coordination had improved under their leadership but one said,

> 'coordination is better but it's still pretty poor! There is too much of a departmental culture. They work as separate companies and they are not joined up. This is very challenging – I have to bang on the table all the time!'

One of his successors argued that "services need to dovetail, not overlap". However, another mayor said that "everyone works well together here – there is no problem with coordination". A third claimed that coordination is better: "the role is clearly defined. I engage across [departmental] relationships rather than working in silos – work across the officers – counteract the silo mentality". Claims to have improved coordination were common but several admitted to having problems in overcoming poor cross-departmental relations: the mayor who declared that "officers and councillors often work in silos and fail to represent the people" expressed a common and enduring problem. One mayor claimed that the issue was wider: "joined up integration is more important than internal coordination – work with Department of Work and Pensions, need to coordinate the whole public sector". Several mayors saw the creation of 'one stop shops' – where a range of services and advice are made available to the public at a single, convenient location – as important.

Relations between mayors and their councils and the party groups within them were highly variable. Several mayors reported problems with getting councillors to accept that their roles had changed: They ranged from the mayor who was also leader of his party group on the council, with a majority of 52 of 54 members – he had no problems: "I lead it – there is no longer a separate Leader of the Group" – to the independents, all of whom had difficulties with their councils, including having their budgets rejected. One mayor found getting councillors to accept that their roles had changed was difficult because:

> 'many members saw [the mayoral system] as a way to replace the old system by making the new system as like the old as possible but the elected mayor focuses attention on one individual … Some members understand it but others are not running as quickly as they should to catch up with it.'

An independent mayor – the former football mascot – said that "the biggest challenge has been to prove that I take the job seriously, that I am not a joke". The continuing challenge for him was to work with the various groups on the hung council: "All the parties have gone against me at one time or another. I need to work with the parties and the councillors." His office has now been abolished by referendum. A Labour mayor had no problems with her own party group but found that "the Conservatives are difficult because they don't want us to succeed, the Liberal Democrats are better".

An important aspect of relations with councils and their party groups was the appointment of the mayoral cabinet or executive. Some mayors appointed single party cabinets but others tried appointing cabinets consisting of members of most or all the parties represented on the council. However, these arrangements were not always successful. Appointing leading members of party groups should help to ease approval of mayoral decisions and policies by councillors where the mayor's party has a small or no majority on the council. An independent mayor who had appointed a cross party cabinet said that

> 'the mixed cabinet is useful. I try not to make enemies of the parties … A hung council makes it easier because if there was one party in control and if they were against me, it would be more difficult'.

Another independent mayor advertised his executive positions among councillors and got members who were not members of the former leadership groups to apply: he offered executive jobs with conditions to those who were successful. "They all talk like managers now."

Elected mayors' relations with their Chief Executive Officer (CEO) were very varied. One declared his intention to abolish the post before he gained office and promptly deleted the CEO post and made the incumbent redundant once he was elected, demonstrating his firm intention to become the CEO himself. Some other mayors had dismissed one or more CEOs or downgraded the office to ensure that the mayor had control over politics and policy. One declared that "The mayor has to prevail over the CEO – politicians must win every time!" His successor claimed to have had "four Chief Executives to far. The first was likeable but useless, was bullied by the chief officers … The second was a complete disaster." This officer was followed by an appointee (Joan) nominated by the Local Government Association to advise the council for three months. Then, "the Government imposed a CEO who lasted 18 months – he was a scribe, a typical civil servant. No ideas, then Joan came back … she is good and we get on well". Another respondent declared that the buck stops with her, in particular "*policy* stops with me". By contrast, a female mayor stated that "I would NOT want to get rid of the CEO. My relations with him are really good. I asked him to look at [the borough] and then work to improve it". Others maintained good relations with their CEOs and relied on them heavily. They saw the CEO as a valuable ally and colleague: good relationships are ultimately important. One mayor said that on Friday afternoons he would drop in to wish his CEO a good weekend but would leave an hour and a half later. An independent mayor lost his CEO to another council after a year which caused him concern: "He was my right hand man, when he went, I felt on my own" but he established "an excellent relationship with the new guy".

Relations with chief officers were again variable but always important. Most mayors maintained management teams, which were important in maintaining coordination of services. Some mayors attached importance to having all the chief officers in the same building; one declared that because of this "We deal with issues of concern to the public. We don't need regular formal meetings", while others maintained regular management team meetings. By contrast, an independent mayor told us that "I meet the CEO three times a week, the Chief Finance Officer twice a week during budget preparations. I meet the service directors every Monday".

Mayors' roles in council budget, strategies and policies raise the issue of their relations with the council because the budget and the council's strategies require approval by the full council: one mayor acknowledged that only the budget and three of four other strategic documents need to go to the full council. The council's agreement is usually achieved easily when the mayor and the council majority are from the same party, although one Labour mayor reported tension with his Labour group. Otherwise mayors, especially independents, ran into difficulties in getting their strategies and budgets approved. One independent had had his budget rejected at least twice. An independent mayor "prepared my own budget but this was rejected almost unanimously by the council. This was a challenge!" The early mayoral elections produced a significant number of independent mayors but many of them have since been displaced by party nominees (see Game, 2003), hence an initial weakening of the party system was gradually replaced by its renewed strengthening.

Effective overview and scrutiny was important for mayors, who generally acknowledged the importance of developing and maintaining effective scrutiny of themselves and the authority's other office holders. They stressed the importance of maintaining their accountability to citizens and their elected representatives through overview and scrutiny and in other ways, thus confirming Anna Randle's early finding that scrutiny 'has grown to play an increasing role in mayoral councils, as arguably it should do where there is a very powerful executive' (n.d.: 19). One respondent declared that "good scrutiny equals good governance" but he felt that in his authority the scrutiny councillors had been "not valued and not resourced and not independent". They were also too reactive; "We have to get them away from that". Another mayor complained that his scrutiny committee "has not found what it should be doing – it is not particularly proactive or challenging". Some mayors had sought actively to develop the role of overview and scrutiny committees, especially by encouraging them to take a proactive role in developing council policies rather than just reacting to the mayor's or the cabinet's proposals. One mayor has got them to develop "task and finish" groups to consider three or four specific policy areas.

Thus, mayors especially wanted scrutiny committees to take a more proactive role in proposing and influencing policies, rather than only examining them in retrospect or when something went seriously wrong. One mayor said that "I am trying to get Scrutiny to understand policy development. I ask for a view about what we should do". Some mayors were concerned about the effectiveness of overview and scrutiny arrangements and felt that councillors were not fully developing them. One was concerned about partisan influences on scrutiny committees: "Scrutiny chairs are opposition members – they try to use it politically, which is a source of weakness."

For several respondents developing the role of councillors as community champions was important, especially for those who were not given seats on the cabinet or executive. However, some mayors found getting councillors to accept their new and different roles difficult: "some members understand it but others are not running as quickly as they should to catch up with it ... Many lament the passing of the old structure". However, many studies of councillors have demonstrated that the majority of them are not primarily interested in policy but are content to concentrate on representing their wards, dealing with the constituents' needs and problems and playing their role in their local communities (see Elcock, 1994, Chapter 3).

Governance

Elected mayors generally attached great importance to their governance roles, developing networks of contacts with business communities, the voluntary sector, other public authorities and central government, although the nature of these relationships varied considerably. One mayor had given priority to addressing the governmental issues in his own authority before concentrating on developing external networks but most mayors had begun developing their networks as soon as they gained office. Most saw themselves as network managers. Several mayors had set up liaison groups or were having regular meetings with their local Chambers of Commerce, other business communities or individual firms, as well as with trades unions, the voluntary sector and many others. Two mayors stressed the importance of the churches in their communities.

Mayors commonly approached their relations with outside organisations in two ways. One was to set up a formal organisation involving members from other public services, businesses and others: a "team", advisory committee or regular meetings. One mayor said of the business community and the voluntary sector that "I meet them around this table or elsewhere". Another held regular business breakfasts. Most mayors also engaged in informal discussion; one said casually that "the Bishop dropped in yesterday!" Relations with the business community were generally important to mayors, especially in economically depressed communities where regeneration was a priority task. One respondent told us that she "met the Chamber of Commerce monthly". Another said that "the key priority is regeneration of the Borough". An emphasis on partnerships with the business community and other organisations was a common priority. One declared that "the mayor leads on external relations, on borough wide, sub-regional, regional and national matters. The mayor leads – that is my raison d'être – the ambassadorial role, whatever!" Relations with outside organisations were important for all mayors. Their roles on local bodies such as Local Strategic Partnerships (LSPs) varied but they all took some part in them. One was vice chairman of his LSP but he was unusual in adopting such a formal role.

Increased individual visibility was generally claimed by mayors who felt that they were more visible than traditional leaders of the council, a view confirmed by Anna Randle (n.d.: 28), who found that elected mayors achieved 57% name recognition in their communities whereas council leaders scored only 25%. Sometimes there was almost too much recognition. One mayor could not walk 100 yards down the street without someone recognising him. Face recognition was an important aspect of their personal roles. One mayor declared that "I can't walk for ten minutes without getting stopped!" Another mayor stressed the importance of dealing with citizens who telephoned him or wrote to him: "the public needs actually to see that getting involved does lead to a change in their circumstances and has a real impact on their lives".

Several mayors adopted specific community projects. One initiated cleaning up areas within the borough: his "Operation Clean Streets" where council departments and other agencies "pool resources to go into a specific area, clean the street, repair street furniture, remove graffiti and fly-tips … and go to schools, talk to dog wardens". Others concentrated on developing the best possible services especially in austere times, or creating personal projects. One mayor published a series of policy Green and White Papers intended to promote public discussion of ways of meeting the community's needs. As a result, "the public is engaged hugely". Another respondent said that he had made 100 promises during his election campaign and 98 of them had either been achieved or were being worked on.

Relations with other governments were important. There was some chafing with the central government; one mayor referred to "Pickles's diktats", while another described her relations with the central government as "businesslike". Relations with other local authorities were conducted through collaborative and more formal meetings. Meetings with other local representatives, including MPs and MEPs, were generally frequent and useful. Relations with the National Health Service and local utilities were also important and usually good. Coordination in the delivery of services was essential for many mayors. Several stressed the importance of regional arrangements during the Labour government's regional reforms and after. One respondent talked enthusiastically about the City Region arrangements in her locality: when asked about working with other councils she declared "very much so, in the … City Region. We work with [other councils in the former metropolitan county] and further afield". She clearly felt the need for a regional or sub-regional tier of governance.

Contact with citizens and local communities were crucially important for mayors. Many respondents stressed the usefulness of area or neighbourhood committees and parish or town councils where they exist. Meetings with citizens and communities were an essential part of mayoral and cabinet life: at least two mayors held their cabinet meetings in different locations within their boroughs. Another common initiative was the establishment of 'one stop shops' that made a range of local services available to local residents close to their homes. One mayor had published a "Making a difference to your neighbourhood" White Paper: each neighbourhood would have a Neighbourhood Action Plan and "one stop shops, where residents can go and have everything dealt with". Another mayor stressed that she visited all 21 wards in her authority area at least once a year and had also sought to create neighbourhood committees and one stop shops.

Allegiance

Keeping election promises and delivering manifesto programmes are generally regarded as very important. One mayor had made 100 pledges during his election campaign and within two years of election he claimed that the authority had implemented or was working on 98 of them. This respondent also declared that his campaign for re-election had begun on his first day in office.

Views on whether they should be party politicians or be above politics varied, from determined political partisans to those who tried to develop and maintain a cross-party consensus. Views about the value of party groups varied considerably. Some mayors were wary of them and shared Copus's (2004) doubts about their value because they make decisions behind closed doors but others followed the more benign view taken by the Widdicombe Committee (1986) that they ensure clear, predictable decision making. In terms of partisanship, views varied but there was a widespread sense that the mayor represents the wider community, not just his or her own party. One mayor declared firmly that "I am a Labour mayor so I'm not above politics. I believe in Socialist policies but I'm here for the whole community". Another Labour incumbent said

> 'I came up with and am loyal to my party but I have never been tribal. It is not difficult to be loyal to the party and work with respect and cooperation with others. Politics is not the most important aspect of this job.'

A third saw his role as "leading – and telling my own party what I plan to do", so having the scope to act independently of his party. These mayors thus saw themselves as promoting their party's views but also recognised that they had a responsibility to the wider local community to represent their views and fight for their interests and that they have their individual right and power to do so.

This raises the wider issue of how far the introduction of elected mayors has weakened or strengthened the hold of the political parties on local authorities. The election of a surprisingly large number of independent candidates in the first round of mayoral elections indicated that the national parties' hold on local councils might be weakening but several of the independents have been replaced by partisan candidates, thus strengthening the parties' control over council policies, priorities and services. However, the mayor is to a large extent independent of the council by virtue of his or her election and can therefore develop his or her own policies, as well as making his or her own decisions on individual cases or specific choices. Elected mayors also have extensive powers and discretion delegated to them by the relevant legislation. Hence they are by no means wholly beholden to their party groups, unlike council leaders elected and subject to re-election by councillors, although four year terms of office are becoming common, which gives leaders more security of tenure and therefore more scope for independent action but still less so than elected mayors.

One respondent declared that "the elected mayor focuses attention on the individual". Another, a Liberal Democrat, said that he had good relations with his party's council group: "they are never unhappy with me but it might get tenser – I have to be pragmatic". Mayors will usually wish to work with their party groups but one Labour respondent with a Labour council reported difficulties in doing so, mainly because councillors were reluctant to accept that their roles had been changed by the introduction of the mayoral system: "some people create uncertainty and make mischief, in that change has come about because of the mayor". However, this problem seemed to have resolved itself by the time the second Labour mayor was elected. Generally, mayors work more or less effectively with party groups but they have asserted their individual rights and responsibilities to make decisions on behalf of their communities.

By contrast, an independent mayor saw his role as "speaking about and for the town, not for himself". He also did not see himself as a politician, although he did see himself as providing political direction that was not in evidence before his election. Another independent declared rather bluntly that "I'm anti-party. Party politics should not have a big role in local politics any more". However, he has not only lost office but the office itself has been abolished by referendum. Some mayors had dealt with partisan politics by creating cross party cabinets but one mayor who had done this said that "we still struggle with the political groups, especially Labour ... Councillors should represent their wards, not their party, raise local issues, represent local people rather than local political groups". Generally maintaining support in the council may be done through a friendly party group but independents need to build relations with councillors and their groups in order to secure support for their policies: the independent mayor cited earlier in this paragraph had had his budget defeated in his council several times. A mayor from a minor party firmly declared that "party politics plays no role in this job".

Contact with individual citizens was generally recognised as important even if, as one respondent declared, it is the "micro" aspect of the job. One respondent declared that "I am the Good Samaritan – I deal with people's problems!" Another thought it was important to stress that mayors achieved this in a wide variety of ways, from making sure that they got "out and about regularly" to having regular meetings with neighbourhood committees, parish and town councils, as well as having extensive informal contacts with the citizenry. Many mayors also thought it was essential to maintain effective administration and services in order to retain their credibility and satisfy their electors: "I get things done", one declared. Sometimes mayors needed to address possible threats to their tenure or the office itself.

Media relations were a considerable preoccupation for mayors and varied considerably. One wrote a weekly column for his local newspaper and another said that he had established a link with his local fortnightly paper. Many respondents made use of their local and regional radio stations but television appearances were less frequent. Views of the importance of the media varied: one respondent said that "I'm not a great believer in the media: you don't achieve a lot that way. I prefer to get things done". She sends out a monthly round-up setting out the authority's recent achievements. A recent edition included setting up an energy supplier switching scheme and the regeneration of a local seaside resort that had fallen on hard times. Overall, "I'm sure you will agree that this represents good progress in our first year. It will be essential, however, to focus on the continued delivery of our priorities in our second year". Some mayors stressed their use of new social media as a means of increasing their contact with the public. One mayor who highlighted this also stressed the importance of holding public meetings: "I hold 5–6 surgeries a month ... Village tours in the summer – announce by leaflet, 300 people may turn up".

When asked whether they would stand for re-election and how they would prepare for it, several mayors declared that they started campaigning for re-election on day one of their terms of office: one declaring that "I started this the day I got elected". They attached importance to ensuring that their manifesto commitments would be carried out. However, one mayor, who was only just completing her first year in office, declared that it was too early for her to make such a decision: "I get things done. People need to see results – get people on board, get things done so I haven't thought about that!". Running an effective local government was her priority and if she was successful her re-election would surely follow.

Conclusion

Mayors make a difference, at least in their own estimation, and all our respondents claimed to have done so, in terms of both the internal government of their authorities and the governance role of network management. The extent of this difference varies because of differences in how they came to office and what they hope and try to achieve. There is no evidence so far of the Lord Acton problem of power tending to corrupt. In this context, several respondents stressed the importance of effective scrutiny and one specifically mentioned the Audit Commission as an essential auditor of his actions and behaviour but the Commission has now been abolished.

There is much to be said about the elusive concept of leadership, to which our respondents had a wide range of attitudes and approaches. Here judgements must be made about their formal and informal power and influence, as well as their personal attributes. In terms of their formal powers, many mayors stressed the wide extent of the powers vested in their offices by the legislation establishing them, including their individual responsibility for determining the council's policies. One mayor emphasised his role as the community leader. Another asserted that "I have the power to be directive – much more so than I had as (council) leader because of the overall responsibility I have". Objective assessment of mayors' impact on their communities is beyond the scope of this chapter and of the research methods applied to develop it. This is a suggestion for further research but it may be that the only way to assess this will be to compare a series of detailed case studies of elected mayors in particular communities.

Another common assertion was related to the governance role, particularly that elected mayors constitute a highly visible source of local leadership which they saw as resulting from the nature of the mayoral office. Their methods of doing this range from formal meetings with business and other leaders, either in forums set up by themselves or using existing institutions such as LSPs, to using informal personal contacts, like the mayor who had received a casual call from the local bishop the day before.

Several mayors were determined to be judged by their achievements, others by their personal efforts. Many mayors stressed their local origins as an important reason for their success: their claim to be born and bred in their community was a vital aspect of their support. One declared it important for people to see that he is "still the same bloke". Generally, mayors regarded their visibility positively. All of them certainly believed that they had made a difference. Some mayors set out to be as transformative leaders who set about radically changing the personnel and management structures of their councils, while others adopted a more incremental approach. This difference applied especially to their relations with the council's Chief Executive Officer: the more radical mayors dismissed their CEOs or clipped their wings, while others developed cordial relations with them. All saw themselves as highly visible leaders that other local actors could identify, access and work with easily.

References

Copus, C. (2004) *Party Politics in Local Government*, Manchester: Manchester University Press.

Copus, C. (2006) *Leading the Localities: Executive Mayors in English Local Governance*, Manchester: Manchester University Press.

Elcock, H. (1994) *Local Government: Policy and Management in Local Authorities* (3rd edn), Oxford: Routledge.

Elcock, H. (2009) 'Elected Mayors: Lesson dewing from four countries', *Public Administration*, 86(3), 795–811.

Elcock, H. and Fenwick, J. (2012) 'The political leadership matrix: a tool for analysis', *Public Money and Management*, 32(2), 67–94.

Fenwick, J. and Elcock, H. (2014) 'Elected Mayors: Leading Locally?', *Local Government Studies*, 40(4), 581–99.

Game, C. (2003) 'Elected mayors: more distraction than attraction?', *Public Policy & Administration*, 18(1), 13–28.

Randle, A. (n.d.) 'Mayors mid term: lessons from the first eighteen months of directly elected mayors', New Local Government Network.

Svara, J. H. and Watson, D. J. (eds) (2010) *More than Mayor or Manager*, Washington DC: Georgetown University Press.

Widdicombe Committee (1986) *The Conduct of Local Authority Business*, Cmnd 9797, London: HMSO.

FIVE

Directly elected mayors: necessary but not sufficient to transform places? The case of Liverpool

Nicola Headlam and Paul Hepburn,
University of Liverpool, UK

Introduction

Interest in mayoral models as key to the many challenges of subnational governance and as a way around 'traditional' local government has reached a high water mark with the institutionalising of the 'northern powerhouse' policy within the machinery of government in the 2015 Queen's Speech. Therein a metropolitan mayor model is presented to local government by the Conservative government as a condition for investment. It is fair to say, however, that the enthusiasm for mayoral models is far from an 'evidence-based' policy; data on the effect of such changes is empirically equivocal, patchy and partial.

Mayoral authorities exist in 17 single local authorities in England. The combined authority 'metro mayor' for Greater Manchester will be the first UK mayor, outside London, to cover multiple boroughs. The Mayor of London sits atop a whole assembly structure in the Greater London Authority and the extant London boroughs in an uneasy distribution of power. This chapter explores the experience of the adjacent city region to Greater Manchester, Liverpool City Region (LCR), which although sharing space within the 'northern powerhouse' has a different governance story to tell. Research evidence offers little to demonstrate the vaunted connection between positive economic outcomes and strong modes of executive leadership. The aim of this chapter is to address this lack of empirical clarity through the lens of a case study on the directly elected mayor for the city of Liverpool. However, the key role of a figurehead in embodying a credible narrative around a place may provide the basis for changing received wisdom about that place with a concomitant impact on investor confidence, from both private and public sectors. We argue that getting this story straight provides the foundation for transforming a place, and yet that this narrative is wider and broader than simply can be framed by and around a directly elected mayor.

Presenting the case of Liverpool, our argument is based on a study of the perceptions of the shift from a leader and cabinet model to a directly elected mayor model in 2013. We argue that the potentially radical potential of the introduction of the mayoral model was engulfed by the conjunction of this change with an aggressive austerity agenda that has undermined the scope of the local authority to operate effectively in the city of Liverpool. We survey the possibilities for co-working across the boroughs of Merseyside and argue that the development of political cohesion (within whatever leadership arrangements are appropriate) is the biggest challenge for an often fractious local political elite.

Notwithstanding this, the Conservative government is committed to the policy of directly elected mayors for the UK's urban centres. It is resolute in its insistence that mayors are a 'good thing' and that combined authorities for city regions must adopt a directly elected 'metro mayor' as part of their governance structures if they want to receive devolved powers and responsibilities.

> The case for mayors is founded on their having the potential to make a greater contribution to achieving successful economic, social and environmental outcomes in their cities. This is particularly important for our larger cities that should be key drivers of economic growth in this country. The Government believes that strong leadership of these cities by executive mayors can also benefit local citizens by improving the clarity of municipal decision-making, boosting democratic engagement and enhancing the prestige of their city. (DCLG, 2011: 1)

These expected outcomes reflect what can be viewed as a shift in thinking about urban problems (see, for example, Buck et al, 2005). Put simply, this perspective sees cities as pivotal to wider societal success and for cities to thrive they require new forms of urban governance to drive a sustainable economic competitiveness, achieve social cohesion and a more engaged citizenry.

Democratising devolution

In expecting mayors to improve local democratic engagement, the UK government is tapping into a well of concern about the contemporary legitimacy of the political establishment generally illustrated by falling levels of electoral turnout and growing levels of civic disenchantment within liberal democracies. Castells (1997) saw this as a crisis of democracy, others as a legitimacy crisis (Borraz and John, 2004). However, as Borraz and John point out, while electoral turnout is generally falling to varying degrees in most European countries – and has been falling in the USA since the 1950s – it is falling at all levels of government and it seems 'reformers are looking towards local institutional reforms for appropriate answers' (Borraz and John, 2004: 115). In such circumstances directly elected mayors are expected to animate local democracy by reconnecting voters with politicians and providing 'a clearer connection to the electorate and a persistent focus on building and developing a story of place' (Gash and Sims, 2012: 11).

The shift towards this new style of leadership has also coincided with a move towards local governance which may be defined as 'a flexible pattern of public decision-making based upon loose networks of individuals in key public and para-public and private bodies at various territorial levels' (Borraz and John, 2004: 112). This situates public policy decision making and service delivery in a complex pattern of networks where the powers of locally elected officials are often constrained by higher tiers of government. Here mayors are expected to act as a focal point in the network, setting goals and coordinating decision making and service delivery. It is context that brings into sharp relief the style of leadership and the question of what powers a mayor should wield.

Higher tiers of government have been created by the process of globalisation, which is also considered to frame the momentum and policy development for the new urban leadership. Harding and Le Gales (1998) argued that cities are granted a particularly influential role by the politics of globalisation. In hollowing out the powers of the nation state, so the argument goes, powers and responsibilities are pushed up to supranational bodies while at the same time passed below to subnational governance bodies. As such, cities and their mayors 'have acted less as administrative arms of a centralised states ... and more as independent political actors. They can engage in aggressive place-making and competition for investment' (Judd, 2000: 959). Similarly, within the European Union institutional framework mayors have emerged as significant political players beyond the immediate confines of their cities (McNeill, 2001).

However, the resilience of the nation state, the influence of national governments and the specificities of local politics and economies in shaping the contours of local economic development should not be understated. Different political constitutions and the particular role of central government is one reason given (Harding, 1997) why, for example, the tenets of local economic development from US urban political economy literature cannot be imported wholesale into the European context. While notions of 'urban regime' (Stone, 1989) and 'growth-machine' (Logan, 1976) might explain local economic outcomes in the US, it is the decisive role of national government in central–local government relations and the absence of a 'rentier class' of local land developers that make them a weaker template for explaining urban outcomes in Europe. Nonetheless, urban areas outside the US are becoming more outward facing. Increasingly local governance is often characterised by a 'political entrepreneur' style which focuses on context – 'local leadership' and 'intergovernmental' effects – in order to mobilise and attract resources, generate new policies or establish cooperative networks.

Such imperatives were recognised by enduring political entrepreneur Michael Heseltine, who as UK Secretary of State for the Environment called for a mayor for Liverpool as early as 1991, even though directly elected mayors were only introduced in the UK by the Local Government Act 2000. At that time, they could only be created following a referendum in favour in the relevant local authority. In 2008–09, while in opposition, the Conservatives pledged to hold mayoral referendums in England's 12 largest cities outside London, and as part of the coalition government introduced legislation to do so in 2011. Both Leicester and Liverpool subsequently acquired mayors following resolutions by their respective city councils, without referendums. Joe Anderson, previously leader of Bristol City Council, became Liverpool's first directly elected mayor.

The stakes were raised considerably in 2015 by the 'Devo-Manc' deal offered by the government to the Greater Manchester Combined Authority (GMCA). Here, a directly elected mayor for the city region – a metro mayor – would have control over a devolved transport budget, strategic planning powers and a £300 million housing investment fund. Alongside this the Chancellor signed a deal to devolve £6 billion worth of health spending per annum to the GMCA.

In this context it becomes more important to understand the impact or difference a mayoral model of governance might make to various urban outcomes. We have stated that the empirical evidence on the impact of a directly elected mayor on urban outcomes is equivocal at best. However, for our purpose here it is relevant to highlight the work of those commentators who insist that directly elected mayors are not in and of themselves a panacea for urban ills.

Within this context Schragger (2006) argues that mayoral leadership alone is unlikely to generate significant changes in a city's economic and social circumstance. Instead he places emphasis on the capacity of the mayor to invoke executive power on behalf of the entire polity. It is a democratic argument which sees the city as having:

> a collective identity and interests independent of the particular ends of the citizens who inhabit it, then the embodiment of those interests in one executive office becomes more attractive. The articulation of the city's interests by a single executive official is particularly important for urban municipalities which experience the most significant gaps between resources and responsibilities (Schragger, 2006: 2576).

Following this, McNeill discusses the potential for mayors to stimulate 'the place specificity of a city, as embodiment of its mythical "character", and as narrator and animator of its futures and urban spaces' (2001: 356). In a more recent article Jayne (2011: 805) argues that mayors should be seen 'as avatars who embody abstract concepts of ideologies of place, community and politics that are both territorial and relational'. This notion is, in many respects, empirically grounded in case studies of the mayors of Rome, Madrid and Budapest by Martins and Alvarez (2007).

The mayoral bandwagon is, then, far from exclusive to the UK and there is a proliferation of bodies at European and international level promoting knowledge exchange between elected officials, not to mention the activities of mayors and officials in boosting places internationally. The activities of mayors on the international stage are fairly opaque, though Beal and Pinson (2014) have explored this research agenda in 'When Mayors go Global'. They argue that there have been substantial changes to the international stage for local political actors as entrepreneurial governance strategies have taken hold, and they argue that there has been a growing importance of international strategies in interurban competition and in the elaboration of urban policies. Yet, what is less known is how urban political leaders make use of their international activities and connections and to what extent these are linked to their legitimacy strategies.

Finally, it is important to frame the scope for action at the scales over which the mayors operate. Allmendinger and Haughton (2007) in their discussion of the reformulation of spatial regulation argue for an empirical focus which combines scope and scale of operation and state it is always necessary to examine the politics of scale and scope as integrally related aspects of the processes of state restructuring. Although we argue the case here in terms of spatial planning, we would also want to assert that a more explicit consideration of issues of 'scope' would be useful in other spheres of state regulation. (Allmendinger and Haughton, 2007: 1431).

The role of the English urban directly elected mayor, despite the 'Devo-Manc' deal, remains unclear in policy terms. Policy appears to signal a disruptor to local government 'business as usual' through clear and visible leadership and further that this has some relationship between leadership style and economic development outcomes for places. (See Hambleton, 2014, for a full exposition of the notion of place-based leadership.)

The circuits of influence of the Mayor of Liverpool

In this section we explore perceptions of the mayoral model of governance in Liverpool. It concentrates on the ability to build coalitions of interest and action with a wide range of external organisations and interests, operating at different scales, that currently or might in future contribute to the development of the city.

The data presented here came from documentary sources and 37 semi-structured interviews with key informants. Given their important roles as demonstrations of the different ways of working that have been created under the mayoral regime, we begin with the roles of the newly constituted Mayoral Development Commission (MDC) and the first round of Mayoral Commissions that were established in order to draw on external expertise and knowledge. In addition to these interviews we conducted two online surveys, one of this same group from the city and city regional elite, and another aimed circulated by social media, which was answered by 400 (admittedly self-selecting) members of the public.

Interviewees were chosen on the basis of their expertise across a range of relevant issue areas and their different degrees of exposure to the mayor. Where feasible, interviewees were asked to contrast their perceptions and experience of the mayoral regime with their previous experience of dealing either with Liverpool City Council when it had an indirectly elected council leader or with other local authorities. Interviewees were guaranteed anonymity in order to provide them with the freedom to offer personal views that could be critical, supportive or neutral with respect to the difference that the mayoral model has made or might make. Further to these mixed methods we conducted an analysis of the diary of the mayor, comparing the time he allocated as leader of the council and as directly elected mayor.

There are significant changes of emphasis associated with the shift from the council leader model to the functions of the mayoral model in Liverpool. One change can be discerned from looking at the proportion of the total appointment time spent by Joe Anderson on particular activities formerly as leader and while being mayor, as shown in Figure 5.1. The figure combines an analysis of absolute time spent on various activities (in hours on the x axis) with the overall proportion of time spent.

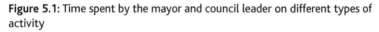

Figure 5.1: Time spent by the mayor and council leader on different types of activity

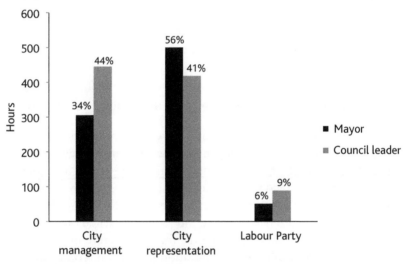

The mayor has started to spend a smaller proportion of his time in the day to day activities we have classified as city management (34%) than he did as council leader (44%) and more than half of his time (56%) representing the city at various meetings and functions (compared to 41% before). Interestingly, he is also spending less time on Labour Party related activity than he did as council leader. These findings may have consequences for the mayor's style and mode of operating but we find that this changing focus requires more qualitative exposition. For this we explore in depth attitudes and sentiments from interview respondents. From these elite groups there were some people highly sceptical about the mayoral model (and its incumbent) while others expressed hope and optimism that a figurehead or focus could help the city make a wider case for itself. A third group was cautiously optimistic and herein came the quotation which forms the title of this chapter. A directly elected mayor, they argued, was either necessary but not sufficient for Liverpool to face its specific challenges, or irrelevant in comparison with the scale of these challenges.

There was a sense that having a directly elected mayor was seen to have increased access to government ministers, senior civil servants and European Commission officials. Many of the political elite referred to "ministers on speed-dial" and bilateral relationships vastly improved between the mayoralty and the centre. Sceptics were quick to point out, however that "more chat has not led to more for the city" – with the most damning critique of the current governance regime complaining that "nothing in Liverpool is ever under-strategised but boy is it under-delivered". This view was given a clear illustration as the embedding of Joe Anderson as mayor coincided with the announcement of the route of a new high speed train (HS2) with "stops at the most significant cities of the north-west, Manchester airport and Manchester – nothing for Liverpool, again…"

Governance innovations: the MDC and policy commissions

Establishing the mayoralty, Joe Anderson did not have much in way of resources to draw on, admitting in interview that he was reticent about spending due to the financial pressures on the city. As a consequence, a highly inventive (and resource neutral) set of governance innovations were developed as a way of supporting the mayoralty with wider policy expertise than existed within the city council itself. Potentially the most significant of these has been the formal structure of the MDC.

The MDC is an important innovation in terms of connecting the mayor to private sector and other institutional expertise, but has not been able to take on the role originally envisaged for it in spearheading the delivery of new economic development. This is largely due to the fact that, while it is formally established as a development corporation, it has not been afforded the national resources given to its predecessors through which it might fund a large scale development programme. Instead, it has functioned mainly as a sounding board and source of external, independent expertise and constructive challenge to the mayor.

Members perceived both strengths and limitations to this role. It was described, for example, as: "Excellent on paper, combining good people but (it is) not a development corporation in the sense that it links through to delivery". Another interviewee reported "Not sure how useful the board is. Lots of talk. If anything is going to happen as a result, it probably demands activity outside these structures." Another found it "… a 'not bad' discussion group, half of whose members have connections with the city rather than live in it". And further "(It is a) talking shop but not meant pejoratively. Stimulating for members; not clear what it adds for the mayor and chief executive. (It is) another scrutiny committee but not assembled through the political process." A further observer drew attention to the contrast between the way the board operates and private sector decision making, particularly in respect of the intelligence that underpins it:

> '[There is a] piece of work still to be done on the 'why, where, what' of business development. [They] don't find it as easy as businesses to do overview/horizon scanning. Liverpool Vision [the economic development strategy body, reporting to the mayor] is not looking at the overall business environment. They generate intelligence but don't look at it from a business perspective. This is one function of the private sector members of the Mayoral Development Board.'

In a sense the MDC is a hostage to fortune. Development corporations have a rich history in Liverpool, such as those assembled for the regeneration of the Albert Dock and the building of the Convention Centre. Without significant resources the MDC struggles to be transformative in the sense that these projects have been.

In addition to the MDC, the mayor convened a set of ad-hoc policy commissions. These were viewed from people familiar with their remit (not the general public) generally more positively. The Health Commission, and the Fairness Commission, in particular, were seen as having been effective at evidence gathering, and to have broadened the sources of expertise available to the mayor in areas of policy that are critical to the city but for which responsibility falls across a variety of agencies and organisations. There was general consensus that the commissions could not have been assembled, particularly with the levels of seniority and status they drew upon, but for the additional convening capacity that a directly elected mayor could bring.

The commissions were also seen as highly cost effective ways of overcoming some of the capacity constraints that have resulted from public expenditure reductions and the perceived need to protect statutory service delivery. During a period in which information, intelligence and policy development functions, together with the delivery of non-statutory services, have been cut, the commissions, along with the MDC, have proved to be useful vehicles for intelligence gathering and the sourcing of specialist advice for the mayor. This chimes with the concern that was expressed by many interviewees about the capacity of the council in general and the mayor's immediate executive support arrangements in particular: "that the city council had already been denuded of senior executives before he became mayor – this isn't unusual, given the bigger local government context – but there's a feeling that its policy development capacity is weak".

Where interviewees were less convinced by the commission model was in its ability to ensure the delivery, by partner agencies, of many of the policy initiatives with which individual commissions were associated. This 'implementation gap' has been reduced, in some cases, by the signing of memoranda of understanding between partners, for example in relation to health and wellbeing.

Many of the connections that have been brokered with local agencies have come about through the work of the commissions. In our interviews with individual city-based organisations, however, there was a general perception that the mayor was accessible and approachable, that he could deliver on the promises he made and that he had an instinctive grasp of the importance of key 'anchor institutions' beyond the city council to the performance and prospects of the city. An example is among city universities, where there was a perception that the mayor understood that the value of higher education to the city was not just a matter of the spending power of students and staff but that it extended into the civic activities of both of those groups, the role of academics in thought leadership, the spin-offs generated by university research in terms of economic development and health and wellbeing, and the value of university 'brands' for the international image of the city. The designation of the 'Knowledge Quarter' as one of the Mayoral Development Zones, and the level of trust placed in university leaderships in taking it forward, were seen as evidence of a deepening relationship with the mayor. We were told that:

> 'The Mayoralty made things simpler for the university. [It is] clear who to go to talk to … In practice, the mayor has been more consultative … From outside … [the] targets are the mayor and chief executive who are seen to work well together and seamlessly. If you want to float an idea, get a decision made, it's the mayor or chief executive.'

Governance of the city region

It is notable that some of the capacity and implementation issues relate to operating within the city of Liverpool only, and some are stretched further by the need for city regional, cross conurbation working in the government's preferred metropolitan mayor governance fix. Cooperating in the creation of new governance arrangements for the city region around the city was regarded by many interviewees as one of the biggest challenges facing the mayor. The challenge is made more formidable by the perception that the LCR lags behind those centred on other large provincial cities in formalising and making effective a new set of governance arrangements for the city region that may be critical to the future devolution of power and decentralisation of resources from the national level. The creation of a combined authority (CA) in 2014 – a move that is credited by many to the lobbying of the mayor – is an important first step but as yet the CA is an empty shell awaiting a purpose that has yet to be adequately defined and remains a somewhat vexed political space.

During our interview programme, we were informed that: "While [government is] not prescribing a CA model ... if local authorities come up with a proposal you put a big tick in the governance column..." this quote stood out as interesting in that talk of governance as emergent, as interactive or as a process was reduced to a tick-box by this official. There was little doubt, however, that functioning CA models "give a sense of pooling sovereignty". In the Merseyside example, however "Liverpool-ing sovereignty" is controversial. While interviewees tried to be bullish about the possibilities for designing their own arrangements – "if core cities can sort out their functional geography and come with a clear agenda it makes it impossible for government to say no" – none were in much doubt about the ways in which the "deck was stacked in favour of the centre".

A further complicating factor in the LCR, according to some, was that the advent of an elected mayor for Liverpool had created a further obstacle to making a success of the CA in the sense that there is concern, among other LCR local authorities, that Liverpool's voice carried greater weight with government ministers and could "scoop the pool". We were told, for example, that:

> 'It's great we've got a prominent person at the centre of the city region, but we have to just ensure that that's not at the expense of the city region as a whole. ... one of the problems he faces actually is his title ... the Mayor of

Liverpool ... there's always a danger that the leaders of the other boroughs will both think, he's no more than our equal but because of his title, he's going to look as if he's the first amongst equals, and you could imagine some sort of personal sensitivity around that sort of stuff.'

This poses a particular challenge to the mayor and the leaders of other LCR local authorities, of crafting arrangements that recognise Liverpool's strategic importance as the central city, the recognisable global brand and the location of much of the more innovative economic activity within the city region, but also to acknowledge the strengths and assets of the surrounding areas. It was suggested, for example, that this was particularly manifested in the lack of agreement about using Liverpool as the "attack brand" for marketing the LCR. This was captured in the comment that "Merseyside has never been seen as Greater Liverpool". There were also a number of (unprompted) references to how Greater Manchester had dealt with this issue by spreading responsibility between the constituent local authorities in terms of strategic and policy area leadership. By contrast the relationship between LCR local authorities was viewed by some as "dysfunctional", characterised by "internecine strife" and held back by a tendency towards "lowest common denominator" solutions.

Many interviewees expressed frustration about "that bit where you fundamentally care about your city but your orbit is bigger because you recognise that your destiny is linked to all these other guys" and "there is a little too much of local authorities putting the interests of their own slightly artificial local authority boundaries beyond the interests of the city region as a whole". And further,

'Others in the core cities have clocked the significance of the functional economic geography ... have clocked the fact that Manchester happily extract loads out of government because they seem coherent, because they seem united, because they don't air their dirty laundry ... they come to government with this united coherent voice with clear vision.'

The creation of the CA provides the potential for resolving some of these tensions, but only if the constituent local authorities embrace it as a vehicle through which they can pursue genuine common purpose and not as a government hurdle they were required to clear. The mayor has confirmed his ambition for the LCR by signalling that he is in favour, ultimately, of a 'metro mayor' for the whole of the city region but sees a successful CA model as a necessary first step along that road. This longer term possibility is recognised as a legitimate aspiration by many of our interviewees who reported, for example, that "Ministers have got confidence in that model and I think that it drives the thought, well, if it works in London, surely it can work elsewhere." However, until 'Devo-Manc', neither the range of powers, nor the institutional largesse of the Mayor of London had ever been on offer to the provinces.

The key question for the LCR that was implicitly raised by contrasts with Greater Manchester is where the leadership that might begin to recreate some of the elements of Greater Manchester's success – a common vision and narrative that all the CA authorities can buy into, strong metropolitan institutions, a common investment framework and sufficient political maturity to accept that not all areas can benefit equally from strategic choices but are nonetheless better served by collaboration than by outright competition – can feasibly come from.

A further complicating factor in the building of collaborative city regional relationships is the institutional separation between the Local Enterprise Partnership (LEP) and local authority structures. A number of interviewees acknowledged that there appeared to be some tension between a nominally business-led LEP and the political leadership of Liverpool and the LCR. "The mayor does not appear to be meshing particularly well with the LEP – his preferred vehicle is Liverpool Vision which is under his control." And the more direct challenge to the mayor's turf was because "the LEP had seemed to be picking up many of the issues and powers and opportunities that the mayor himself might have wanted to see at his disposal".

Despite some fears about the strength of the LEP and its performance, it is an important building block in more thoroughgoing city regional relations as it does operate across the conurbation. The LEP was clearly not helped by the delay appointing a chair and its lack of capacity and resources. It has the strength of a unique subscription model with major private sector buy-in which gives it legitimacy. Conversely, it was contended that it did not have the "carrying capacity" to do what the government expected.

> 'The jury's still out on LEPs ... the LEPs come with nothing ... businesses who give up their time will only do that for so long ... seemed to have the same mission as Mersey Partnership but with no budget and no powers.'

This criticism chimes with that of the MDC, and begs the question of what these bodies are supposed to *do* in the absence of significant funding streams comparable to those available for regional development under the old Regional Development Agencies. All these strategic entities have struggled under austerity measures to the point that the LEP and the local authorities were said to be facing "horrendous capacity issues" in relation to the strategic and delivery challenges facing the LCR and "none have the critical mass to deal with them but will not cede authority on anything".

Whether this particular critique is fair or not it is particularly apposite in relation to the establishment of a CA for the LCR if the same capacity and strategic policy issues remain. The fragmentation of city regional leadership between the mayor, the CA and the LEP risks complicating the process of securing external resources through competitive bidding processes and clear delivery mechanisms.

Conclusions

In this chapter we have sought to introduce the challenges of place-based forms of leadership within the LCR as a counter to the government case that visibility and accountability and a direct mandate from the electorate can cure all ills. There is a concern that altering executive models of local government leadership may be seen as a panacea for all manner of perceived criticisms of local government and further that under conditions of severe local government spending restraint mayoral models implemented 'on the cheap' may further compromise the strategic leadership challenge in places with concentrations of poverty and inequality. The mayoral model appears to suck the oxygen out of thoroughgoing questions about appropriate levels of resourcing, continuity of some local services and, in effect, the appropriate ambit of the public sector itself. There is no controversy within Liverpool over the need for constructive relations with the wider city and sub-region. The outstanding question is the role that a directly elected mayor might feasibly play in influencing the further development of this more extensive space both institutionally and in terms of strategy. The issues facing the LCR are huge and extend well beyond the capabilities of a single person, irrespective of their political acumen, networks or will. The mayoralty is necessary but not sufficient to bring about the transformation of Merseyside over the longer term. Refocusing reform of local government around a sense of purpose and mission, financing models and investment in the place, streamlining the ways in which private sector voices are courted and for what purpose, and working across the boundaries of the conurbation are all far more urgent tasks for the local political regime than seeking "ticks in governance boxes" conveyed from beyond the city region.

References

Allmendinger, P. and Haughton, G. (2007) 'The fluid scales and scope of UK spatial planning', *Environment and Planning A*, 39(6), 1478–96.

Beal, V. and Pinson, G. (2014) 'When mayors go global: international strategies, urban governance and leadership', *International Journal of Urban and Regional Research*, 38, 1.

Borraz, O. and John, P. (2004) 'The transformation of urban political leadership in Western Europe', *International Journal of Urban and Regional Research*, 28(1), 107–20.

Buck, N., Gordon, I., Harding, A. and Turok, I. (eds) (2005) *Changing Cities: Rethinking Urban Competitiveness, Cohesion and Governance*, Basingstoke: Palgrave Macmillan.

Castells, M. (1997) *The Power of Identity*, Oxford, Blackwell.

DCLG (2011) 'Localism Bill: creating executive mayors in the 12 largest English cities – Impact assessment', https://www.gov.uk/government/uploads/system/uploads/attachment_data/file/1829754.pdf

Gash, T. and Sims, S. (eds) (2012) *What can Elected Mayors do for our Cities?* London: Institute for Government.

Hambleton, R. (2014) Leading *the Inclusive City: Place-Based Innovation for a Bounded Planet*, Cambridge: Polity Press.

Harding, A. (1997) 'Urban regimes in a Europe of cities', *European Urban and Regional Studies*, 4(4), 291–314.

Harding, A. and Le Gales, P. (1998) 'Cities and states in Europe', *West European Politics*, 21(3), 120–45.

Jayne, M. (2011)' From actor to avatar: the place of mayors in theories of urban governance', *Geography Compass*, 5(11), 801–10.

Judd, D. (2000) 'Strong leadership', *Urban Studies*, 37(5–6), 951–61.

Logan, J. R. (1976) 'Logan on Molotch and Molotch on Logan: Notes on the growth machine-toward a comparative political economy of place', *American Journal of Sociology*, 82(2), 349–52.

Martins, L. and Alvarez, J. M. R. (2007) 'Towards glocal leadership: taking up the challenge of new local governance in Europe', *Environment and Planning C: Government and Policy*, 25, 391–409.

McNeill, D. (2001) 'Embodying a Europe of the cities: geographies of mayoral leadership', *Area*, 33(4), 353–9.

Schragger, R. (2006) 'Can strong mayors empower weak cities?', *The Yale Law Journal*, 115(6), 2542–78.

Stone, C. L. (1989) *Regime Politics: Governing Atlanta 1946–1988*, Lawrence: University Press of Kansas.

SIX

Embracing social responsibilities through local leadership: comparing the experience of the mayors of Bristol and Liverpool

Nasrul Ismail,
University of Bristol, UK

Introduction

The concept of social responsibility in leadership has not been frequently articulated in the policy and politics debate. I argue such a concept emerges from, and entails notions of, accountability (Cameron and Caza, 2005), integrity (Badaracco and Ellsworth, 1989), dependability (Meindl and Ehrlich, 1987), and authenticity (Freeman and Auster, 2011), exercised within precise powers and boundaries, as ensured by supportive political networks and local communities.

By positioning the concept of social responsibility in leadership in the centre of the mainstream political debate, this chapter will evaluate the following question: To what extent have the Mayor of Bristol, George Ferguson, and the Mayor of Liverpool, Joe Anderson, embraced socially responsible leadership within urban governance?

Mayors Ferguson and Anderson present a unique, dual case study on socially responsible leadership. Both Bristol and Liverpool are part of the English Core Cities forum, which comprises large second-tier English cities where, for two decades, they have shared best practice in political governance and have lobbied the national government on issues relating to economic development (Meegan et al, 2014). Yet, both leaders are different in their social leadership approaches. Their applications are context driven and locally contingent. As such, the comparative perspective that this chapter adds nuances how we theorise social responsibilities in leadership.

Using Hudson and Lowe's (2004) model of governance, the chapter will explore the convergence of the socially responsible leadership concept from three levels: the macro level (national level), meso level (city governance) and the micro level (city electorates). It will use several broad framing principles, such as accountability, integrity, dependability and authenticity, to support the comparative analysis.

The chapter begins by mapping out the emergence of socially responsible leadership from the statutory framework at the macro level. It will highlight a tension in the legal structure between, on the one hand, the Localism Act 2011 in addressing the prevailing fiscal austerity and, on the other hand, the battle against the real lack of power conferred from Whitehall and the risk averse framework under the Public Sector (Social Value) Act 2012.

It then goes on to explore the relationship of the mayors with their political networks at the meso level, particularly with non-state actors. Here, consideration will be given to how successful both Mayors Ferguson and Anderson have been in transforming the two-way relationship from a mere co-production of local services to co-determination of local decision making with stakeholders.

In the final section, the discussion will shift towards the local electorates' perception at the micro level. As such, both Mayor Ferguson's and Mayor Anderson's leadership experiences will be benchmarked against the three traits of social leadership, namely paving the way, inspiring a shared vision and challenging the status quo within the urban governance context.

The analysis within this chapter will draw upon publicly available evidence, documents and statements to operationalise the public representations of the mayors from an external point of view. While this may be viewed as a limitation of the study, it provides a fair depiction of the mayors in observing their social responsibilities in their local leadership, taking into account the distinct variations reflecting the political conditions and the individual aspirations of the mayors for their city.

Macro level: facing the reality of localism

At the macro level, social responsibility in leadership is enshrined through the statutory framework of the Localism Act 2011, which devolves the central responsibilities back to the local realm, albeit bucking the trend of the UK constitutional landscape. The government opined:

> [W]e share a conviction that the days of big government are over; that centralisation and top-down control have proved a

failure. We believe that the time has come to disperse power more widely in Britain today; to recognise that we will only make progress if we help people come together to make life better. In short, it is our ambition to distribute power and opportunity to people rather than hoarding authority within government. (HM Government, 2010: 7)

In effect, the 2011 Act codifies the notion of socially responsible leadership, whereby such a concept no longer enjoys a normative, non-binding and soft power status. Section 1(1) of the 2011 Act mandates a 'general power of competence', where directly elected mayors are given more freedom to work with their political networks, to deliver creativity, authenticity and innovation to meet local people's needs.

The autonomy to act is key. Rather conveniently, this apparatus was established at the critical time when, following a 'baptism of fire', both Ferguson and Anderson faced an uphill struggle in mitigating the impact of urban austerity across Bristol and Liverpool. Consequent to the central government's proposal of a £5.5 billion reduction in the budget for local government (HM Treasury, 2010), the budget cuts were set at £83 million in Bristol, after accounting for greater tax revenues and changes to government funding (BBC, 2014). The cuts in Liverpool were almost double that of Bristol, with Mayor Anderson being tasked to find a further £156 million of savings by March 2018 (*Liverpool Echo*, 2015).

As a response, Mayors Ferguson and Anderson may exercise the mandated general power of competence by delegating the service delivery functions of the councils to non-state actors. Section 81(1) of the same Act can be triggered by non-state actors to acquire the right to express an interest in taking over the running of a local authority service, where the local authority must consider and respond to this challenge; and where it accepts it, runs a procurement exercise for the service in which the challenging organisation can bid. Here, there is a movement towards co-production, which ensures greater collaboration in urban governance, claimed to become 'a hegemonic discourse' (Skelcher and Sullivan, 2008: 41), with the use of partnerships as the mechanism of choice when it comes to implementing most public initiatives (Turrini et al, 2010). Some scholars argue that integrated service delivery increases the capacity to respond to local challenges and thus should be the way forward in local urban governance. Hambleton and Howard (2012) are even optimistic that if public services can be co-delivered by state and voluntary and community sector organisations working in partnership more effectively, there is no reason for the alliances not being able to grow the resources available to improve the quality of life in an area, even in a time of fiscal austerity.

Nevertheless, it can be argued that the 2011 Act's provisions remain too aspirational, and run the risk of being an example of political rhetoric from the former coalition government. None of these statutory provisions has been formally activated by any mayors across England, nor by non-state actors since receiving royal assent on 15 November 2011. Perhaps they are too ambitious for mayors and other network actors to implement. Furthermore, along with provisions in the Cities and Local Government Devolution Act 2016, which introduces directly elected mayors to combined local authorities in England and Wales, it can also be viewed as a tool of convenience for the coalition, used to delegate the neoliberal politics of austerity, rather than a genuine apparatus that can be used by both mayors to further embrace social responsibilities and make real differences to the local areas.

The failure of the localism agenda in this context is two-fold. Perhaps tellingly, the over-centralised state remains deeply entrenched within local government, without a major increase in local power for mayors to exercise. This has, to a certain extent, hindered the implementation of localism rhetoric, not only in Bristol and Liverpool, but across the areas of urban governance. Hambleton and Sweeting (2004) explained that while we seem to notice the lift and shift of the US-style local leadership and decision making model into the UK political landscape, central government still dictates the majority of local decision making. This then leaves very little room for mayors to manoeuvre: directly elected mayors in England still lack the taxation and spending powers to make a real difference, compared to their transatlantic friends such as New York Mayor Bill de Basio – in New York, 69% of city income is generated through the local regeneration of funding (Harding et al, 2013).

At the same time, the wide power for mayors under Section 1(1) of the 2011 Act is hampered by the introduction of the Public Services (Social Value) Act 2012, just 68 days after the 2011 Act was enacted. The 2012 Act chiefly confines the interpretation of the socioeconomic impact of local mayors' decisions to the matters pertaining to commissioning and procurement of local services only. Furthermore, the 2012 Act encourages mayors to be risk averse, by requiring them to conduct assessments of the impacts on the local community of their commissioning decisions. It was therefore not surprising when a survey found that 83% of English local authorities did not quantify social value within procurement practices (Dobson, 2012), which resembles lack of coherence in embodying the social value virtues under the 2012

Act, reinforcing the rhetoric of the localism agenda at the macro level of governance.

Without a real sense of devolution of powers to mayors, and with the constriction of innovation under the 2012 Act, it is impossible to see the applicability of the localism concept as advanced under the 2011 Act to mayoral governance, especially in Bristol and Liverpool. In this respect, it is highly questionable whether the provisions under the 2011 Act, which was once seen to be capable of 'delivering a radically different form of local governance' (Lowndes and Pratchett, 2012: 22), can aid the mayors in embracing socially responsible leadership in their urban governance context.

Meso level: making the leap of faith from co-production and co-determination

Compared to the macro level, the concept of socially responsible leadership moves more organically and, arguably, more effectively at the meso level through the evolution from 'co-production' of local services to the 'co-determination' of local decision making.

Such a movement is catalysed by steering from Whitehall, through the idea of the 'Big Society' by central government, based around social action, public sector reform, community enablement, direct financial aid from the central government to charities, and removing the roadblocks that hinder the implementation of local initiatives (Cabinet Office, 2010). Such an aspiration inevitably renews the shift in paradigm from 'local government' to 'local governance', and emerges through the reduction of the functions for local authorities, which is axiomatic of the growth of other bodies at the local level (Stoker, 1998). Here, we seem to witness the increasing trend of voluntary and community sector organisations in acting extra-politically to deliver local services.

Mayors Ferguson and Anderson have fully embraced co-production of public services with non-state actors, which runs parallel to the principal–agent relationship discourse (Buse et al, 2012). With this model in mind, particularly during a time of prevailing austerity, partnerships inevitably have to 'engage in difficult conversations, about what is going on in local communities, what a shared response could entail, how creativity can overcome defensiveness, and what truly collaborative city leadership might look like' (Lowndes and Squires, 2012: 408).

Here, Bristol chooses a conventional mode of governance: co-production of local services through pooled budgets with strategic partners and delivery of services through voluntary and community sector organisations. In contrast, the movement in Liverpool is even bolder. Mayor Anderson established the Mayoral Development Corporation, which unites partners from the private, voluntary and other public sectors to drive growth and development in the city (Liverpool Vision, 2013), which signifies the transformation from co-production to co-determination of the local decision making process.

Distinguishing Bristol and Liverpool mayors' experience illuminates an underlying struggle that requires decision makers to embrace 'a paradigm shift ... to ensure that the non-state actors can take part in the co-determination of the decision-making process' (Pugh, 2011: 14). At the same time, there is a question whether non-state actors are capable of submitting themselves to the Big Society challenges. The leap of faith in question perhaps stems from what Hayman (2011) proposes: there are still doubts about whether social enterprises are capable of delivering public services on a scale that the government wishes, which requires a change in the mayors' mindsets. Trust and confidence are key to the success of the relationship to transform from co-production to co-determination, with the mayors still maintaining the chain of accountability within local governance, as witnessed in the Liverpool context.

We also witness the emergence of voluntary and community sector organisations as the new pathway of social consciousness by local people, to translate individual interests into collective and public issues. These organisations act as a 'sounding board' for a specific cause that seeks to influence public policy design and operation (Grant, 1989).

This can be seen from analyising media content by the extent to which the voluntary and community sector organisations have been successful in articulating the impacts of fiscal austerity to both mayors. Based on national and local newspaper reports between May 2012 and December 2015, there were 39 news items in Bristol with the voluntary and community sector organisations representing the extent to which financial cuts had affected their users. For example, a Bristol-based domestic abuse charity, Missing Link, launched aggressive media campaigns (using local newspapers, e-petitions and Twitter) against the funding cut proposals for services for homeless vulnerable women with mental health and complex health needs (Change, 2014). Overwhelmed by negative responses to the proposals, Mayor Ferguson overturned his initial decision (Change, 2014), which reflects the notion of dependability of the mayor during austerity. In contrast, there were only 21 new items in Liverpool on the same subject, with unknown impacts compared to Bristol.

In this instance, the use of voluntary and community sector organisations as the social consciousness mechanism demands the mayors be accountable for their decisions, which, in turn, equalises the bargaining power between mayors and local residents. It also summons mayors to address the strategic leadership challenge facing the locality, and empowers them to make tough decisions that call on their dependability and integrity. On the other hand, this apparatus is generally a passive mechanism that must be activated by citizens; it requires a commitment of time and resources. People may feel intimidated using such mechanisms unless they are widely institutionalised (Danet, 1981). They may have little interest in participating in the democratic debate, which outweighs the benefits (Osmani, 2007). Perhaps, the social consciousness concept is still at its infancy with some continual growth witnessed in Bristol and Liverpool. The social consciousness concept may develop further in the future, along with its impact on urban governance.

Micro level: theorising electorate expectations

At the micro level, it is contended that the social responsibilities in leadership arise from the expectations of the local electorate. Borrowing from Kouzes and Posner (2007), both Mayor Ferguson and Mayor Anderson will be benchmarked against three universal keys of social leadership traits: paving the way; inspiring a shared vision; and challenging the process. These traits indicate a measure of good governance for mayoral leadership, which may reassure some ardent critics that there is enough evidence of the positive benefits of elected mayors for local residents (Marsh, 2012; Fenwick, 2013).

Paving the way

Paving the way refers to the expectation of local residents that mayors will make things happen in their cities. This can be seen from Bristol's and Liverpool's regeneration plans, demonstrating the mayors' authenticity and creativity in managing the cities' resources.

For instance, recognising the financial hardship landscape in Bristol, Mayor Ferguson made a courageous decision by selling the council's freehold interest in the docks and surrounding areas at Avonmouth for a £10 million profit (*Bristol Post*, 2014b). Similarly, in Liverpool, Mayor Anderson formulated a long-term £1.5 billion regeneration plan for Kings Dock and Lime Street in the city centre, which includes an Olympic standard ice rink, an extreme sports complex, as well as restaurants and domestic properties (*Liverpool Echo*, 2014). Within this context, both Mayors Ferguson and Anderson have been observed to lead their areas into new, uncharted territories and make things happen in their cities through an authentic local regeneration plan, in an attempt to safeguard the cities from the brunt of financial cuts. While both Mayors Ferguson and Anderson have been successful in their local regeneration plans, they have also been unsuccessful in lobbying financial support from the central government, evidenced through their failure in persuading central government to consider the funding for a high-speed railway scheme in both cities (*Liverpool Express*, 2014; *Bristol Post*, 2014a). On reflection, the unwillingness of the central government to listen to these mayors' quests for high-speed rail is contradictory. Despite the political endorsement in the roles of mayoral leadership at the macro level, the lack of courage to support these local leaders indicates the reluctance of central government to listen to local areas, which shows the lack of a real sense of devolution of powers from Whitehall to both Bristol and Liverpool. In fact, there should be a scope for a bargain between the mayors and central government, which requires more persuasion and mature discussion at the national level in order to sustain the longevity of mayoral governance in local areas. Without political support and appropriate incentives for these mayors, conducive and sufficient conditions for effective observation of socially responsible leadership are not provided at the micro level, and it will be difficult for central government to maintain its position given public endorsement for the mayoral prefecture in urban governance.

Inspiring a shared vision

Inspiring a shared vision involves aligning the local residents and strategic partners with the mayoral visions for local areas. Hambleton and Bullock (1996: 8–9) assert that a good leader is able to express a clear vision for the area, by setting out an agenda of what the future of the area should be, by formulating a strategic policy direction, and by listening to local people and leadership.

Mayor Ferguson is seen to be more creative in engaging with the local electorates than his Liverpool counterpart. An interactive, two-way collaborative approach between Mayor Ferguson and the local residents transpired when the former launched Ideas Lab in 2013, which generated more than 300 innovative ideas from the residents for the city (Bristol City Council, 2013b). The mayor empowered the local residents to come up with innovative ideas in the hope of informing the Mayor's Vision for Bristol, a plan that sets out his priorities to make

Bristol better for its citizens: a healthier city, with improved transport, better connected neighbourhoods, a stronger focus on education and training, more jobs and homes, more involved citizens, and more power to make decisions locally (Bristol City Council, 2013a; 2013c). Such an authentic move at the micro level is also congruent with Stoker's contextualisation of soft power in inspiring a vision, which is 'the power to get other people to share your ideas and vision via framing, influencing, bargaining and diplomacy' (Stoker, 1998: 27–8).

Mayor Anderson, on the other hand, followed the conventional top-down approach in which he formed a local regeneration plan, along with the establishment of a number of commissions to examine specific local issues, including health, education and fairness (Liverpool City Council, 2012).

Despite differing approaches, both of the mayors have managed to inspire a shared vision for the local area, albeit for different audiences. Both methodical approaches have proven to be fruitful when Ferguson and Anderson were both nominated and shortlisted for the World Mayor Award in 2014, along with 24 other mayors from across the globe (World Mayor, 2014a). They did not win; nevertheless, the following submissions were testimony of their public engagement and support, and the local electorates' understanding and acceptability of the mayors' visions.

For Bristol's Mayor:

> [George Ferguson] has really energised the city and more people are aware of and take an interest in our local democracy. As with any leader or decision maker, not everyone agrees with everything George does but they have definitely heard of him. (World Mayor, 2014b)

For Liverpool's Mayor:

> Joe Anderson is an inspiration … because of his commitment to the people of Liverpool … he has time for everyone, and building of new housing, schools and supporting health provision for everyone in our City despite swingeing cuts by Government. [This] is admirable beyond belief. (World Mayor, 2014c)

Challenging the process

Finally, challenging the process refers to the capability of the local mayors to challenge the status quo of the political architype. Challenging the status quo is particularly pertinent to Mayor Ferguson, who stood as an independent candidate, compared to Mayor Anderson who was a Labour Party candidate. Freedom from group discipline provides 'a basis for a stronger, more proactive and individualised style of leadership than over models of local government leadership' (Leach et al, 2005), despite the fact that partisanship politics is a crucial characteristic of English local government (Mouritzen and Svara, 2002) and that scholars have insisted that it remains a dominant feature (Leach et al, 2005).

Here, Mayor Ferguson used his independence as a strategy to convince the public that the citizens are at the heart of the decision making process rather than implementing self-serving activities that may resemble loyalty to the governing parties, which is notably in line with the notion of integrity and accountability.

However, while being free from the need to form tactical coalitions to stay in power and be able to provide clear and decisive leadership, the problem also presents itself when a candidate is party neutral. Evidenced through his struggle in forming a 'rainbow cabinet' after being elected, Mayor Ferguson was met with initial rejection by the Labour Party, when they refused to be part of his leadership team, insisting it would create a healthy political environment by acting as a self-elected scrutiny group (*Bristol Post*, 2012).

Benjamin's (1988) theory on self-identity contextualises Ferguson's experience:

> In trying to establish itself as an independent entity, the self must yet recognise the other as a subject like itself in order to be recognised by the other ... In its encounter with the other, the self wishes to affirm its absolute independence even though its need for the other and the other's similar wish to undercut that affirmation. (1988: 32)

In this context, Mayor Ferguson had a challenge in mediating between the acceptability of his political network and his freedom from political affiliation, while being able to use his departure from partisan politics to challenge the status quo in the governance of urban polity, something that was not an issue for Mayor Anderson. Hambleton and Sweeting (2004) have aptly reasoned that despite being unconstrained by party discipline, an independent mayor (such as Ferguson) has to appeal to popular sentiment if he wishes to be re-elected. Thus, a balancing act is required to behave neutrally, which reflects the nature of integrity, and to appeal to popular sentiment.

Table 6.1 shows a comparison between the Bristol and Liverpool mayors according to the broad framing principles of social responsibility in leadership of accountability, integrity, dependability, and authenticity at the macro, meso and micro levels.

Table 6.1: Social responsibility for Mayors Ferguson and Anderson

Framing principles of social responsibility in leadership	Mayor George Ferguson, Bristol	Mayor Joe Anderson, Liverpool
Accountability	Section 1(1) of the Localism Act 2011 gives the general power of competence to the mayors to deliver innovations to meet local needs. However, this is partly constricted by the Public Services (Social Value) Act 2012.	
	Opted for a conventional model of co-production: pooling of budgets with public sector partners and commissioning of services through voluntary and community sector organisations.	Adopted a bolder approach compared to Bristol by establishing the Mayoral Development Corporation to unite private, voluntary and public sector partners, shifting towards co-determination of local decision making process.
Integrity	Pertinent to Mayor Ferguson who ran as an independent candidate, and had to manage a delicate balance between party neutrality and management of the political network in the absence of political affiliation.	Loyalty to the affiliated party, in line with the notion of integrity. Less scrutiny by political peers as decision making is expected to be broadly in line with the party visions.
Dependability	Overturned initial decisions relating to financial cuts on critical services, such as homelessness, following voluntary and community sector media campaigns, demonstrating dependability in leadership at a critical time of austerity.	Mitigated impacts of cuts through a local regeneration plan in Liverpool City Centre and established commissions to examine specific community issues. Mayor Anderson's financial decisions had not been subject to an aggressive challenge as the decisions were made via the Mayoral Development Corporation, which is more inclusive of all partners in the city.
Authenticity	Relinquished the council's freehold interest in the docks for a £10 million return to mitigate the impact of financial austerity.	Devised a long-term £1.5 billion regeneration plan for Kings Dock and Lime Street in Liverpool city centre.
	Creative engagement with local residents; launched an interactive Idea Lab in 2013. The project generated over 300 innovative ideas from residents, which informed the Mayor's Vision for Bristol.	Adopted a conventional top-down approach through a local regeneration plan and established commissions for health, education and fairness.

Conclusions

The story of socially responsible leadership is more nuanced than may have been appreciated previously. Turning to the initial question of this chapter: To what extent have Mayor Ferguson and Mayor Anderson embraced the social responsibilities of leadership within their urban governance context? This chapter has demonstrated the extent to which both of the mayors have embodied the core values within responsible leadership – accountability, integrity, dependability and authenticity – within their urban governance context, albeit with different political trajectories, due to the context driven nature and locally contingent issues.

At the macro level, while the statutory framework under the Localism Act 2011 has the capability of challenging both mayors to deliver authentic innovative solutions in Bristol and Liverpool during a time of austerity, there is no real sense of devolution of powers from Whitehall to these mayors. This, along with the limitations under the Public Sector (Social Value) Act 2012, have reinforced the political rhetoric of the localism agenda of the coalition government.

More development of the socially responsible leadership doctrine is seen at the meso level. It has been argued that Mayor Anderson in Liverpool has moved his political relationship with non-state actors from a co-production of the public services towards a co-determination of the local decision making process, through the Mayoral Development Corporation, compared to his Bristol ally who opted for a more stereotypical mode of governance. At the micro level, socially responsible leadership has been examined from the citizens' expectation viewpoint. First, in terms of paving the way, both Bristol and Liverpool mayors have made things happen in their cities through regeneration plans, demonstrating their inventiveness in managing the cities' wealth. On the other hand, both of them failed in attracting national funding for high-speed rail connections. Such a struggle demonstrates the central government's lack of courage to listen to local mayors, which can stem from reluctance to devolve more powers to local areas, contradicting political rhetoric regarding localism.

Second, Mayor Ferguson has been praised in being creative in inspiring his leadership vision by collaborating with his local electorate through the Ideas Lab, where more than 300 innovative ideas were generated by Bristol's residents. In contrast, Mayor Anderson opted for the conventional top-down approach in uniting local residents, businesses, voluntary and community sector organisations, and other public sector organisations in delivering his political vision in Liverpool.

Despite appealing to different segments of their electorates, both of the mayors have managed to inspire their visions for the local area, testified through their nominations for the World Mayor Award in 2014.

Finally, challenging the status quo within the political landscape comes naturally for Mayor Ferguson who stands in as an independent candidate, compared to Mayor Anderson who is a Labour politician. Mayor Ferguson in this context faced nearly unsurmountable challenges in balancing the management of his political network while appealing to popular sentiment.

Leadership is an expansive activity. There have been various developments around the mayoral leadership that will either expand or diminish their powers. 'Metro Mayors' and devolution deals may be a threat to mayoral power. This may be politically challenging for Bristol, where the devolution deal for the West of England could unveil a political dynamic between the mayor and the leaders of other participating councils, such as South Gloucestershire, Bath and North East Somerset, and North Somerset (West of England Local Enterprise Partnership, 2015). Such spaces offer the potential to move the mayoral debate beyond the micro level, towards the impact of mayoral governance onto the institutional, societal and global political outlook. Although social responsibility values are relational, and they may only offer partial motivating forces, both Mayor Ferguson of Bristol and Mayor Anderson of Liverpool have embraced social responsibility in their local leadership, albeit via different trajectories, as mediated by their context and locality.

References

Badaracco, J. and Ellsworth, R. R. (1989) *Leadership and the Quest for Integrity,* Massachusetts: Harvard Business School Press.

BBC (2014) 'Reprieve for Bristol's public toilets in Mayor's revised budget cuts', www.bbc.co.uk/news/uk-england-bristol-25733377

Benjamin, J. (1988) *The Bonds of Love: Psychoanalysis, Feminism, and the Problem of Domination,* New York: Pantheon.

Bristol City Council (2013a) 'A vision for Bristol', www.bristol.gov. uk/page/mayor/vision-bristol

Bristol City Council (2013b) 'George's Ideas Lab encourages brightest and boldest Bristol innovations', http://news.bristol.gov.uk/georges-ideas-lab-encourages-brightest-and-boldest-bristol-innovations

Bristol City Council (2013c) 'State of the city: Mayoral priorities', www. bristol.gov.uk/documents/20182/34748/State+of+the+City+2013-+Mayoral+vision+v8.pdf

Bristol Post (2012) 'Labour in turmoil over decision on mayor's cabinet', 27 November, www.bristolpost.co.uk/Labour-turmoil-decision-mayor-s-cabinet/story-17433731-detail/story.html

Bristol Post (2014a) 'Mayor says Bristol must not miss out on high-speed train plans', 24 June, www.bristolpost.co.uk/Mayor-says-Bristol-miss-high-speed-train-plans/story-21280758-detail/story.html

Bristol Post (2014b) 'Plenty of ideas for how to spend £10m windfall from sale of freehold at Avonmouth', 27 March, www.bristolpost.co.uk/Plenty-ideas-spend-10m-windfall-sale-freehold/story-20859267-detail/story.html

Buse, K., Mays, N. and Walt, G. (2012) *Making Health Policy* (2nd edn), Berkshire: Open University Press.

Cabinet Office (2010) 'Transcript of a speech by the Prime Minister on the Big Society', 19 July, https://www.gov.uk/government/speeches/big-society-speech

Cameron, K. and Caza, A. (2005) 'Developing strategies and skills for responsible leadership', in J. P. Doh and S. A. Stumpf (eds) *Handbook on Responsible Leadership and Governance in Global Business,* Cheltenham: Edward Elgar Publishing.

Change (2014) 'Petition update – women-only services protected', www.change.org/p/bristol-city-council-protect-women-only-homelessness-services-in-bristol/u/7361130

Danet, B. (1981) 'Client-organisation relationships', in P. C. Nystrom and W. H. Starbuck (eds) *Handbook of Organisational Design*, New York: Oxford University Press.

Dobson, J. (2012) 'Commissioning for social value: What the Public Services (Social Value) Act 2012 means in practice', York: Housing Quality Network, http://urbanpollinators.co.uk/wp-content/plugins/downloads-manager/upload/Commissioning%20for%20social%20value.pdf

Fenwick, J. (2013) 'Elected mayors: Slumbering deeply', *Policy and Politics*, 41(1), 123–25.

Freeman, E. and Auster, E. R. (2011) 'Values, authenticity, and responsible leadership', *Responsible Leadership*, 98(1), 15–23.

Grant, W. (1989) *Pressure Groups, Politics and Democracy in Britain*, Hertfordshire: Philip Allan.

Hambleton, R. and Bullock, S. (1996) *Revitalising Local Democracy – The Leadership Options*, London: Local Government Management Board.

Hambleton, R. and Howard, J. (2012) *Public Sector Innovation and Local Leadership in the UK and the Netherlands*, York: Joseph Rowntree Foundation.

Hambleton, R. and Sweeting, D. (2004) 'US-Style leadership for English local government?', *Public Administration Review*, 64(4), 474–88.

Harding, A., Anderson, J., Jones, A., Le Gales, P., and Flamson, J. (2013) *Do Global Cities Need a Mayor?*, Liverpool: University of Liverpool.

Hayman, A. (2011) 'LCG view – social enterprises', *Local Government Chronicle*, 14.

HM Government (2010) 'The Coalition: Our programme for government', London: HM Government, https://www.gov.uk/government/uploads/system/uploads/attachment_data/file/78977/coalition_programme_for_government.pdfHM Treasury (2010) *Spending Review 2010*, Cm 7942, London: HMSO.

Hudson, J. and Lowe, S. (2004) *Understanding the Policy Process: Analysing Welfare Policy and Practice*, Bristol: The Policy Press.

Kouzes, J.M. and Posner, B. Z. (2007) *The Leadership Challenge* (4th edn), San Francisco: Jossey-Bass.

Leach, S., Hartley, J., Lowndes, V., Wilson, D., and Downe, J. (2005) *Local Political Leadership in England and Wales*, York: Joseph Rowntree Foundation.

Liverpool City Council (2012) 'Mayor's priorities', https://liverpool.gov.uk/mayor/pledges/

Liverpool Echo (2014) 'Mayor unveils ambitious £1.5billion plans for Liverpool City Centre', 16 May, www.liverpoolecho.co.uk/news/liverpool-news/liverpool-city-centre-15-billion-7128109

Liverpool Echo (2015) 'Exclusive: Liverpool mayor Joe Anderson 'confident' of saving some of Liverpool's SureStart centres from closure', 18 February, www.liverpoolecho.co.uk/news/liverpool-news/exclusive-liverpool-mayor-joe-anderson-8668955

Liverpool Express (2014) 'Mayor's statement about high speed rail', 27 October, www.liverpoolexpress.co.uk/mayors-statement-high-speed-rail/Liverpool Vision (2013) 'Liverpool Vision business plan', www.liverpoolvision.co.uk/wp-content/uploads/2014/01/Liverpool-Vision-Business-Plan-2013.pdf

Lowndes, V. and Pratchett, L. (2012) 'Local governance under the Coalition Government: Austerity, Localism, and the 'Big Society', *Local Government Studies*, 38(1), 21–40.

Lowndes, V. and Squires, S. (2012) 'Cuts, collaboration and creativity', *Public Money and Management*, 32(6), 401–8.

Marsh, A. (2012) 'Is it time to put the dream of elected mayors to bed?', *Policy & Politics*, 40(4), 607–11.

Meegan, R., Kennett, P., Jones, G. and Croft, J. (2014) 'Global economic crisis, austerity and neoliberal urban governance in England', *Cambridge Journal of Regions, Economy and Society*, 7(1), 137–53.

Meindl, J. R. and Ehrlich, S. B. (1987) 'The romance of leadership and the evaluation of organizational performance', *Academy of Management Journal*, 30, 91–109.

Mouritzen, P. E. and Svara, J. (2002) *Leadership at the Apex: Politicians and Administrators in Western Local Government*, Pittsburgh: University of Pittsburgh Press.

Osmani, S. R. (2007) *Participatory Governance: An Overview of the Issues and Evidence in Participatory Governance and the Millennium Development Goals*, New York: United Nations.

Pugh, P. (2011) 'It's just the state of the third sector', *Local Government Chronicle*, 14.

Skelcher, C. and Sullivan, H. (2008) 'Theory-driven approaches to analysing collaborative performance', *Public Management Review*, 10(6), 751–71.

Stoker, G. (1998) 'Governance as theory: Five propositions', *International Social Science Journal*, 50(155), 17–28.

Turrini, A. D., Cristofoli, F., Frosini, F. and Nasi, G. (2010) 'Networking literature about determinants of network effectiveness', *Public Administration*, 88, 528–50.

West of England Local Enterprise Partnership (2015) 'West of England proposes ambitious devolution deal worth £2bn to economy', www. westofenglandlep.co.uk/news/ambitious-devolution-deal

World Mayor (2014a) 'World Mayor 2014: The 26 finalists', www. worldmayor.com/contest_2014/shortlist-2014.html

World Mayor (2014b) 'Testimonials for George Ferguson, Mayor of Bristol, UK', www.worldmayor.com/contest_2014/bristol-mayor-ferguson.html

World Mayor (2014c) 'Testimonials for Joe Anderson, Mayor of Liverpool, UK', www.worldmayor.com/contest_2014/liverpool-mayor-anderson.html

Part II
International perspectives

The two worlds of elected mayors in the US: what type of mayor should cities choose?

James H. Svara, University of North Carolina at Chapel Hill, US

Introduction

In the US, the issue of electing mayors is complex and segmented, and it has changed over time. It is linked to additional issues related to form of government and professionalism in the governmental structure. The questions about mayors and the settings in which they operate have been raised can be summarised as follows in historical order:

1. Whether to change from a weak mayor-council form with fragmented authority to a strong mayor-council form arose in many cities particularly larger ones in the 1880s and was advanced by the Model City Charter in 1900.
2. Whether to shift from the mayor-council form to the council-manager form starting in the 1910s. A mayor chosen by the council from its members was part of the Second Model City Charter approved in 1915.
3. Whether to shift from council selected to directly elected mayor in council-manager cities was a continuing question. Direct election cities were a majority by 1965, but selection from within the council was still advocated by some traditional municipal reformers.
4. Whether to shift from council-manager to mayor-council form of government has been considered particularly in cities over 100,000 in population since 1990, although the conversions have been rare.

This chapter briefly reviews the arguments that supported the two major forms of government in points one and two from this list. There is a short discussion of point three – the choice between selection of the mayor within the council and direct election in council-manager cities. The chapter primarily examines the arguments made in support of the two major sets of alternative form of government and two types of elected mayors – point four. The choice is between a form of government based on unified authority as found in a parliamentary system – the council-manager form – or one based on separation of powers between the mayor with executive authority and the council with legislative authority – the mayor-council form. In other words, the question is not whether to have an elected mayor but rather about the institutional setting in which the mayor operates and the style of leadership associated with each setting.

The arguments advanced for each structure in recent referendums to change the form of government in large cities analysed by Svara and Watson (2010) are expanded by an in-depth analysis of the opposing campaigns in Sacramento, California, during a six-year effort to adopt the strong mayor form of government that ended unsuccessfully in 2014. This drawn out process provided a setting for a full debate of the advantages and disadvantages of two types of elected mayors in particular and of the two major models of governance in general. Drawing on Svara and Watson's (2010) 15 cases, a summary set of arguments is provided to address the major question about directly elected mayors in the US – which type of elected mayor associated with the differing governance structures is preferable?

The early period of competing reforms

Most city governments in the US incorporated principles of the national and state constitutions from their inception. Separation of powers and 'checks and balance' – offsetting powers to prevent a single official or branch of government from possessing uncontrolled authority – were common to all the governance frameworks. In local governments, the mayor's executive powers were shared with the council, boards and commissions, and other elected officials. In the late 19th century, municipal reformers concerned about improving the performance of city governments identified fragmentation of authority as a major cause of ineffectiveness, inefficiency and excessive influence of the dominant political party. Some cities changed their charters starting in the 1880s to concentrate more authority in the mayor's office. Organised in the National Municipal League, reformers drafted the Model City Charter in 1900. The recommended charter made the elected mayor a strong executive who exercised control over administrative offices and interacted with the city council that had separate legislative powers (Banfield and Wilson 1963: 140–1.)

Others favoured a different approach to reform. Frank Goodnow, the leading scholar in the newly emerging field of public administration, criticised the changes that occurred in cities that strengthened the mayor. Speaking specifically about the experience in Brooklyn, New York, Goodnow argued that it was unlikely that greater power in the mayor's office would lead to better administration of city government. 'Certainly since 1888,' he concluded, 'the government has been oftener bad than good' (quoted in Brazeau 1897: 81).

Goodnow like other reformers favoured a simplification of the government structure, but he preferred that authority be concentrated in the city council. The 'council system,' he wrote in 1908, 'has the great advantage that it avoids all possibility of conflict between municipal authorities' (Goodnow, 1908: 180). He referred specifically to the 'British principle of concentrating all administrative power in a popularly elected council' (188). With the British council as the model and experience with a new appointed executive referred to as the 'city manager' in a few cities in the first decade of the 20th century, reformers in the Municipal League revised the Second Model Charter in 1915. It included the council-manager form that included a top administrative official with centralised executive authority appointed by the council (Woodruff, 1919). Preferably, the mayor would be selected by the city council from its members. This was one of a number of provisions that reduced the political dimension in local government along with nonpartisan and at-large elections, a small council, a civil service system and of course a professional city manager.

Thus, the two models of reform reflected differing governance principles and reflected differing conceptions of the nature of the mayor's office and the relationship of this official to the public.

Changing logic and declining support for the non-elected mayor

The council-manager form as a new option for organising local governments in the US attracted a lot of attention and many adoptions during the 1920s. Growth in the use of the form declined during the economic depression of the 1930s and the Second World War, but it accelerated in the 1950s and 1960s in part because of the expansion of suburban city governments in urban regions. Little attention was given to how the mayor was selected until 1945 when the International City/County Management Association (ICMA) reported that almost two in five council-manager cities elected their mayors (Childs, 1965: 38-39). The proportion continued to grow and reached a majority in 1965. In the previous year, the National Municipal League in the sixth edition of the Model City Charter included direct election of the mayor as a recommended alternative (Childs, 1965: 39).

To a traditional reformer like Richard Childs, the election of the mayor was a deviation from the 'pure' council-manager form of government (Childs, 1965: 39). He acknowledged that direct election attracts 'vigorously assertive personalities' to run for the office but argued that it did not enhance the mayor's leadership: 'leadership ... cannot be ordained since for outsiders to select one man to be the leader of a council is to tell the others to be followers' (Childs, 1965: 43). This argument indicates that Childs and those who supported selection of the mayor by the council viewed the office in narrow terms. The mayor was to be the leader of the council serving as its presiding officer and acting as its spokesperson, and was not expected to provide leadership to all residents and secure a broad base of popular support for government initiatives. There was also the presumption that putting mayors on 'separate pedestals' (Childs, 1965: 40) in council-manager cities would encourage them to go their own way, generating resentment from other council members and potentially producing conflict between the mayor and city manager. Other terms associated with the council-manager mayor – figurehead, ribbon cutter and simply weak mayor – suggested that the mayor was an insignificant leader outside the council.

Despite these arguments, the proportion of directly elected mayors continued to grow in council-manager cities, and a positive and broader conceptualisation of the position began to emerge in the 1970s. At the present time, according to a detailed classification of all cities above 10,000 in population in the US,[1] 63% of the council-manager cities have an elected mayor and 81% of these cities over 100,000 in population elect the mayor (Nelson and Svara, 2010). The mayor came to be viewed as a facilitator who contributed to the performance of the government by linking the parts of the council-manager form, improving their interaction, and fostering a shared commitment to goals (Svara and Bohmbach, 1976; Svara, 1987; 1994). The mayor in the council-manager form occupies a strategic location at the centre of communication channels with the council, the city manager and outside actors (Svara, 1990).

Mayors can fill a broad range of roles beyond the traditional roles of presiding officer, serving as a link to the public and representative/ promoter of the city (Svara, 1994: 219–27). The mayor promotes coordination and communication as an articulator/mobiliser of issues for the city and liaison with the city manager. The mayor can strengthen teamwork on the council by working to coalesce the council into a cohesive team and establishing a positive 'tone'. In addition, the mayor can build networks beyond the government that connect individuals, groups, organisations, and other governments inside and beyond the community. Additional roles deal with policy leadership and guiding the way the council works.

As delegator/organiser, the mayor helps the council and manager understand and maintain their roles. As goal setter, mayors engage in activities to create a sense of direction or a climate for change. Finally, in the policy initiator role, the mayor develops programmes and policies to address problems. If active in these roles, the mayor is instrumental in shaping the city's policy agenda and creating a shared vision. There is new recognition of the importance of the mayor as a visionary who helps shape the goals for the city and builds popular support for initiatives (Svara, 2009). A leader who lacks vision or fails to foster a process for creating a vision leaves council members and the public in a state of uncertainty and confusion. By enlisting others, leaders seek to inspire a 'shared vision' (Kouzes and Posner, 2002) that provides 'a clear picture of what it would look and feel like if [the organisation] were achieving its mission' (Crosby and Bryson, 2005: 89). Beyond its content, a shared vision creates an emotional connection between people and the leader (Denhardt and Denhardt, 2006: 89).

All these roles are mutually reinforcing and success in one enhances success in others, and they are filled concurrently. Facilitative and visionary leadership do not depend on direct election, but particularly the link to the public, network builder, and policy initiator roles are enhanced by campaigning and the implied mandate that comes with winning an election. Direct election makes the mayor a more visible and better known figure in public affairs and increases the likelihood that the mayor is a visionary. In a survey of council members in 2001, 46% of the council members with a directly elected mayor agreed that the mayor is a visionary compared to 35% when the mayor is selected within the council (Svara, 2009: 14).

There are interconnections between a facilitative style and vision. Leaders who base their leadership on formal or informal powers may have some advantages in promoting their ideas and securing the support of some backers, but ultimately a leader is not viewed as a visionary by offering rewards or threatening sanctions. Mayors and other leaders cannot 'impose a self-motivating vision on others' (Kouzes and Posner, 2002: 113). Denhardt and Denhardt (2006: 89) argue that we increasingly recognise that 'broad participation in setting the goals, directions, and vision of a group or organization is helpful in arriving at the most comprehensive and creative statement, as well as the one most likely to be implemented'. Still, facilitation is not enough by itself. According to Kouzes and Posner (2002: 113), 'before you can inspire others, you have to be inspired yourself'. Although the facilitator without vision can move the organisation forward by helping to get the ideas promoted by others accepted as shared goals, it is also possible that others will not have the ideas that generate widespread support or are not able to reach the public in the way the mayor can. The mayor must be able to step forward, articulate goals that incorporate the views of other council members, and persuade others to support them.

This model of leadership based on facilitation and vision contrasts with an alternative model that stresses power and control based on formal resources and the capacity to invest them wisely to enhance the resource base of the office (Dahl, 1961). The importance of overcoming resistance arises in part from the presence of separation of powers that gives council members the resources to check the mayor. From this perspective, mayors increase their ability to set the direction of city government by rewarding supporters and punishing opponents using their budgetary, personnel, and administrative resources. There is no reason why mayors should differ in their potential for visionary leadership based on form of government, but they differ in the resources and authority at their disposal and in the presence or absence of offsetting powers in the council.

Council-manager mayors cannot choose to be power-based leaders who use material and political resources to secure their vision. However, they are not dependent on using material resources to win support on the council, and they do not need to organise the governmental administration and secure support from administrative staff for their agenda. The council-manager mayor can incorporate the goals of council members into a shared vision that provides direction to the manager and staff. With a sense of the goals that the mayor and council want to achieve, the manager is able to provide independent recommendations of actions to take and to align departments to meet the goals of the mayor and council.

Thus, the debate in the US is over the powers and institutional setting of the elected mayor. These characteristics shape the kind of leadership that the mayor is likely to offer.

Referendums to change form of government in large cities

The choice of form of government can be an issue in larger cities. Overall, the number of council-manager cities over 100,000 in population is growing and represents 58% of the total. Still, the underlying question about the appropriateness of the council-manager form to the large city context is often raised,[2] and the debate has intensified in the past two decades (Gurwitt, 1993). Since 1990, local governments in 26 of America's 243 large cities have grappled with the question of whether they should change from one form of government to the other and held a referendum to change the form of government – over 10% of the large cities. The council-manager form has been replaced with the mayor-council form in ten cities.[3] On the other hand, the council-manager form replaced the mayor-council form in two cities and replaced the commission form in one city. Abandonment of the council-manager form was rejected during this period in 11 large cities. In addition, charter changes from the commission to strong mayor form and from a weak mayor-council form to the strong mayor form were rejected in two cities.

With these cross-currents of change, there is not a clear trend regarding public preferences for each form in large cities, but it is apparent that the issue of change in form is more likely to be raised in large council-manager cities. They represented 21 of the 26 large cities in which the referendums to change form of government have been held in the past 25 years. It is likely that other cities will consider a change but experience suggests that retention of the council-manager form will be as or more likely than rejection.

Summarising arguments in support of facilitative versus executive mayors

The debate in the past 25 years in larger cities in the US has not been over whether mayors should be directly elected, but rather what powers mayors should have within a separation of powers or unified authority form of government. Along with Douglas Watson, I reviewed the arguments identified by authors of case studies of the referendums campaigns in 14 cities (Svara and Watson, 2010).[4] In addition, the referendum campaign in Sacramento, California, that was unsuccessful in bringing about a charter change to strengthen the mayor's office is examined to discover the wide array of arguments that made in that six-year long discussion. Two reports – Eye on Sacramento (2014) and Dugger and Kelly (2014) – provide detailed accounts.

Sacramento has a population of almost half a million people and is the capital of California. The effort to change the form of government was promoted Kevin Johnson – a well-known former professional basketball star and native of Sacramento who defeated a two-term incumbent in by 15 percentage points to be elected as mayor in 2008. As a candidate, he had campaigned for a revision of the city charter to a strong mayor form and in January 2009 he launched a petition drive to get the charter change on the ballot. The draft charter would have given the mayor extremely broad executive powers including hiring authority for several hundred senior level managers and staff and contained no limits on the number of terms the mayor could serve. Over 34,000 signatures were acquired to put the initiative on the ballot, but state courts ruled that a vote to replace a city charter rather than simply amending it could only be put on the ballot by action of the city council or an elected charter review commission. A scheduled vote on the initiative in 2010 was cancelled. In 2011, the mayor proposed to the city council a new version of the charter revision but once again the council did not approve a referendum. The elections held in November 2012, however, brought a new majority to the city council that supported the change to a strong mayor form. By late 2013, there was support on the council to approve a referendum.[5] The proposed charter was labelled the Sacramento Checks and Balances Act of 2014, or 'Measure L'. The referendum was held on 4 November 2014.

After a vigorous and expensive campaign in which supporters spent over US$800,000, Measure L was defeated by the voters 57–43% (Lillis, 2014). Despite endorsement of the change by the *Sacramento Bee* newspaper and many other organisations, the opponents had support from civic groups such as the League of Women Voters and a statement of opposition from the ICMA along with financial support from the ICMA Fund for Professional Management and the California City Management Foundation (Duggan, 2015). The opponents benefitted from a catchy slogan – 'L No: Stop the Power Grab'.

The extended debate in Sacramento generated a wide range of arguments supporting both the current and the proposed form of government. These points along with those covered in the 14 case studies of earlier referendums provide insights into the strengths and weaknesses of the major forms of government in the US and the kinds of mayors associated with each form. The summary of the two sets of opposing arguments includes the points made in *favour* of each form of government along with the *criticisms* of the alternate form.

The arguments made by supporters of the mayor-council form are summarised in Table 7.1. The city in which the argument was made is noted in the table. Table 7.2 details some of the criticisms of the council-manager form. The presentation continues with Table 7.3 summarising arguments of supporters of the council-manager form and Table 7.4 detailing criticisms of the mayor-council form. After listing the arguments that were made on each side, there is identification of potential points that have not been clearly articulated in the 15 referendums and might be developed more fully in the future.

It is interesting that the Sacramento campaign did not dismiss the mayor in the council-manager form as a figurehead. Clearly, Kevin Johnson as mayor was demonstrating that the mayor could exert considerable influence within the council-manager form. Also, it was unusual the extent to which the city manager in Sacramento was criticised as an unchecked executive. This point was the key argument for the need to have 'checks and balances'. The ability of the mayor to view the needs of the city as a whole was another central theme in Sacramento. The mayor's new veto power was another new 'check' on the city council that was added to the governmental process. The

Table 7.1: Major themes in support of the mayor-council form

Arguments/claims	City
Strong leadership; mayor is 'in charge' or 'stronger' vis-à-vis council and manager; mayor can forge coalitions with use of incentives and sanctions	Cincinnati, Dallas, Grand Rapids, Kansas City, Oakland, Portland, Richmond, St. Louis, St. Petersburg, San Diego, Spokane
One person who can be held accountable by voters	Cincinnati, Dallas, Oakland, Richmond, St. Louis, Sacramento
Greater capacity to initiate major policy changes	Dallas, Richmond, Spokane, Sacramento
Chief administrative officer (CAO; in Sacramento, still called 'city manager' but appointed by the mayor) provides administrative expertise • Mayor required to present qualifications of the person selected at a public hearing	Grand Rapids, Oakland (1998)[6], Sacramento Sacramento
City can produce effective political executives and capable department heads experienced in business and state government	Sacramento
Council can be supported by Office of Independent Budget Analyst to serve as counterweight to the mayor	Sacramento
Mayor represents the whole city to offset the parochial perspectives of council members elected from districts	Sacramento

requirement that a three quarters vote – six of eight members of the council – was needed to override the veto presumably appealed to some groups who were opposed to council activism on behalf of neighbourhoods

Table 7.2: Criticisms of the council-manager form

Criticisms	City
Mayor is figurehead; does not have enough power to set direction, form coalitions, or overcome opposition	Cincinnati, Dallas, Hartford, Topeka
Mayor does not have sufficient freedom to initiate policy changes; cannot direct staff to complete tasks, for example, get a pot hole fixed	Sacramento
City council is prone to dissension, and there is no one who can overcome it; potential for deadlock	Cincinnati, Dallas, Kansas City, Richmond, Spokane
Diffusion of power, accountability; too many masters	Cincinnati, Dallas, Kansas City, Richmond
Diffusion of responsibility • No one responsible for overall level of performance • Form is efficient in small matters but does not take on major initiatives	Sacramento
City manager acquires too much influence; is not properly supervised Checks on the power of city manager who is an unelected executive are needed	St. Petersburg, San Diego, Spokane Sacramento
City manager turnover; city council can arbitrarily remove manager	Hartford, Topeka
Having city manager does not guarantee competence and high ethical standards	Hartford, Richmond, St. Petersburg, San Diego, Spokane
The council-manager form is out of date, and the strong mayor form will be 'just better'	Sacramento

Additional traditional criticisms of the council-manager form include the charge that the city manager is narrowly focused on improving efficiency and ignores broader values, the form is efficient in small matters but not effective in taking on major initiatives, and the city manager is an outsider whose decisions do not reflect community values (Banfield and Wilson, 1963). These points had not been made in the earlier case studies, but a combination of the first two points was raised in Sacramento. The diffusion of responsibility criticism was expanded there. The Vote Yes on Measure L campaign claimed that no one was empowered to move the city from 'Good to Great' in a council-manager government where 'nobody is in charge because everybody is in charge' (Vote Yes on Measure L, 1994). The presumption was that only a powerful mayor could produce this change. The concern about outsiders does appear to be declining, although proponents of Measure L in Sacramento emphasised that local managers with experience in business and state government could be recruited.

There are additional arguments that were not fully developed or clearly expressed. The leadership role of the mayor has not been examined in depth in most campaigns. Sacramento is a partial exception. The Charter Review Commission (2009) that studied the charter for the council observed that in council-manager cities 'the Mayor is both the political leader of the community and the City Council'. Successful mayors have the 'qualities necessary for successful leadership generally'. The fact that the current mayor in a certain council-manager city is an active leader is acknowledged. In Sacramento, observers noted the mayor could have made even more contributions if not so focused on changing the form of government. Chester Newland, faculty member in public administration and member of the Charter Review Commission, stated that the 'Boss Mayor proposal was not in the interests of Sacramento or the success of Kevin Johnson as Mayor' who could accomplish more 'with thoughtfully collaborative leadership' (Newland, 2010). Still, the full potential for the mayor to be a facilitative and visionary leader has not

Table 7.3: Major themes in support of the council-manager form

Arguments/claims	City
Mayor is leader; a visionary who provides facilitative leadership and builds partnerships; leader of the council and symbol for the community	Grand Rapids, Kansas City, Sacramento
Council is a governing board that focuses on coherent policymaking and oversight of administrative performance • Benefits of 'unified structure' (see related claim regarding separation of powers below)	El Paso, Grand Rapids, Portland Sacramento
Shared leadership is valuable; better than centralised power	Portland, Richmond
Decisions reflect universal values such as equality, fairness, social equity, inclusiveness, responsiveness, efficiency and effectiveness	Dallas, Richmond (fairness to minorities)
City manager brings professionalism to day-to-day operations and stresses effectiveness and efficiency	El Paso, Oakland, Sacramento
City manager is continuously accountable to the council for performance	El Paso, Sacramento, Sacramento
Benefits of a 'unified system'	Sacramento
Sound corporate structure provides for board of directors with its own chair to which the CEO reports	Sacramento

been well articulated in these campaigns. It is correct but incomplete to say that the 'mayor serves as the political leader and "face" of the community' (Edgar et al, 2014).

Table 7.4: Criticisms of the mayor-council form

Criticism	City
Performance of form is too dependent on one person; effectiveness can rise and fall with qualities of the mayor; lack of continuity; when faced with obstacles, mayors seek more power; strong mayor weakens council	El Paso, St. Louis, Sacramento
Mayors have excessive power and are more prone to cronyism, favouritism and corruption • Charter change is 'power grab' that will create a 'boss mayor'	Cincinnati, Dallas, El Paso, Grand Rapids, Spokane, Topeka Sacramento
Mayors will strengthen business, downtown power due to importance of monetary contributions to mayoral candidates • Risk of 'crony capitalism'	Cincinnati, Dallas, Portland, Richmond, St. Louis, Sacramento
Political inference in administration; no chief administrative officer (CAO) or professionalism of the CAO depends on whom the mayor appoints; mayor can bypass the CAO and undercut his/her professionalism	El Paso, Grand Rapids, Oakland (1996), Spokane, Sacramento
Waste and inefficiency	El Paso
Centralised power weakens minority groups and neighbourhood groups and offsets their representation on the council	Dallas, Richmond, St. Louis, St. Petersburg, Sacramento

Academic research demonstrates that city managers provide policy advice based on knowledge, experience, and objective assessment of trends, needs, and community goals (Nelson and Svara, 2014; 2015), but this contribution is largely ignored. The focus remains on the manager's role as an internal manager. California leaders in the ICMA repeated the partial description of the manager's role as managing the city's day-to-day operations (Edgar et al, 2014) with no acknowledgement of the advisory role or the important strategic management involved in planning and assessing future trends, needs, and opportunities. The city manager not only speaks 'truth to power when the mayor makes a mistake,' as Newland indicated (Bento, 2009), but provides a broad range of information and advice including identifying options that elected officials may not want to hear. They are free to ignore the advice, but elected officials and the public deserve to be fully informed. Shifting to the strong mayor form entails giving up the independent professional analysis of policy options and recommendations by the city manager as well as complete reporting to the council on performance to support its oversight role.

A major theme in the Sacramento referendum was the debate about changing the nature of the governance process, although the implications of a shift to a separation of powers form were not fully elaborated. Separation of powers has long been associated with conflict among officials as the earlier statement from Goodnow indicates. In Sacramento, the Charter Review Commission (2009) distinguished the separation of powers model – or the 'divided system' – and the current 'unified system'. The increased likelihood of conflict between the mayor and council with separation of powers (Svara, 1990) was not discussed extensively in the campaigns. The League of Women Voters expressed their support for 'a collaborative council-manager form of government', although the reasons why a cooperative relationship is likely with the council-manager form were not stressed.

The superior performance of council-manager governments in promoting efficiency was stressed in many campaigns, but little attention is given to the record of council-manager cities in establishing long-term goals, maintaining continuity of commitments and introducing innovative practices (Nelson and Svara, 2012). Although proponents argued that charter change would make Sacramento a 'hub for innovation' (Vote Yes on Measure L, 2014), supporters of the council-manager form could have done more to demonstrate that the city already has these characteristics and that they are more likely to expand under the council-manager form.

Among criticisms of the mayor-council form, the weaker performance of the council as a governing board and its domination by the mayor was noted in Grand Rapids, but conflict between the mayor and council and the risk of impasse between the two seats of power appear to be rarely mentioned. Although the superior accountability of city managers under the continuous control of the city council is a well-developed theme in the campaigns, the shortcomings in the accountability of the strong mayor and this form of government generally were not well developed. The Eye on Sacramento (2014) report noted the focus of strong mayors on their supporters and potentially limited attention to the requests of officials or groups that oppose the mayor. The mayor in Sacramento said publicly that he wanted the power to get a pothole fixed, but the mayor can do so now through a manager accountable to the council. In addition, council members also transmit complaints to staff and should be able to expect an appropriate and prompt response. The constituents of mayoral supporters on the council may get better treatment than the constituents of mayoral critics in the strong mayor form of government (Eye on Sacramento, 2014). Relying on elections to keep the mayor accountable requires waiting for up to four years and is not relevant in the mayor's final years in office if the mayor is term limited. There is the potential for diffusion of responsibility for the failure to act when a proposal has majority support on the council, but not a sufficient majority to overcome a mayoral veto.[7]

The impact of the strong mayor form on governing capacity of the council is another theme that could be developed more fully. Some council members may recognise that they can make deals with the mayor to exchange their support for favours whereas they cannot make deals with the city manager. With the extensive control by the strong mayor of jobs, budgets, and determining which specific projects and requests from council members will be accepted, the mayor is in a position to make deals with council members to get their vote, their support or their silence. Favouring some members over others gives the mayor the ability to divide the council into factions (Newland, 2010). This possibility adds to the limited capacity of the council to independently review and question the mayor. In filling its oversight role, the council can have a great deal of difficulty getting information from the mayor's office and departments whose directors are controlled by the mayor. The supposed independence of legislators in a separation of powers form is substantially limited in practice.

Finally, there is an integral transparency in council–manager form that has not been adequately recognised in the campaigns. There is a failure to recognise that the manager communicates with the whole council in public. To be sure, the manager has one-on-one meetings with the mayor and individual council members. These are fundamentally different, however, from the meetings between the strong mayor and the chief administrative officer (CAO) in which the mayor determines whether an issue will be shared with the council, what options will be provided, and what information will be made available.

Conclusion

The discussion of options for local government structure in the US appears at times to be a comparison of a mayor-centred structure and a professional manager-centred structure, but this is not the case. The mayor's leadership is integral and essential to both forms of government. Douglas Watson and I titled our book on form of government referendums *More than Mayor or Manager* because the choice of form determines what kind of mayor, council and top administrator a city is likely to have as well as shaping the interactions among officials in the governmental process.

Mayors in the council-manager form whose link to the public is strengthened by direct election are leaders of the city council and the community, and they liaise for the whole council with the city manager. Direct election increases the likelihood that the mayor provides visionary leadership compared to the mayors in council-manager cities that are selected by the council. Council-manager mayors can make an important contribution appropriate to their governmental structure just as the mayor in the mayor-council form can. A council-manager city may function capably with an inept mayor because others can handle parts of the leadership role, but it can excel with an effective one especially when directly elected. These elected mayors, however, must be aware that they are enhancing the performance of the government as a whole. They improve performance by helping the council function better, by assuring a high level of communication and cooperation with the city manager and staff, and by building support in the community. And they contribute to the city government's success by proposing initiatives and working to create a shared vision in the council. Despite their electoral mandate, these mayors cannot be effective by going their own way and seeking to accomplish their own agenda, by suppressing the independent advice received from the manager and staff, or by unilaterally intervening in the administrative process to secure preferred actions.

These characteristics clearly apply to council-manager mayors. It is possible for mayors in mayor-council cities to use the same approaches rather than relying on their formal powers and political resources (Wheeland, 2009). Some of these mayors can be effective as assertive leaders who use their powers to advance their agenda, but they run the risk of failing to get council support for proposals and limiting their accomplishments by diverting resources to handling conflicts with the council. They could have independent CAOs who assess a full range of policy options for addressing problems as city managers typically do and who share information freely with the council and the public, but executive mayors are likely to expect their CAO to demonstrate loyalty and deference to the mayor.

In selecting the council-manager or the mayor-council form, citizens are typically choosing different types of mayors who in different ways can be effective political leaders.

Notes

[1]   K. Nelson, faculty member at the University of North Carolina at Chapel Hill, has combined multiple data sources to develop a comprehensive database for all cities in the US over 10,000 in population.

[2]   The largest cities in the US did not adopt the council-manager form in the early decades of the municipal reform movement. It was found in smaller cities and during the 1950s disproportionately in suburban cities. Banfield and Wilson (1963) advanced the argument that it was well suited primarily for smaller, more homogeneous cities. As council-manager cities have grown and become more diverse, the form is now being used in cities of all kinds including four cities over 1 million in population – Dallas, Phoenix, San Antonio, and San Jose.

[3]   The cities in each category are listed here. The case study cities in Svara and Watson (2010) are underlined.

[a]   Change from council-manager to mayor-council: Colorado Springs, Colorado; Fresno, California; Hartford, Connecticut; Miami, Florida; Oakland, California; Richmond, Virginia; St. Petersburg, Florida; San Diego, California; Spokane, Washington; and Toledo, Ohio.

[b]   Change from mayor-council to council-manager: El Paso, Texas, and Topeka, Kansas.

[c]   Change from commission form to council-manager: Cedar Rapids, Iowa.

[d]   Abandonment of the council-manager form was rejected: Corpus Christi, Texas; Cincinnati, Ohio; Dallas, Texas; Grand Rapids, Michigan; Kansas City, Missouri; Little Rock, Arkansas; Pasadena, Texas; Pueblo, Colorado; Sacramento, California; Tucson, Arizona; and Worcester, Massachusetts.

[e]   Change from commission to strong mayor form rejected: Portland, Oregon.

[f]   Change from weak mayor-council form to the strong mayor form rejected: St. Louis, Missouri.

[4]   The case study cities are listed in Note 3.

[5]   Compared to the version proposed in 2011, the council dropped terms limits for council members and limited the mayor to three terms (not counting Johnson's first two terms). A requirement of voter approval for council and mayor pay raises that exceed 5% per year was dropped, a provision was added that provides that the city council 'may' create an ethics commission and a neighbourhood advisory committee. A budget analyst position hired by the council was added.

[6]   A trial change in form began in Oakland in 1998, and it was finalised in 2004. Points made only in the first round of change are identified.

[7]   In addition, the Sacramento charter change created the possibility of impasse due to tie votes on the even-numbered council.

References

Banfield, E. C. and Wilson, J. Q. (1963) *City Politics*, New York: Vintage Books.

Bento, A. (2009) 'Town Hall Suspicious of Strong Mayor Proposal', *Sacramento Press*, 11 October, https://sacramentopress.com/2009/10/11/town-hall-suspicious-of-strong-mayor-proposal/

Brazeau, T. W. (1897) *Mayor Vs. Council: Should a System of Municipal Government, Concentrating All Executive and Administrative Powers in the Mayor, be Adopted in Cities of the United States?* The Twenty-seventh Annual Joint Debate of the University of Wisconsin.

Charter Review Commission (2009) *Final Report: City of Sacramento*.

Childs, R. S. (1965) *The First 50 Years of the Council-Manager Plan of Municipal Government*, New York: National Municipal League.

Crosby, B. C. and Bryson, J. M. (2005) *Leadership for the Common Good: Tackling Public Problems in a Shared-Power World* (2nd edn), San Francisco: Jossey-Bass.

Dahl, R. A. (1961) *Who Governs?* New Haven: Yale University Press.

Denhardt, R. B., and Denhardt, J. V. (2006) *The Dance of Leadership: The Art of Leading in Business, Government, and Society*, Armonk, NY: M.E. Sharpe.

Duggan, K. (2015) 'Preserving Professional Management: Lessons Learned in Sacramento, California', *PM Magazine*, June, http://icma. org/en/press/pm_magazine/article/105818

Dugger, C. and Kelly, A. (2014) *Measure L: Sacramento Checks and Balances Act of 2014*, Sacramento: University of the Pacific, McGeorge School of Law, www.mcgeorge.edu/Documents/Publications/ Measure%20L2014.pdf

Edgar, W. H., Gaebler, T. A., Gould, R. S. and Martel, P. E. (2014) 'ICMA Issues Statement of Sacramento's Measure L', 17 October, http://icma.org/en/icma/newsroom/highlights/Article/105121/ ICMA_Issues_Statement_on_Sacramentos_Measure_L

Eye on Sacramento (2014) *Policy Report on Measure L—The Sacramento Checks and Balances Act of 2014*, Sacramento: Eye on Sacramento.

Goodnow, F. J. (1908) *City Government in the United States*, New York: Century Company.

Gurwitt, R. (1993) 'The Lure of the Strong Mayor', *Governing*, 6(10) (July), 36–41.

Kouzes, J. M. and Posner, B. Z. (2002) *The Leadership Challenge* (3rd edn), San Francisco: Jossey-Bass.

Lillis, R. (2014) 'Strong-mayor plan defeated, Kevin Johnson concedes', *Sacramento Bee*, 5 November, www.sacbee.com/news/local/news- columns-blogs/city-beat/article3583619.html

Nelson, K. L. and Svara, J. H. (2010) 'Adaptation of Models Versus Variations in Form: Classifying Structures of City Government', *Urban Affairs Review*, 45 (4), 544–62.

Nelson, K. L. and Svara, J. H. (2012) 'Form of Government Still Matters: Fostering Innovation in U.S. Municipalities', *American Review of Public Administration*, 42, 257–81.

Nelson, K. L. and Svara, J. H. (2014) 'Upholding and Expanding the Roles of Local Government Managers: State of the Profession 2012', *The Municipal Year Book 2014*, 81: 3–20, Washington: ICMA.

Nelson, K. L. and Svara, J. H. (2015) 'The roles of local government managers in theory and practice: a centennial perspective, *Public Administration Review*, 75: 49–61.

Newland, C. A. (2010) 'USC Exclusive with Dr. Chester Newland: discussing the strong mayor,' PublicCEO, 20 July, www.publicceo. com/2010/07/usc-exclusive-with-dr-chester-newland-discussing-the-strong-mayor/

Svara, J. H. (1987) Mayoral leadership in council-manager cities: preconditions versus preconceptions, *Journal of Politics*, 49: 207–27.

Svara, J. H. (1990) *Official Leadership in the City: Patterns of Conflict and Cooperation*, New York: Oxford University Press.

Svara, J. H. (1994) *Facilitative Leadership in Local Government: Lessons from Successful Mayors and Chairpersons in the Council-Manager Form*, San Francisco: Jossey-Bass.

Svara, J. H. (2009) *The Facilitative Leader in City Hall: Reexamining the Scope and Contributions*, Boca Raton, FL: CRC Press.

Svara, J. H. and Bohmbach, J. (1976) 'The Mayoralty and Leadership in Council-Manager Cities', *Popular Government*, 41: 1-6.

Svara, J. H. and Watson, D. (2010) *More than Mayor or Manager: Campaigns to Change Form of Government in America's Large Cities*, Washington: Georgetown University Press, 2010.

Vote Yes on Measure L (2014) 'Importance of Charter Revision', www.facebook.com/voteyesonl/

Wheeland, C. M. (2009) 'The Power to Persuade: Philadelphia, Pennsylvania', in Svara, J. (ed.) *The Facilitative Leader in City Hall: Reexamining the Scope and Contributions* (ASPA Series in Public Administration and Public Policy), Boca Raton, FL: Routledge, pp 327-52.

Woodruff, C. R. (1919) *A New Municipal Program*, New York: D. Appleton and Company.

EIGHT

Popular leaders or rats in the ranks? Political leadership in Australian cities

Paul Burton, Griffith University, Australia

Introduction

In 2000–01 I spent a significant amount of time chairing the Bristol Democracy Commission, a body set up by Bristol City Council to review the political management structures of the council and to make recommendations on which of a number of options pre-determined by central government the council should adopt in the future; we were also charged with reviewing the current state of engagement in local democratic politics in the city and to recommend ways in which this might be improved, enhanced and stimulated, especially at the neighbourhood level.

Just over one year later, we presented our report (Burton, 2001) to the Lord Mayor of Bristol, at that time Councillor Graham Robertson, a longstanding Labour member of the city council and a former leader of the council. While we were not in absolute agreement, there was a high degree of consensus on the Commission that a new approach to political leadership and management within the council was worthy of serious consideration and indeed that there was a strong case for taking a new approach. In particular, we believed there was merit in moving to a new system in which the mayor of the city would no longer be limited to playing a mainly ceremonial role but would have some autonomous executive powers, including the power to form a cabinet of their choosing to help lead the city, and would be directly elected by the electors of Bristol.

Some years later I moved to Australia to join Griffith University and work within the jurisdiction of the City of Gold Coast. As well as being the sixth largest city in Australia, it is the second largest local government authority (by population) in the country, led by a council of 14 divisional councillors and a directly elected mayor, all of whom are expected to work full time in the role and are well paid to do so.[1] Party politics is not a significant feature in the election of councillors and while the political allegiances of councillors and candidates standing in local elections may be known, this does not figure prominently in their campaigning. Thus, in the city where I now work there is a local political management structure that delivers most of the measures I advocated as a member of the Bristol Democracy Commission. Does this Australian system deliver the benefits anticipated some years ago when reviewing the political management arrangements of Bristol City Council and is the experience of the City of Gold Coast and Queensland of relevance to the rest of Australia?

A very brief history of local government in Australia

The Adelaide Corporation, created by the province of South Australia (the predecessor of the current state of South Australia) in October 1840, is widely recognised as the first formal entity of local government in Australia – which of course was not at that time a nation, but a collection of British colonies. It was followed soon after by the establishment of the City of Sydney council in New South Wales and the Town of Melbourne council in Victoria in 1842 and thereafter by a series of councils and other bodies designed principally to build roads and provide a limited range of other public services and utilities for their localities. There are now approximately 560 local government bodies in Australia, almost half the number that existed at the time of Federation in 1901 (Sansom, 2012).

The creation of the Commonwealth of Australia in 1901 involved the newly formed states giving up certain powers over such matters as defence, immigration, foreign policy, customs and excise, and general taxation to the new Commonwealth government. Local government was not seen as a Commonwealth responsibility and has remained a state and Northern Territory responsibility ever since (Australian Government, 2013) and as a result different systems of local government apply across the country. Nevertheless, most local government bodies are responsible for the provision of a similar set of services, including engineering works (roads, bridges, sewerage and storm water systems and so on), planning and development approval, building works certification, recreation facilities (parks, sports centres, camping grounds, community halls), cultural and educational facilities such as galleries and libraries, public health functions (licensing, noise control and animal control) and some community services such as age care, meals on wheels and so on. Local government in Australia is not responsible for primary and secondary education, most social services, social housing, most health services or for policing. In recent years the Commonwealth government has provided an increasing volume of funding to support the provision of local services through a number of specific purpose payments (SPPs), each subject to a National Agreement. These funding streams are mainly channelled to the states and territories although some funding programmes such as Roads to Recovery allow money to go directly to local councils.[2] Across the whole of Australia, local governments typically raise 37% of their revenue through local rates (property taxes), 33% from a variety of user charges and fees, 13% from grants made by state and federal governments and 17% from a plethora of miscellaneous sources including interest payments. These proportions vary substantially across the states and territories and according to the size and characteristic of each council.

Although constitutionally dependent on their respective state governments, local government is now represented through the President of the Australian Local Government Association on the main body charged with managing relations between all three levels of government, the Council of Australian Governments (COAG). The National Agreements described above are the product of policy debate initiated at COAG and indicate some degree of increased recognition of the role of local government, especially the larger councils and some informal groupings of local governments.

The current state of local political management structures across Australia

In their recent exploration of local government political management arrangements in Australia, Martin and Aulich (2012) describe the varied state of play across the country. Two of the most important features of these arrangements are the ways in which mayors come to office and the powers they are able to exercise once in office. In New South Wales mayors are indirectly elected (that is by their fellow councillors) and a local referendum is required to move to a system of direct election. Less than 20% of councils have adopted the direct election of their mayor, who in either case serves principally as the chairperson of council meetings and performs ceremonial functions. The council as a whole is responsible for making policy and providing local civic leadership. All Victorian councils (except the cities of Melbourne and Geelong) indirectly elect their mayors for two year terms, who then chair council meetings but have no other specified powers. Like New South Wales, Western Australia defaults to indirect elections and requires a local referendum to move to a system of direct election. The Mayor of Perth must, however, be directly elected but in all cases the full council retains responsibility for policy decisions and local leadership. In South Australia, each council can decide (without the need for a local referendum) which model to adopt, and almost three quarters have chosen to directly elect their mayors, who can in some circumstances provide advice to the chief executive officer on the implementation of policies that remain the collective responsibility of the whole council. The Lord Mayor of the state's capital city, Adelaide, has additional executive powers and responsibilities. Tasmania gives a substantial local leadership role to its mayors, who are directly elected (along with their deputy) every two years. They oversee their fellow councillors in carrying out their functions and are able to liaise closely with the council's general manager in overseeing the performance of the council and the implementation of policies. Only in Queensland are all mayors directly elected for a full four-year term and enjoy a semi-executive as well as a ceremonial role. They are able to liaise directly with and provide strategic direction to the chief executive officer, to propose a budget and to provide local leadership. The Lord Mayor of Brisbane has even more extensive powers, although the current Brisbane model has changed significantly over the years since 1921 when the system of directly elected mayors was first introduced in Queensland.

Most councils, therefore, choose their leader from within their own ranks and the public has only an indirect influence on this selection process. Although consistent with the ways in which the prime minister of the federal government, state premiers and the chief minsters of territory governments are determined, this process remains prone to local coalition politics and internecine conflict within political parties and factional groupings (Grant et al, 2015; Kiss, 2002). These machinations were famously captured in the 1996 documentary film *Rats in the Ranks*, which followed the internal election of the Mayor of Leichardt Council in Sydney's inner west in 1994. The film is highly regarded for its portrayal of Australian local politics and served as the inspiration for the ABC satirical series about local government, *Grass Roots*, broadcast initially between 2000 and 2003.

It is noteworthy that many of the capital city councils are able or required to directly elect their mayor, regardless of the system prevailing in the rest of the state. But of greater significance is the fact that some of these councils (Sydney and Melbourne in particular) cover only a small part of the greater metropolitan area, such that the lord mayors of Sydney and Melbourne are, in effect, lord mayors only of their respective central business districts. The exception to this is the capital city of Brisbane, which has since 1921 enjoyed a political management regime markedly different from the rest of Australia and which, in a country that has so often taken its political cue from the UK, prefigured developments there by around 80 years (Stockwell, 1995). From its establishment in 1860, Queensland had a bicameral parliament, comprising an elected Legislative Assembly (lower house) and an appointed Legislative Council (upper house). The Labor government formed after the 1915 state elections embarked on a programme of reform that included the abolition of what it saw as the undemocratic Legislative Council and substantial changes to the management of local government, including the introduction of direct elections for (urban) council mayors and (rural) shire chairmen who were granted new executive powers. As noted by the Hon. William McCormack, then Home Secretary in the Queensland government:

> The idea of electing a mayor as chief executive was certainly new, but there were good reasons why the mayor should not be an ordinary alderman ... The mayor was the chief executive officer of the whole of the ratepayers in that particular area. (quoted in Tucker, 1994: 510)

This process also saw the amalgamation of 18 existing councils into the Greater Brisbane Council in 1925, with the mayor becoming the CEO of the new council. Over the coming years this arrangement was amended on numerous occasions (Tucker, 1994) in the face of arguments about democratic accountability, the concentration of power and the need to adopt modern business management methods. Sometimes the mayor's powers were weakened by making him (and they have with the exception of Sallyanne Atkinson always been men) subject to oversight by a committee of aldermen, or by giving control of the staff of the council to a town clerk or CEO, but in a number of cases the Lord Mayor (since 1930) has been able to exercise considerable power and influence through their political skills and forceful personality. Clem Jones (1961–75), Sallyanne Atkinson (1985–91), Jim Soorley (1991–2003) and Campbell Newman (2004–11) are widely regarded as the most influential of Brisbane's mayors by dint of their charismatic personality, political skills and wider experience of management (Tucker, 1994) and all were able to capitalise on the legitimacy offered to them by being directly elected by the people at large.

The case for directly elected mayors in Australian local government

In his review of what Australian mayors can now and should do in the future, Sansom (2012) presents an argument put forward by many (including other contributors to this volume) that there is a need for more effective local political leadership that is both 'facilitative' (Stoker et al, 2007) and 'place-based' (Hambleton, 2015), and grounded in the office of mayor. As already described, mayors in Queensland have as a matter of course a greater range of executive powers and responsibilities than their counterparts in other states and territories as well as the greater legitimacy that goes with direct election. But Sansom (2012: 15) also notes that many Queensland mayors and the directly elected mayors of the major capital cities often 'exercise power or influence significantly greater than indicated by the relevant provisions of the local government Act' and that 'there are many other mayors across Australia who, regardless of their method of election, exercise considerable authority and provide forceful leadership, irrespective of the precise wording of the legislation' (Sansom, 2012: 17). Nevertheless, Sansom argues that having a personal mandate to serve as leader for at least two years (if not four) is an essential foundation on which a raft of other mayoral attributes must be built if we are to see more effective place-based leadership in Australian cities.

Of course there is also a set of counter arguments that point to the danger of mayoral elections becoming little more than a personality contest between those either with a very high media profile or a bank balance that allows considerable expenditure on campaigning, but where neither has any particular experience of local political leadership or community involvement. The election of Darryn Lyons (former paparazzo photographer) to the mayoralty of Geelong in Victoria and of Stuart Drummond (former soccer club mascot) to the mayoralty of Hartlepool in the UK can be seen as the epitome of these concerns. While Drummond was re-elected for a second term and can therefore claim that concerns over his capabilities were somewhat misplaced, the Lyons-led government of Geelong was recently dismissed by the Victorian government after only three years in office following a commission of inquiry into allegations of mismanagement and bullying (ABC, 2016). Other concerns focus on the possibility of mayors failing to secure the support of other members of their council and having to deal with political stalemate, although it is worth noting that in the UK an increase in the number of councils on which no one party secures overall control has led to similar outcomes over the past 20 years (Local Government Association, 2014).

There is also an argument, although not in my view an especially compelling one, that because councillors must usually relinquish their divisional seat in order to contest the mayoralty, if they lose the mayoral election their experience is lost to council altogether until at least the next election. While this may well be the case, it is merely one of many difficult choices to be made by any aspirant mayor and is no good reason in itself for avoiding direct elections.

The other mayoral attributes and activities set out by Sansom include playing a prominent role in local community leadership by preparing and presenting a long-term vision for the locality, overseeing the preparation and implementation of council plans and strategies to achieve that vision and leading inter-governmental relations, not only with the state and federal governments, but also in partnership with adjoining councils, especially in metropolitan regional settings. These are explored further in the work of Martin and Aulich (2012), who scrutinise in more detail the relationships between mayors and CEOs in achieving better local leadership.

If these are the theoretical arguments for and against directly elected mayors, how are they received by the public at large? How satisfied is the general public with local government in Australia and do they have strong views on whether their mayors should be directly or indirectly elected? The next section explores these views on more detail.

Satisfaction with local government and mayors/leaders

There are few robust and reliable surveys of public satisfaction with local government across the whole of Australia, and none that focus specifically on local political management arrangements, including the extent of support for directly or indirectly elected mayors. However, the Australian Constitutional Values Survey (ACVS; Brown, 2014) provides some insights into the standing of local government compared with other levels of government. Based on a telephone survey of 1,200 randomly selected adults from across Australia, the latest ACVS (2014) shows a relatively high (69.4%) level of satisfaction with the state of Australian democracy as a whole, although one that has fallen from the 81% satisfaction level recorded in the first survey in 2008. Trust in local government across the country is slightly higher (58.9%) compared with state (54.5%) or national level (52.5%) but there are variations state by state with Queensland showing one of the largest discrepancies between satisfaction with state (44.5%) and local levels

(62.7%). However, it is not clear whether this is associated in any way with the political leadership of local government although the level of satisfaction with the state government in Queensland is the lowest in Australia. For example, in Tasmania, where mayors are also directly elected, the level of satisfaction with local government is comparatively low (53%) and fell considerably (a drop of 18.1 percentage points from 71.1) since the last survey in 2012.

The report of the 2014 ACVS shows there is very little support for giving local government greater responsibility for a wider range of services such as housing, health or environmental protection, and while a majority (71.6%) believe the overall three tier federal system needs to be reformed, a relatively high proportion of respondents (35.9%) felt that this should involve the abolition of local government altogether! This data suggests that for most Australians, the question of how to elect the leader of their local council is not a matter of great importance or significance. There is no evidence of any strong connection in practice or in public opinion between the overall performance of councils, however measured, and the ways in which their leaders are chosen. This is not to say that in many places there is not public criticism of the performance of council and their leaders, but that the method of choosing the leader is not seen as especially relevant.

Mayors in practice: Queensland case studies

But what of the performance of directly elected mayors? Again, there is little or no evidence of mayoral performance resulting from any systematic and rigorous national study, or even from studies within particular states. This section draws, therefore, on the experience and impact of two directly elected mayors in Queensland, presenting their personal views to illustrate some of the practical as well as political challenges facing contemporary mayors of this type.

How do mayors in office describe their experiences of serving in this role? Why did they stand for office and what did they expect of the role? At the time of interview, Tom Tate was in his first term as Mayor of the City of Gold Coast, having stood unsuccessfully on one occasion previously; Pam Parker was in her second term as Mayor of Logan City but did not stand for a third term in the election in April 2016. Both were interviewed as part of the background research for the preparation of this chapter and offer interesting insights on the motivations and ambitions of mayors, their day to day working practices and their relations with fellow councillors.[3]

Pam Parker moved to Queensland from Victoria and worked in an administrative capacity for Logan City Council for 18 months before deciding to stand for election as a divisional councillor: "I ran for council because I saw the calibre of councillors and thought, if I couldn't do a better job than that there's something wrong with me". Initially she found it difficult to strike the right balance between community service and making business decisions about the council as a whole: "I was playing Mother Teresa whilst also trying to play governance."

Having served three terms as a divisional councillor she was confronted by a new set of challenges when council amalgamations in 2008 saw Logan grow considerably in the size of its jurisdiction by taking on a substantial rural hinterland and the nearby urban centre of Beenleigh, neither of which was especially happy to be part of the new Logan City. She decided to run for mayor in order to play a greater role in making the newly amalgamated council function as effectively as possible and was successful in the 2008 election, becoming the first female mayor of the city. Having been a hard-working councillor, Parker believed she was well-prepared for the mayoralty, but soon found herself working 20 hour days because "approachability brings with it an amazing workload". She eventually increased the staff in her office from one to five and believes that employing a 'media person' to write her speeches and presentations saved her 30–40 hours of work per week. She did not, however, have a Chief of Staff mainly because she felt it would be difficult to rely on that person to the extent that it would be worthwhile:

> 'My knowledge won't allow me to let go of a lot of things because I have more knowledge than the people working around me … that's the downside … when you do let go, the ball gets dropped and then I end up, I call myself the fire warden and I end up having to put the fires out.'

When asked about the extent to which she felt able to call on other mayors for advice or support, Parker revealed an interesting although perhaps not surprising gendered perspective. This perspective was shaped when she first became mayor and encountered some less than progressive views about her capabilities, including from among some of her fellow councillors: "you've got some prehistoric dinosaurs … there are some members of the old guard that have taken a while to get used to women in leadership roles". Nevertheless, she did seek advice from her fellow mayors in the state, especially from other female mayors who she feels are more empathetic:

> 'I think the girls communicate on a girl level more so, so we'll share things confidentially with one another because you get a little bit more guarded when sharing with a male, because their way of thinking is different to ours.'

Finally, Parker spoke of the case for mayors having more power and makes an interesting case for being cautious in extending these powers. When asked whether the current number of councillors is about right, she believed the current 12 is workable and provides a good balance in the desire for efficiency and representativeness. While claiming to favour benevolent dictatorships (and seeing herself as benevolent) she also believed in the importance of taking her fellow councillors "on the journey" with her. She would be happy for more constitutional power being given to leaders with "humility and compassion" and whose ultimate goal "was just about their community", while stating firmly that "I would not like people who are dismissive of others to have [more] authority". Mayor Parker was less clear of how to ensure or guarantee the benevolence of any "local dictator" or how to test candidates' claims of "humility and compassion" in advance of them taking office. However, it is worth noting that in the most recent elections in Logan (March 2016), Parker eventually gave a public endorsement of the winning candidate, having previously said she would not endorse any candidate.

Tom Tate became Mayor of the City of Gold Coast in 2012 at his second attempt. He first contested the mayoralty in 2008 believing that a party political approach was called for and stood, therefore, as an endorsed candidate of the Queensland Liberal National Party (LNP), along with a full slate of LNP divisional candidates. This belief proved unfounded and neither he nor any of his candidates was elected as the conservative vote split between his team and that of another conservative candidate and team. Four years later Tate stood again, this time as an independent and without a slate of divisional candidates and won with 49% of the vote, almost twice that of his nearest rival.

With a background in engineering, property development and tourism, he decided to enter local politics for two mains reasons: first, he was already spending a considerable amount of time on community and local business groups (Lions, Chamber of Commerce, Surfers Paradise Alliance and so on); and, second, he had the financial security to be able to devote himself to local politics and to be able to fund a major local campaign in support of his candidature. He also declared a strong commitment to improving the fortunes of the city by transforming the council from what was widely portrayed (in the local media at least) as dysfunctional into a more business-like operation. In this he drew also on his engineering background: "My engineering mindset helped in the corporate world, it's output oriented … but having said that, there was a learning curve from being a business leader to a political leader." He speaks also of the significance of an egotistical drive to seek the leadership of the council, rather than becoming a divisional councillor in the first instance and then looking to step up to the mayoralty:

> 'there's a bit of ego involved, I've run my own businesses which have employed over 300 people and I haven't had to report to anyone else … and all those community boards I was on, I was either chairman or president so the idea of chairing committees was second nature to me. Also, I really feel that as mayor you can make the most difference for the time spent … and get things moving.'

Tate had campaigned, like many of his competitors, to deal with what was portrayed in the media as a divided and dysfunctional council and a 'bloated bureaucracy'. As some of the more critical divisional councillors had given up their seats to the contest (unsuccessfully) the mayoralty, the new council he led was less fractured and many first time members were more amenable to the various reforms to its operating procedures initiated by the new mayor. He believes that most of these reforms have been successful, even if some were viewed with scepticism at the outset:

> 'I made a motion, first up, that I'm going to have fortnightly meetings [of the full council] and I remember all the returning councillors going, well that's not going to work, but now we have fortnightly meetings and yesterday's meeting lasted 48 minutes [rather than the weekly meetings that used to regularly last for 5–6 hours]'.

He also developed a new working relationship with the CEO, who many of his mayoral competitors had promised to sack immediately if they won office. Tate's view was to move forward more pragmatically.

'I had a meeting and said, let's see if we can work together for six months, but I know one thing: after six months I will still be mayor, it's your call whether you still want to be the CEO. But in saying that, the working relationship is good in that for the first time in eight years the CEO has clear direction from the elected wing.'

Like Mayor Parker, Tate was somewhat ambivalent about mayors having greater powers. He would like more authority to prepare an approved budget but is wary of mayors having more widespread power and authority in case they misuse it, "As mayor I trust me to do the right thing, but I can't say that if a different mayor comes in, that person would also do it right."

Tate described one of the biggest challenges he has faced as mayor to be managing his own health and wellbeing, rather than any substantive political issues. During his first year in office he found the succession of meetings and official functions began to take its toll on his health and he was unable to find time to visit the gym. He too described the pressures and constraints on his family life and cited a promise made to his wife that he would commit to two terms in office (if re-elected) but not to a third term. He did, however, feel able to call on fellow mayors in South East Queensland, including Mayor Parker, for advice when he needed it, as well as receiving counsel from former Gold Coast mayors that he felt share his political vision for the city and how it should be run.

Finally, he disavowed any move into state or federal politics. "I've always been on the record – radio and television – you'll never see my name on a state or federal ballot paper, I'm not interested." He said he plans to retire from local politics when he has completed what he hopes will be two terms of office.

These two cases illustrate three important elements of contemporary political leadership in Australian local government. First, local political leadership can serve as an effective stepping stone to higher office for those that choose this course, especially when stepping up from the leadership of a large and powerful council. Second, while the formal statutory powers of directly elected mayors are relatively modest in comparison with strong mayor models from elsewhere in the world, experienced and skilled mayors can exercise political leadership beyond these powers. Third, in order to cope with the mental and physical challenges of performing successfully as a mayor, it is important to develop a functioning mayoral office and a productive working relationship with the senior leadership of the council's administrative arm. Of course the experiences of Parker and Tate as directly elected leaders of two of the largest local governments in the country are not typical and in this chapter I have not been able to present the experiences or views of leaders of much smaller councils who have been chosen differently.

Prospects for change

The most significant feature of local government in Australia is that it remains a creature of state and territory governments and hence any change at the national scale is most likely to be partial rather than wholesale. The Australian Local Government Association has for many years campaigned for the recognition of local government in the Australian constitution, arguing that this could take the form of any combination of symbolic, financial or democratic recognition and recognition through cooperation (ALGA, 2014). An Expert Panel on Constitutional Recognition of Local Government (Spigelman, 2011) reported in 2011 that only financial recognition commanded sufficient support among the public at large and other relevant interests to stand any chance of success in the Constitutional Referendum that would be required to achieve this change. It is worth noting that the issue of extending the number of mayors who might be directly elected was raised only as a relatively minor aspect of one of the forms of recognition – democratic – and was discussed alongside concerns about how best to limit the term of office of mayors and avoid dynastic problems. The pattern of political management models is likely, therefore, to remain one of variation as there is no evidence of any great appetite for systematic change and harmonisation. As in many other spheres of politics and governance in Australia, while there may be some recognition of some problems associated with subnational variability, there is much less acceptance of any one model on which to base a less variable system. This is partly a problem of political inertia and partly one of parochialism in which inter-state rivalries can stand in the way of any acknowledgement that somewhere else might have structured their local political management arrangements in better ways.

Conclusions

While the introduction of directly elected mayors in England and Wales represents a relatively recent innovation (Sandford, 2004) and is driven from the top down, in Australia it has been an established form of local political management in some parts of the country for almost

100 years. This allows, in principle at least, a degree of comparative analysis of the impact of directly elected mayors on the performance and legitimacy of local councils, as indeed does the varied pattern of adoption seen within Australia. However, there has to date been very little empirical research on these issues and no detailed investigation of any possible correlations let alone causal explorations of the impact of directly elected mayors. Surveys such as the ACVS provide little or no evidence of any correlation between the prevailing political management arrangements and support or satisfaction with local government. Nor are there many signs that states operating one system are especially inclined to draw on the experience of states with other systems to review and possibly change their own practices. Similarly, there is no evidence of any popular groundswell of opinion in Queensland to move away from its long established practice of directly electing mayors, but there is some debate in other states about moving in the direction of Queensland, South Australia and Tasmania, especially for larger towns and cities.

If anything the Australian experience suggests that the case for directly elected mayors builds as it applies to places of greater political and economic significance. In Brisbane the amalgamation of a plethora of small councils into one large entity in 1925 was accompanied by the direct election of their mayor and if other capital cities were ever to follow suit (which does not appear likely at present) then they might also choose to couple that process with direct elections. Small councils, at least in terms of the populations they serve, are less likely to feel any pressure to introduce direct elections if they do not already have them. In this respect scale of operation becomes the most significant variable in understanding current and future patterns of political management arrangements, so that very small councils not faced with the challenges of trying to manage complex cities can perhaps do so more plausibly with councillors serving in a part time capacity, who in turn choose their own leader and mayor. On the other hand, it is difficult to imagine Lord Mayors of Brisbane only assuming that role at the end of a day's work elsewhere and willingly handing over their selection as mayor to their fellow councillors instead of the public at large.

Perhaps the most obvious conclusion to be drawn from these comparisons is that prevailing practices in any one place can quickly become normalised and taken for granted, to the extent that alternatives appear peculiar or even inconceivable. Indeed, when I have described the political management arrangements of the City of Gold Coast to local councillors in Bristol they find it difficult to imagine how such a system could work in practice, and vice versa. Nevertheless, it is clear that any differences in how local citizens perceive their council between those that directly elect their leaders and those who do so indirectly are not especially noticeable. Public recognition of who is leading the council is probably greater for those councils in both the UK and Australia with direct elections, but there is only limited evidence to support this view.

Although in Australia there is considerable experience of councils led by directly elected mayors, there appears to be little inclination to learn from the experience of Queensland and to a lesser extent from South Australia and Tasmania or any significant political pressure across most of Australia to have more directly elected mayors which might drive such learning. Nor is there any evident suggestion that councils led by directly elected mayors should revert to a system whereby their political leaders are chosen by representatives of the people, rather than the people themselves. While the direction of change in Australia is, if anything, towards more councils choosing direct over indirect elections, the extent and pace of that change is somewhat glacial. In the meantime, the machinations depicted so vividly in *Rats in the Ranks* are likely to continue to characterise the selection of more local political leaders than the open engagement of the electorate as a whole via direct elections. The impact of this on the performance of councils remains to be explored in future research.

Notes

[1]   Basic allowances from July 2014: mayor – A$227,701; deputy mayor – A$157,922; councillor – A$135, 886 (Queensland Government, 2013). The Australian Bureau of Statistics classifies those earning over A$140,000 as high income households, while the national average wage for those in full time employment in 2013 was A$74,724. On 30 July 2014, A$1 was worth £0.55.

[2]   Under the *Roads to Recovery* programme, the federal government will provide A$2.1 billion to Australia's local councils, state and territory Governments responsible for local roads over the period from 2014–15 to 2018–19.

[3]   These mayors were interviewed face-to-face using a semi-structured list of topics during 2015. The interviews were recorded and transcribed and the quotes presented here are verbatim extracts from the transcripts.

References

ABC (2016) 'Geelong Council officially sacked, elections to be held in 2017, as Bill passes Parliament', ABC News, 14 April. Available www. abc.net.au/news/2016-04-14/geelong-council-elections-could-be-held-as-early-as-next-year/7326368

Australian Government, Department of Infrastructure and Regional Development (2013) *2010–11 report on the operation of the Local Government (Financial Assistance) Act 1995*, Canberra: Commonwealth of Australia

Australian Local Government Association (ALGA) (2014) *ALGA Comment on the Reform of the Federation Issues Paper 1*, Deakin, ACT: ALGA.

Brown, A. J. (2014) *Australian Constitutional Values Survey*, Queensland: Griffith University, Centre for Governance and Public Policy. Available at www.griffith.edu.au/__data/assets/pdf_file/0015/653100/Constitutional-Values-Survey-Oct-2014Results-2.pdf

Burton, P. (2001) Local *Democracy in Bristol: Final Report of the Bristol Democracy Commission*, Bristol: Bristol City Council.

Grant, B., Dollery, B. and Kortt, M. (2015) 'Is there a case for mandating directly elected mayors in Australian local government? Lessons from the 2012 Queensland Local Government Elections', *Australian Journal of Public Administration*, doi: 10.1111/1467–8500.12057

Hambleton, R. (2015) *Leading the Inclusive City: Place-based Innovation for a Bounded Planet*, Bristol: Policy Press.

Kiss, R. (2002) 'Democracy or Community? Australian local government electoral reform', in J. Caulfield and H. O. Larsen (eds) *Local Government at the Millennium*, Wiesbaden: Springer Fachmedien.

Local Government Association (2014) *No Overall Control: Learning Further lessons from Councils without a Majority Administration*, London, LGA.

Martin, J. and Aulich, C. (2012) *Political Management in Australian Local Government: Exploring Roles and Relationships between Mayors and CEOs*, Sydney: Australian Centre of Excellence for Local Government, UTS.

Queensland Government (2013) *Local Government Remuneration and Discipline Tribunal Report 2013*, Brisbane: LGRDT.

Sandford, M. (2004) 'Elected Mayors I: Political innovation, electoral systems and revitalising democracy', *Local Government Studies*, 30(1), 1–21.

Sansom, G. (2012) 'Australian Mayors: What can and should they do?', Centre for Local Government Discussion Paper, University of Technology, Sydney.

Spigelman, J. (2011) *Final Report of the Expert Panel on Constitutional Recognition of Local Government*, Canberra: Department of Regional Australia, Regional Development and Local Government.

Stockwell, S. (1995) 'The Brisbane Model: Considering a unique experiment', *Urban Policy and Research*, 13(2), 89–96.

Stoker, G., Gains, F., Greasley. S., John, P. and Rao, N. (2007) *The New Council Constitutions: the outcomes and impacts of the Local Government Act 2000*, London: Department of Communities and Local Government (DCLG).

Tucker, D. (1994) 'Changing practices and conceptions of the executive function in urban government: The Greater Brisbane experience', *Australian Journal of Public Administration*, 53(4), 508–20.

NINE

Directly elected mayors in New Zealand: the impact of intervening variables on enhanced governing capacity

Christine Cheyne, Massey University, New Zealand

Introduction

Direct election of mayors has been established fairly widely in local government in New Zealand since the late 19th century and mandatory since 1989. While unique and specific historical factors led to the widespread adoption of directly elected mayors, the New Zealand experience may offer insights for comparative studies into their effectiveness. New Zealand has units of local government in which the political leader is either directly elected (city/district councils) or is elected by fellow councillors (regional councils), and there is thus also the possibility of making comparisons internally, within New Zealand. Recent legislative reform has encouraged council reorganisation and rationalisation. The creation of a unitary council for Auckland in 2010 is a notable example. Further unitary councils were anticipated and have been encouraged through reorganisation proposals by the Local Government Commission. Interestingly, however, there seems to be a lack of public appetite for larger, unitary councils and amalgamation plans for three regions (Northland, Wellington and Hawkes Bay) have been rejected. For example, in June 2015 the Local Government Commission recommended a unitary council for the Hawkes Bay region. This was subject to a majority vote in a poll held in mid-September 2015. Two thirds (66%) of voters rejected the proposal and the status quo prevails.

Interest does remain in some other regions (such as Waikato and Bay of Plenty) but with local elections taking place across all councils in 2016 further progress has been halted, at least until after new councils are formed in late 2016. In the meantime, therefore, New Zealand local government has a mixed model of regional leadership. Auckland has a directly elected mayor while other regions have chairs elected by councillors.

Alongside this recent legislative reform has been a strengthening of mayoral power. It is clearly intended – at least by the sponsor of the amendments – that the governing capacity of the Auckland 'metro mayor' model, which was expected to become established in other parts of New Zealand, should be enhanced. However, changes to the draft legislation when it was before a select committee weakened some of provisions that would have strengthened the mayor's powers and retained some existing powers of the wider council. As a result, it is argued that the new framework for councils outside of Auckland is different to Auckland because:

> [the] relative roles and responsibilities of mayors and their governing bodies is more dynamic than in Auckland and not as clearly differentiated, being subject to continual negotiation as both mayors and the governing body can use their appointment and over-rule powers at any time during the triennium (Local Government New Zealand, 2015: 6).

Understanding mayoral leadership

Political commentator Chris Trotter (2013) argues New Zealand's mayoral model:

> ... is a very curious constitutional arrangement, because, with the exception of Auckland City, the people elected to lead our local bodies are vested with no special executive powers, do not control their council's budget and may not even enjoy the support of a majority of their fellow councillors.
>
> Quite how New Zealand ended up with these popularly elected but essentially powerless mayors is a bit of a mystery. We certainly didn't inherit the practice from our colonial forebears. In the United Kingdom – and Australia – the mayoral chain goes around the neck of the council's majority leader.

Legislative amendments passed in late 2013 extended some of – though, as noted above, not all – the additional powers bestowed on the

Auckland mayor in 2010 to other mayors. This move appears designed to strengthen governance. The comment by Trotter draws attention to the constitutional framework within which mayors and councillors operate and the effect of other aspects of these arrangements on the exercise of mayor power.

Governing capacity involves the deployment of resources, nongovernmental as well as governmental, by the parties in government (Stone, 1993: 1). Political leadership is a key element in governing capacity. In their analysis of local political leadership, Elcock and Fenwick (2012) developed a matrix that highlights three sets of influences on local political leadership: (i) institutional/formal; (ii) informal; and (iii) individual. The relative importance of these three sets of attributes is not addressed; however, it constitutes an important line of further research, and can assist in assessing the effectiveness of local political leadership. I argue that the dominant set of influences is the institutional/formal set, as these set the parameters for the exercise of leadership, and which may be helpfully represented as the foundational tier of a pyramid (see Figure 9.1).

Figure 9.1: Three sets of influences on local political leadership

Individual influences

Informal influences

Formal/institutional influences

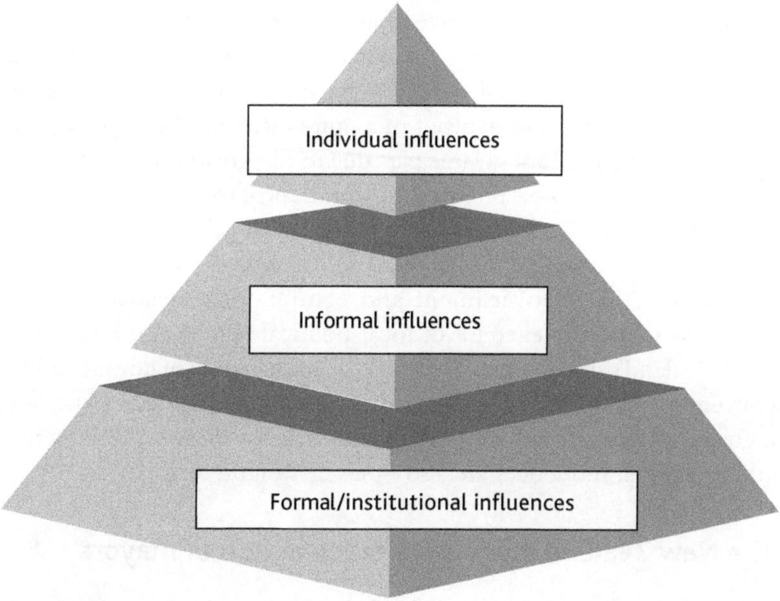

Source: Adapted from Elcock and Fenwick (2012).

The incorporation of the matrix into a pyramid allows the strength/ weight and foundational importance of institutional/formal features to be depicted. These influences reflect the importance of the rule of law, but it is both the existence or absence of legislative and constitutional provisions that demonstrates their importance. A growing body of literature on facilitative leadership and leadership traits testifies to the importance of informal and individual influences but these are exercised within the parameters of the formal and institutional influences. The governing capacity of directly elected mayors can and does vary considerably as a result of these influences. New Zealand's long experience shows that direct election of mayors needs to be contextualised by close attention to the formal and institutional influences that shape the position of mayor.

More detailed analysis of each set of influences can enhance understanding of the impacts of each set. However, it is beyond the scope of a brief chapter such as this to attempt a detailed analysis of all three. Recognising the importance of institutional/formal provisions, this chapter explores that set of influences drawing on the New Zealand experience.

The New Zealand case study is of interest for comparative research because of the recent legislative changes noted above to strengthen the model of direct election of mayors. Despite having its origins in the British system of local government, local government and local political leadership have evolved in a quite different direction to that of the United Kingdom in large part due to the greater degree of fiscal autonomy of New Zealand local government. However, as the New Zealand case will demonstrate, fiscal autonomy does not appear to be a significant variable; rather, it is the constitutional arrangements surrounding local government and central–local relations which appear to shape the exercise of local political leadership. Reflecting New Zealand's strongly unitary state, the importance of constitutional conventions and other variables, in particular central–local relations, arguably constrains the exercise of mayoral power and the informal and individual influences are also of lesser weight.

The New Zealand model of direct election of mayors

While direct election of mayors has been mandated only since 1989 it has long been a feature of local government in New Zealand. Under the Municipal Corporations Ordinance, which established local government in New Zealand in the mid-19th century, mayors were elected by the elected members. However, when Mr Henry Dobson was elected leader of the small South Island town of Blenheim in 1868, he argued that the mayor's authority should come from a wider base than the eight male councillors and instead should come from the ratepayers. The law did not allow ratepayers to elect a mayor but the councillors agreed to elect as mayor the person supported by the ratepayers. This was the system used in Blenheim for several years. It was viewed very favourably by others and eventually was incorporated into a new bill, known as the Blenheim Mayor's Bill, which became the Municipal Corporations Act 1876 and extended to the rest of the country the right of ratepayers to elect the mayor (*Northern Advocate*, 1913).

With this relatively well-established practice of direct election, now extended beyond ratepayers to most of the adult population (with a few categories, such as those serving a prison sentence, not eligible to enrol and vote in elections), the New Zealand model of local government may provide important insights into the effectiveness of direct election of mayors. The model allows comparisons to be made between, on the one hand, regional councils where the political leader, the council chair, is elected by fellow councillors and, on the other, territorial authorities (city/district councils) where the political leader, the mayor, is directly elected by residents. The three influences on mayoral leadership identified above are now considered in turn.

Institutional/formal influences: legislation and constitutional status

An array of statutes shapes local government and local political leadership in New Zealand. Significantly, local government is created by an ordinary statute. Although local government has a degree of autonomy derived from its independent source of finance (property tax) there is limited power attached to this as its purpose and functions are determined by local government statute (not by any written constitutional provision) and some other statutes. Since 1989, direct election of mayors has been mandated for all territorial authorities. However, regional councils are led by a chairperson elected by the members of the council who are elected as representatives of constituencies within the region.

The responsibilities of chief executives are prescribed in detail in Section 42 of the Local Government Act 2002.[1] However, until late 2014 the Act was relatively silent on the matter of the responsibilities of the mayor and elected members other than addressing some obvious areas, such as conflict of interest, and legal and financial probity, and requiring councils to adopt a code of conduct that governs the behaviour of elected members.

Although directly elected by voters at large, until very recently New Zealand mayors have not had any greater formal power than other elected members. Instead, the most that mayors in general have is a 'symbolic' form of power, derived from their figurehead role. In this model, the mayor is a weak mayor (Cheyne, 2004; Leach and Wilson, 2000) but with distinct powers related to four roles discussed by Stoker and Wolman (1992: 245):

• ceremonial/presiding
• coordination and communication
• organisation and policy guidance; and
• external relations.

From 2010 the mayor of the newly created unitary Auckland Council has had some powers additional to those that previously existed, which are clearly intended to strengthen the position. The Local Government (Auckland Council) Act 2009 states that the role of the mayor is to:

a. articulate and promote a vision for Auckland; and
b. provide leadership for the purpose of achieving objectives that will contribute to that vision.

The Act also specifies that the mayor's role is to 'lead the development of Council plans, policies, and budgets for consideration by the governing body; and ensure there is effective engagement between the Auckland Council and the people of Auckland, including those too young to vote'.

In order to carry out this role, the Act specifically gives the mayor the following powers:

a. to establish processes and mechanisms for the Auckland Council to engage with the people of Auckland, whether generally or particularly (for example, the people of a cultural, ethnic, geographic or other community of interest);
b. to appoint the deputy mayor;
c. to establish committees of the governing body;[2]
d. to appoint the chairperson of each committee of the governing body;[3] and
e. to establish and maintain an appropriately staffed office of the mayor.

The mayor is not allowed to delegate any of these powers, which underscores the intention to strengthen the executive power of the mayor.

The explicit statement of the statutory roles and powers of the mayor in the legislation establishing the Auckland Council signals a distinct repositioning of the role of the mayor vis-à-vis both the wider governing body (the other elected members) and also the chief executive (Svara and Nelson, 2008; Svara and Watson, 2010). The move to distinguish the mayor from other elected members is a break from the past, and recognises that symbolic power, while substantial, needs supplementing with formal power. Combined with the legitimacy derived from the much larger electoral base and the expansion of strategic and planning scope arising from the shift to a unitary council, the responsibility of the Auckland mayor to lead planning and, in particular, to adopt a 30-year spatial plan setting out the mayor's vision for the city signifies an elevated role for the Auckland mayor.

At the same time, it is a finely balanced power and designed to

> enable Mayoral leadership while retaining the need for the Mayor to win and maintain the support of the other members of the governing body. Despite the additional powers, the Mayor still has only one vote on the governing body and needs to work with the members of the governing body on issues of common interest (Controller and Auditor-General, 2012: 12).

The Auckland mayor's new powers are exercised within clear parameters, most notably the clear distinction between governance and management roles. As mentioned above, the chief executive's role is clearly spelled out and councils' governing arrangements have had to recognise the separate exercise of the management function by the appointed executive.

Moreover, the Act specifies that the mayor's powers must be exercised in consultation 'with, and acting through, the Council's chief executive; and within the budget in the annual plan'.

Whether informal and individual influences counterbalance, or even outweigh, the institutional/formal parameters is a matter for further research. The Auckland Council is still a relatively new institution, with the first Auckland Mayor Len Brown holding office for two three-year terms (2010–13, 2013–16). In October 2016, a new mayor, Phil Goff took office. As a former Member of Parliament for an Auckland electorate for many years, as well a Leader of the Labour Opposition, senior Cabinet Minister in the 4th Labour Government (1984-90) and 5th Labour Government (1999-2008). Both Brown and Goff have a high political profile in Auckland indicating that individual characteristics of each as mayor are significant but it is the formal statutory roles and powers that are critical.

Further legislation took effect in October 2013 in the form of a new Section 41A in the Local Government Act 2002 which outlined the role and power of mayors. Like the 2009 legislation that applied to the new Auckland Council, the 2013 amendments stated that the role of the mayor is to lead the development of the council's plans, policies, and budgets. Similarly, it gave the mayor new powers to appoint the deputy mayor, establish council committees and to appoint the chairperson of committees (which could be the mayor).

While mayors outside of Auckland now exercise many of the new roles and new powers of the Auckland Council mayor, there are some responsibilities that have not (yet) been extended: specifically, the statutory requirement to undertake spatial planning. Section 79 of the Local Government (Auckland Council) Act introduced a new requirement for a spatial plan which is additional to the requirement that all territorial and regional councils have under the Resource Management Act 1991 to prepare a district or regional plan. The spatial plan is intended to be an integrated and comprehensive strategic year plan that addresses social, economic, environmental and cultural wellbeing over a 20–30-year timeframe as opposed to the Auckland unitary plan, which addresses land use and resource management issues.

Legislative changes in 2012 facilitated the creation of additional unitary councils based on the Auckland model, but as at the beginning of 2017 no additional unitary councils had been created. Although some proposals for amalgamations of city/district and regional councils into unitary councils had failed due to lack of community support, political pressure for rationalisation remains. Co-ordinated action across regions for development requires regional leadership. As yet, a requirement for spatial planning has not been mandated for other councils. Until it is and/or until unitary councils are established in other regions, the role and powers of mayors outside of Auckland are likely to be constrained despite the new statutory powers introduced in 2013. This is because mayors outside of Auckland do not have the responsibility to articulate and promote a vision and provide leadership for the purpose of achieving a long-term vision.

Notwithstanding, there is incremental change in the visibility and influence of mayors outside Auckland. As in Auckland, this increased visibility and influence is seen as important for increasing voter turnout in local elections throughout the country. However, although it has been claimed by the Minister for Local Government (Smith, 2012) that mayoralty elections and by-elections have a higher turnout than for other elected members, local authority election statistics from 1989 to 2013 show no significant difference (Department of Internal Affairs, 2013).

Other legislative provisions affecting the influence of local political leadership includes the remuneration for mayors and councillors, term of office, the electoral system and the responsibilities of councils. Space does not permit a detailed overview of all these facets but a few salient points should be noted. Mayors are elected at the same time as other councillors, in elections held triennially. Councils choose the electoral system with the two options being first past the post and single transferable vote. Mayoralty campaigns receive far greater media attention than other aspects of the election campaign, and while the position of the mayor attracts a relatively high level of interest compared with council positions, turnout is much lower than for parliamentary elections (Cheyne, 2015).

The Local Government Act 2002 provides for an independent government agency, the Remuneration Authority, to set the remuneration, allowances and expenses of mayors, and other elected members on local authorities, community boards and Auckland Council local boards. Mayors and councillors (and chairs of regional councils) are paid a salary from the council budget. Remuneration is set according to a formula that relates to the population of the district/region and elected member's level of responsibility. Rates of remuneration are reviewed annually. The Auckland mayor's salary rate in 2016/2017 was NZ$269,500 (approx. £154,000) compared with NZ$151,850 (approx. £86,560) for the deputy mayor, NZ$125,350 (approx. £71,453) for a committee chair and NZ$105,800 (approx. £60,309) for a councillor without additional responsibilities. The level of remuneration generally allows mayors to work full time.

In addition to the statutory prescriptions of the role of the mayor, and resourcing of the position, the scope of local political leadership is to a large degree determined by the role of local government. In New Zealand, the scope of the responsibilities of local government is determined by the statutory purpose and various other provisions. For a decade from 2002 to 2012 local government in New Zealand operated under a 'broad empowerment' set out in the statutory purpose in Section 10:

    a to enable democratic local decision-making and action by, and on behalf of, communities; and b to promote the social, economic, environmental, and cultural well-being of communities, in the present and for the future.

Essentially, the purpose of local government included promoting social, economic, environmental and cultural wellbeing. In December 2012 that broad empowerment in Section 10(b) was replaced with a new statutory purpose:

b to meet the current and future needs of communities for good-quality local infrastructure, local public services, and performance of regulatory functions in a way that is most cost-effective for households and businesses.

Despite the change of purpose, local government remains engaged in promoting wellbeing, albeit in a less explicit and direct way. It is perhaps too soon to assess whether the scope of local political leadership has been reduced; however, the former 'ultra vires' doctrine has not been re-established and the provisions for spatial planning in Auckland suggest that central government considers local government to have a key role in comprehensive long-term planning.

As well as the Local Government Act 2002, an array of other statutes imposes responsibilities on local government. For example, the Resource Management Act 1991 substantially devolves environmental administration. In contrast with some other jurisdictions, however, education and welfare are functions undertaken by central government while delivery of health services (other than public health) is devolved to district health boards. Land transport planning is a responsibility of local government with funding for infrastructure and services also a shared responsibility.

In contrast with central government, local government's task span is relatively limited and even when it enjoyed a broad empowerment this was constrained in two key ways: (i) the funding base (primarily a property tax); and (ii) the requirement to have public support for proposed activities.[4] The relative financial autonomy of local government in New Zealand may be seen as complementary to and reinforcing mayoral power. It is true that local government has a degree of freedom from central government interference as a result of its lack of dependence on central government transfers and grants. However, central government political leaders exert indirect influence on local government finance through, for example, castigating local government for rates increases beyond the rate of inflation. And being a highly unitary state, New Zealand public expenditure is dominated by central government. In 2012 central government contributed around 19% to the expenditure measure of New Zealand's gross domestic product (GDP) compared with a 4% contribution from local government (Statistics New Zealand, 2012). Local government income is primarily from rates. In the year ended June 2014, over 58% was from rates with around 12% from central government subsidies and transfers (Statistics New Zealand, 2015).

While enjoying some financial autonomy, there are significant statutory encroachments on local political leadership and council autonomy. In the case of the Auckland Council there is the requirement of the Local Government (Auckland Council) Act for a number of functions to be undertaken by arms-length Council Controlled Organisations (CCOs). Prior to 2009, the Local Government Act 2002 made establishment of CCOs a decision of the council. As arms-length organisations, CCOs are not covered by statutory provisions for democratic participation in decision making. Instead of decisions being made by elected members, with requirements for openness and transparency, CCOs are organisations in which councils control 50% or more of the votes or have the right to appoint 50% (or more) of directors or trustees. They typically have boards which conduct business in a manner similar to a private company but with accountability to the council, which determines the objectives for each CCO and monitors their performance.

CCOs are prevalent throughout local government in New Zealand. However, prior to the passage of the Auckland Council legislation, CCOs were established by individual councils. Arguably, the mayor had influence over the number and focus of CCOs. In setting up the Auckland Council, the national government imposed a number of CCOs on Auckland, relating to, among other matters, property, tourism, economic development and transport. The council is able to have influence over CCOs by conveying its expectations in the CCO accountability policy, the mayor's annual letter of expectations, and the *Governance Manual for Substantive CCOs* (Auckland Council, 2015). For example, central government legislated the Auckland Transport governing body, a board of directors which must comprise no fewer than six and no more than eight voting directors (of whom only two may be members of the governing body of the Auckland Council) and one non-voting director nominated by the New Zealand Transport Agency (a government agency). The Local Government (Auckland Council) Act also specified that the board, including its chairperson and deputy chairperson, must be appointed by the Auckland Council. The council is not able to appoint a member of its own governing body as the chairperson or deputy chairperson of the board but it is able to determine the operating rules for Auckland Transport (including the board). There is also a statutory requirement for CCOs to hold at least two public meetings per year for public input. Following strong encouragement from Len Brown, who had campaigned on greater transparency and public accountability of CCOs, Auckland Transport decided at its inaugural meeting to open all meetings to the public. Following his election, Phil Goff also took steps to further strengthen accountability of CCOs to the mayor and governing body.

Local government in New Zealand has no constitutional status. It is established by an ordinary Act of Parliament (as distinct from other constitutional or quasi-constitutional provisions which are entrenched). As long as the governing party in Parliament can command a simple majority of votes in the House, local government legislation can be amended or indeed repealed at whim. Legislative amendments in late 2012 strengthened the powers of the Minister of Local Government to intervene in local government and provided the minister with the option to appoint a Crown Review Team, Crown Observer, Crown Manager or Commissioners to ensure a council's functions are performed satisfactorily.

Institutional/formal influences: public management framework

In 1989, not only was direct election of mayors mandated, local government was reshaped according to new public management principles which had reshaped the core public service at the national level (Boston et al, 1996). Under the State Sector Act 1988, reflecting the principle of managerialism, as well as the principle of the separation of governance and management, a minister appoints the chief executive officer (CEO) of a government department who is accountable to the minister and hence has responsibility for implementing government policy. Similarly, councils are similarly required to appoint a chief executive officer although the CEO is accountable to the council as a whole and not to the mayor. Hence, the New Zealand system of local government can be identified as reflecting the council manager model (Cheyne, 2004; 2010; Hambleton, 1998). As Svara (1990: 51) explains, in the council manager system:

> The mayor and the council occupy the overtly political roles in government, and the manager directs the administrative apparatus, an activity which provides ample room for

influencing and shaping policy without the burdens (or opportunities) attendant to elected leadership status.

Under both the State Sector Act 1988 and the Local Government Act 2002 the chief executive has full responsibility for implementation of policy and employment of staff, and a clear distinction is made between governance and management. Mayors and councillors are also required to maintain the governance/management boundary. Since the 1989 reforms, a corpus of practical guidance has sought to reinforce the 'division of labour' between elected members and appointed staff (see, for example, Controller and Auditor-General, 2002). Although not bound by the code of conduct that staff of core government departments in the public service are bound by, to a large extent the staff of local authorities have operated under a similar set of expectations. While the chief executive is employed by the council on a fixed term contract (normally five years), the legislation and public management framework intends that other staff employment contracts below the chief executive are independent of any political influence. Thus, the workforce in local government has shared the same characteristics of the central government workforce in being grounded in the Westminster principle of a professional public service that operates without political interference (Patapan et al, 2005; Rhodes and Weller, 2005). However, following the strengthening of the powers of the mayor (at first, just in the case of Auckland and then since 2014 elsewhere in local government), a growing number of mayors are appointing their own advisers, arguing that the new legislation increasing their responsibility to lead planning and budgeting has made it necessary for them to have policy and communications specialists. These new staff are akin to the politically appointed 'ministerial advisers' appointed to work in the offices of Cabinet ministers. Arguably, under the new legislation mayors now are individually and publicly more accountable and less able to shift responsibility for unpopular decisions to council as a whole or other councillors, or council staff. Other councillors and the public have expressed concern about the cost of staffing the mayoral office as the staff are remunerated on a level similar to other senior public servants.

Institutional/formal influences: central–local relations

It is clear from the above discussion that local political leadership in New Zealand is exercised within the framework of a unitary state in which central government wields significant power. There are formal institutional arrangements designed to foster collegial central–local relations most notably the Central Government Local Government Forum which is a regular (albeit infrequent) meeting between the prime minister, senior Cabinet ministers, the president of Local Government New Zealand and other senior leaders in the local government sector. In the Auckland region there are new arrangements in the form of the Auckland Policy Office, a new agency that brings together key staff of major government departments all of which have historically been based in the capital city, Wellington, to foster more joined-up working in Auckland. The agency has been expanded considerably since its establishment in 2005, as central government seeks to engage more effectively with local government, business and civil society in Auckland.

However, much of the interaction between the two spheres happens in a more informal way. The imbalance in power between central and local government has meant that central–local relations have not always been as strong and positive as they should and could be. A probing report by the New Zealand Productivity Commission (2013) drew attention to the lack of regard by central government for the role of local government and highlighted the need for improved central–local relations and, in particular, enhanced communication and cooperation between local and central government.

Sweeting (2003) argues that it is important to examine not just the formal powers the mayor has in the local government system (such as the power balance between the mayor and the council) but also the power the mayor has in broader local governance. He proposes a new model which expands the analysis beyond the strong mayor/weak mayor continuum to include an additional dimension of power (power confined to within the office/power extending beyond the office). Using this model, he argued that the London mayor had strong power vis-à-vis the council (the Greater London Authority) but very limited strength outside the confines of the office. He notes that the London mayor

> operates in an environment of central–local relations that limits local autonomy. The UK is a unitary state where sovereign power resides in Parliament. Local authorities only exist because Parliament so desires, and local authorities have no absolute constitutional right to exist. ... Moreover, the functions, structures and sources of finance of local government are all subject to the prescription and proscription of Parliament (Sweeting, 2003: 474).

The same situation applies in New Zealand although there is a significant difference in that New Zealand mayors have largely autonomous funding – although, significantly for Auckland Mayor Len Brown, whose key policy agenda is improved public transport, funding for transport is the one key area where there are financial transfers from the national government. Brown's focus on public transport (in particular, rail) was a direct challenge to the national government which has focused its funding for land transport in Auckland on several major road projects which were ostensibly designed to relieve the city's severe congestion and to create economic growth, but which were widely perceived as increasing car dependence. Without central government subsidies, transport projects planned by local government could not proceed. Brown argued that if central government wants Auckland to have an efficient transport system and to be the national economic powerhouse it needed to support transport projects designed to reduce congestion. Initially, central government considered that Auckland Council needed to fund the project and was unwilling to provide funding that would allow the project to commence at the time Auckland Council wanted. However, in 2016 central government announced a 50% funding contribution which meant the project could be accelerated. This was a major breakthrough that vindicated the leadership and vision of the Auckland mayor.

Conclusion

This chapter has explored institutional/formal variables that have been identified by Elcock and Fenwick as one of three sets of influences on local political leadership. Within this set of influences three particular variables have a significant bearing. *First*, legislation determines the structure, purpose, powers and functions of local government, and the purpose and powers of the mayor, establishes a framework for remuneration of elected members and, in the case of Auckland Council, creates a number of arms-length organisations which are owned by and accountable to the Council. To the extent that both the New Zealand and the English systems of local government are embedded within the Westminster model of government, local political leadership in both places has been shaped by many similar forces including the impact of a dominant central government. However, within these set of influences the two systems demonstrate the scope for variation with New Zealand having adopted a directly elected mayor at an early stage in the development of its local government system. While not a strong mayor, and while also mediated by other variables (including informal and individual), this has been a stable feature of the New Zealand system. Moreover, it has been seen as a model to be emulated especially by some reformers in the UK. At the same time, it needs to be noted that the model of local political leadership found in New Zealand reflects the 'weak mayor' model within the council manager system (Cheyne, 2004). Asquith (2012: 79), for example, noting the power vacuum that characterises the position of mayor, observes:

> There is a perception that mayoral 'power' is something enshrined in law, whereas, in reality, such feats have often been achieved via sheer force of personality and astute coalition building, both within the council and externally amongst diverse groups of stakeholders.

The legislative changes that increased the powers of the mayor from 2013 mean that there is not the same degree of power vacuum that previously existed. If the trend of mayors recruiting political and media staff continues this may further consolidate the power of the mayor. As a result, the *second* set of influences, the public management framework, may undergo some transformation. The public management introduced as a result of public sector reforms in 1989 and which has continued to evolve as public management theory and practice have evolved, emphasised the separation of governance and management. This has been steadfastly maintained over a quarter of a century but the strengthening of the political office of the mayor may lead to a reconfiguration of the relationship between the mayoral office staff and staff in the wider council organisation.

The *third* set of formal institutional influences that has been particularly important in the New Zealand context but which may be less important in non–unitary states is central–local relations. Tensions have often existed in the relationship and the ability of local political leaders to achieve their vision can be easily undermined by central government as the Mayor of Auckland has experienced. Central government leaders are quick to point out that central government expenditure in New Zealand's regions is much greater than local government expenditure and therefore local government needs to have regard for central government policy agendas and objectives if it is to retain existing and attract additional central government investmemt.

Nevertheless, the creation of the Auckland Council represents a major shift in thinking about local political leadership. Table 9.1 summarises the preceding assessment of the system before and after the shift on the key dimensions of local political leadership in 2010.

Table 9.1: Summary of changes to local political leadership following Local Government (Auckland Council) Act 2009

Dimension of local political leadership	Auckland region before November 2010	Auckland Council from November 2010
Political leadership	8 political leaders, visible in their own city/district in the case of cities/districts, or not very visible in the case of the regional council No single regional leadership	One single directly elected mayor, highly visible region-wide leadership
Electoral mandate	Mayors of city/district councils directly elected by population of city/district Regional chair elected by regional councillors	Mayor elected by population of region
Role of mayor	Not spelled out in legislation	Statutory requirement for mayor to lead development of plans, policies and budgets; articulate and promote a vision for Auckland and provide leadership to progress the vision
Powers of political leader	Weak mayor – mainly symbolic power related to ceremonial role, presiding at council meetings, leading external engagement	Modified weak mayor model – mayor has budget for own office staff Symbolic power but with additional legislative powers to engage the people of Auckland, to appoint deputy mayor, establish committees, appoint chairpersons of committees; these powers cannot be delegated

The introduction of a unitary council with a directly elected mayor to govern a region which is home to a third of New Zealand's population (and which is rapidly growing) and a dominant force in the country's economy has elevated *local* political leadership and its formal/institutional supports. In New Zealand's evolving model of local political leadership, both powers and power are enhanced. As indicated above, enhancement of the role and powers of mayors throughout the rest of local government in New Zealand is now part of a bill amending the current Local Government Act. While this may be positive from the perspective of advocates of strong local political leadership further attention needs to be given to the wider institutional framework in which local government is located in particular central–local relations and constitutional arrangements.

By its very absence, the importance of this formal/legislative influence of constitutional protection is demonstrated. The constitutional weakness of local government in New Zealand means that it is vulnerable to reform by the national government. That vulnerability has meant that local government reforms have occurred periodically which are largely ideologically driven. This was clearly the case when Auckland governance was reformed. To provide some distance from the government an independent investigation was instigated by a centre-left government. Although independent, the Royal Commission's membership was undoubtedly influenced by the government that established it and in turn influenced its subsequent recommendations. The election of a centre-right government in November 2008 resulted in a package of governance reforms announced in March 2009 that substantially modified the Royal Commission's proposals. The policy and legislative review process that resulted in the creation of the Auckland Council demonstrate the power of central government to impose its will on local government and local communities. In light of this, and especially in places where central government does not trust or have a commitment to a strong local government sector, the need for constitutional protection for local government becomes particularly important.

Notes
[1] See also clauses 33 and 34 of Schedule 7 of the LGA 2002.
[2] The mayor is required to be a member of each committee.
[3] This can be the mayor himself or herself.
[4] Stringent requirements for public consultation and a relatively demanding regime of open government underpin public scrutiny and accountability.

References

Asquith, A. (2012) 'The Role, Scope and Scale of Local Government in New Zealand: Its Prospective Future', *Australian Journal of Public Administration*, 71(1), 76–84. doi:10.1111/j.1467–8500.2012.00751.x

Auckland Council. (2015) *Governance Manual for Substantive CCOs*. Retrieved from http://www.aucklandcouncil.govt.nz/EN/AboutCouncil/representativesbodies/CCO/Documents/governancemanualforsubstantiveccos.pdf

Boston, J., Martin, J., Pallot, J. and Walsh, P. (eds) (1996) *Public Management: The New Zealand Model*, Auckland: Oxford University Press.

Cheyne, C. M. (2004) 'Changing Political Leadership: the New Zealand Mayor in Contemporary Local Governance', *Political Science*, 56(2), 51–64.

Cheyne, C. M. (2010) 'Strengthening local government?' in R. Miller (ed) *New Zealand Local Government and Politics* (5th edn), Melbourne: Oxford University Press, pp 269–83.

Cheyne, C. M. (2015) 'Local Government', in J. Hayward (ed) *New Zealand Government and Politics* (6th edn), Melbourne: Oxford University Press, pp 190–201.

Controller and Auditor-General (2002) *Managing the Relationship Between a Local Authority's Elected Members and its Chief Executive*, Wellington: Controller and Auditor-General, www.oag.govt. nz/2002/chief-execs/docs/chief-execs.pdf

Department of Internal Affairs (2013) 'Local Authority Election Statistics 2013', www.dia.govt.nz/diawebsite.nsf/wpg_URL/ Services-Local-Elections-Local-Authority-Election-Statistics-2013?OpenDocument

Elcock, H. and Fenwick, J. (2012) 'The political leadership matrix: a tool for analysis', *Public Money & Management*, 32(2), 87.

Hambleton, R. (1998) 'Strengthening political leadership in UK local government', *Public Money and Management*, January–March, 41–58.

Leach, S. and Wilson, D. (2000) *Local Political Leadership*, Bristol: The Policy Press.

Local Government New Zealand (2015) *Local Leadership: The Role of Mayors and the Impact of the LGA 2002 Amendment Act 2012*, www. lgnz.co.nz/assets/Uploads/The-Role-of-Mayors-and-the-Impact-of-the-LGA-2002-Amendment-Act-2012.pdf

New Zealand Productivity Commission (2013) *Towards Better Local Regulation*, Wellington: Productivity Commission, www.productivity. govt.nz/sites/default/files/towards-better-local-regulation.pdf

Northern Advocate (1913) 'Origin of Present Mayoral System', 9 August, p 4.

Patapan, H., Wanna, J. and Weller, P. (eds) (2005) *Westminster Legacies: Democracy and Responsible Government in Asia and the Pacific*, Sydney: University of New South Wales Press.

Rhodes, R. A. W. and Weller, P. (2005) 'Westminster transplanted and Westminster implanted: Exploring political change', in H. Patapan, J. Wanna and P. Weller (eds), *Westminster Legacies: Democracy and Responsible Government in Asia and the Pacific,* Sydney: University of New South Wales Press, pp 1–12.

Smith, N. (2012) 'Better Local Government', New Zealand Government, www.beehive.govt.nz/sites/all/files/Better-Local-Gvt-pr08.pdf

Statistics New Zealand (2015) 'Local Authority Statistics: March 2015 quarter – tables', www.stats.govt.nz/browse_for_stats/government_finance/local_government/LocalAuthorityStatistics_HOTPMar15qtr.aspx

Stoker, G. and Wolman, H. (1992) 'Drawing lessons from US experience: An elected mayor for British local government', *Public Administration*, 70, 241–67.

Stone, C. N. (1993) 'Urban Regimes and the Capacity to Govern: A Political Economy Approach', *Journal of Urban Affairs*, 15(1), 1–28. doi:10.1111/j.1467–9906.1993.tb00300.x

Svara, J. H. (1990) *Official Leadership in the City. Patterns of Conflict and Co-operation*, New York: Oxford University Press.

Svara, J. H. and Nelson, K. L. (2008) 'Taking Stock of the Council-Manager Form at 100', *Public Management Magazine*, 90(7), 6–14.

Svara, J. H., and Watson, D. J. (2010) 'Introduction: Framing constitutional contests in large cities', in J. H. Svara and D. J. Watson (eds), *More than a Mayor or a Manager: Campaigns to Change Form of Government in America's Largest Cities*, Washington DC: Georgetown University Press, pp 1–22.

Sweeting, D. (2003) 'How strong is the Mayor of London?', *Policy & Politics*, 31(4), 465–78. doi:10.1332/030557303322439353

Trotter, C. (2013) 'Election of NZ mayors 'curious'', *The Press*, 17 December, www.stuff.co.nz/the-press/opinion/columnists/chris-trotter/9524637/Election-of-NZ-mayors-curious

TEN

Directly elected mayors in Germany: leadership and institutional context

Björn Egner, Technische Universität Darmstadt, Germany

Introduction

A common issue in political science is the extent to which rules affect behaviour. This chapter takes a variation on this theme and explores the extent to which different institutional rules around the competences of the mayor and council in various German states lead to different perceptions about the power of the actors involved. This chapter first explains why Germany has different municipal codes by sketching the history of local self-government of German municipalities after 1945. Then, the different institutional rules inscribed in the municipal codes of the *Länder* are presented, which are used to elaborate an index of mayoral power. The index will then be correlated with the perception of local actors about the balance of power in their municipality and, finally, explanations will be offered about why mayors and councillors perceive the exercise power as they do. In this analysis, only 13 of the 16 German states are covered, as three 'city states' are special cases that are not comparable to others in relation to local government.

The evolution of local government in Germany

Local government does not have a prominent place in the German constitution. In Article 28, two short sentences prescribe the principles of the German local government system:

1. Municipalities and counties have the right to govern themselves within the framework of the law.
2. In counties and municipalities, the people must have a representative body which emerges from general, direct, free, equal and secret ballots.

Everything else concerning municipalities may be decided upon by the *Länder*, which have considerable discretion over their own organisation. German municipalities are considered 'creatures of the Länder' (Wollmann, 2004: 109), since they can be founded, merged, re-organised and abolished by state legislation without their consent. The *Länder* have so far followed different approaches in organising their municipalities.

The postwar configuration

During the postwar reorganisation, the four allies followed a top-down process by reinstating the local level of government. In each occupational zone, the occupying power chose a different local government system for its zone. Those systems were kept largely intact by the newly founded German states (*Länder*), which formed the federal republic.

In the Soviet zone, municipalities were created without strong local discretion; from the beginning, they mainly exercised their role as local units of the central state, having to implement laws without their own sphere of political judgement.

In the French zone (containing mainly Rhineland-Palatinate and the Saarland), a dualist system of local government was introduced, consisting of a council elected, long-term, institutionally weak mayor and a strong council, which very much resembled the French style of organising municipal government (Knemeyer, 1999: 107). Despite of the weak position of the mayor, this kind of municipal code later was called 'the mayoral model'.

In the British zone (containing Lower Saxony, North-Rhine Westphalia and Schleswig-Holstein[1]), a council manager system was introduced, where a strong council chose a politically neutral 'director' to head the city administration, and the council elected mayor was mainly a ceremonial figure. This municipal code was later called 'the northern council model'.

In the US zone (containing Bavaria, Baden-Wurttemberg and Hesse), the occupying power did not intervene into the design of the municipal code. Therefore, the three *Länder* adopted a democratic version of their traditional municipal codes from the pre-war era. This included a directly elected strong mayor in Baden-Wurttemberg and Bavaria, later called the 'southern council model'. Hesse adopted a unique institutional arrangement with a council elected mayor who is supported by a council elected executive board, the latter being collectively responsible for the leadership of the administration (called 'the magistrate model').

   With the exceptions of Baden–Wurttemberg and Bavaria, all states therefore installed a 'parliamentary system of government' (Wollmann, 1999: 45) at the local level.

Institutional change in the wake of German unification

The codes in the eight *Länder* of the Federal Republic of Germany (FRG) were essentially unchanged until the German unification in 1990, when the five new states from the East were incorporated into the German Federation. In the transitional period between the democratisation of the German Democratic Republic (GDR) and the incorporation into the Federation, the GDR parliament decreed an all-GDR municipal code where it enshrined the principles of the 'peaceful revolution' by introducing three key features, namely directly elected mayors, preferential voting for councils and local referendums. After the transitional period, the five new states had to adopt new municipal codes for their cities and towns.[2] At the same time, the debate about efficiency at the local level was on the rise in the West, originally initiated by proposals for the introduction of new public management schemes in municipal administrations (Banner, 1982). Inspired by the debates about democratic and management reforms, a wave of change began, in which nearly all Western states made changes to the institutional practices of their municipalities.[3] After the reforms, all municipal codes had aligned to the former 'southern model', which is why the term 'triumph of the southern model' was coined (Knemeyer, 1999: 109). After those reforms, the three key elements from the southern model were common in all the modified codes. However, despite the alignment, there are still remarkable variances between codes.

Institutional Index of mayoral power

I have previously established an index of institutional power for German mayors (Egner, 2007: 77ff), which will be used in this chapter. The index measures the power of the mayor as the central actor in local politics and is based on the differences in the formal competencies of mayor and council in the 13 states considered here. For the construction of the index, I used only those institutional rules that: (a) are derived from laws; (b) are comparable with each other; (c) can be coded numerically; (d) vary between states; and (e) relate to the two main municipal organs, namely mayor and council. The institutional indicators of mayoral power will be consolidated into an aggregated index by giving each indicator the same weight. In the following paragraphs, the power of the mayor will be measured by using 38 indicators which relate to six areas of the mayor–council relationship, which form the subsequent sections. All indicators are dichotomous (0 and 1) or trichotomous (0, ½ and 1), where '1' indicates a strong mayor, '0' indicates a weak mayor and '½' indicates the medium position. The indicators are included in Table 10.1A in the Annex.

Election of the mayor

For the power of the mayor concerning his/her election, there are two indicators: the length of the term of office (IN01) and access for candidacy (IN02). A mayor with a longer term of office is more powerful, because they can wait for another council to be elected. If mayors have short term connected to the council term (elections for mayor and council are held on the same day), the campaigns can be strongly connected and the mayor may not present himself as an independent figure. Access for candidacy is important because the independence of a mayor is higher (and thus, his institutional power is greater) if it is possible to stand as an independent candidate.

Recall of the mayor

Though the direct election of the mayor has been introduced in all 13 states, the rules for recall are very different. There are two states where there is no recall at all (Baden-Wurttemberg and Bavaria); in all the other states, a recall can be initiated. If a recall is to be conducted, only the electorate can remove the mayor from office. But the question remains whether the recall can be initiated by the council (IN03), which weakens the mayor. The decision in the council can vary on two dimensions: First, it has to be determined if there is a requirement of a certain majority for a recall to be *proposed*, that is there must be a certain share of councillors actually signing a formal proposal to start the process (IN04). Second, it has to be assessed whether a certain majority is needed to actually initiate the process of removal (IN05). If the recall can be initiated by the citizens (IN06), a mayor is weaker as there is the 'threat' of a citizen recall. For the recall vote itself, the codes provide different quotas for a successful recall. The first quorum is the definition of the majority (IN07). In some states, the share of the voters participating in the recall is decisive (IN08).

General distribution of powers between mayor and council

Twelve indicators are used to assess the distribution of power between mayor and council. The most important characteristics of the mayor concern the general competences of the two organs. The most decisive is the 'gap competence'; the decision about issues that are not assigned by law to either one of the organs (IN09). Scholars distinguish between the council having 'general responsibility' (it may decide over everything which is 'in the gap'), and the 'competence of interception' (it has to actively grab for decisions). The second criterion is if the council holds the right to restore its competencies over issues formerly delegated to the mayor (IN10). If the council can take back the competences, the mayor is considered weak, otherwise s/he is institutionally strong. The next three indicators operationalise the degree of information control. The more information rights the council has, the weaker the mayor is, because discretion for strategic moves are thus restricted. The general information rights of the council (IN11) can be distinguished from the right for inspection of records for the council minority (IN12) or even for single councillors (IN13). Sometimes, there might be critical situations in a municipality where the council is not able to reach a decision, for example if it lacks the quorum councillors in a session. In some states, the mayor has the right to make 'substitution decisions' – he may take decisions in lieu of the council (IN14). Another important issue is 'emergency decisions' that may be taken by the mayor if a quick decision in the competence realm of the council is needed, but the council cannot convene in time (IN15). Additionally, he may also object to council decisions if public welfare is threatened (IN16). There are also differences between the municipal codes of the states concerning the recruitment of municipal personnel. It is possible to distinguish between the decision to hire somebody as an employee in the local administration (IN17) and the formal implementation of the decision by signing an employment contract (IN18). The last indicators in this section concern the competences for day-to-day management in the administration. This concerns both tasks assigned to the municipalities by upper levels of government (IN19) and tasks of administration emerging locally (IN20).

External representation of the municipality

The external representation of the municipality is operationalised by four indicators. The first indicator concerns the political representation of the municipality (IN21), which may be assigned to the mayor or another actor, such as the president of the council. The second aspect covers legally binding contracts between the municipality and economic partners (IN22). The mayor here can act on his own, but in some states may require the consent of another actor (for example, the council president). The other two indicators refer to the competence of representing the municipality in joint associations (IN23), typically providing water, waste disposal, etc., for more than one municipality and companies where the municipality holds shares (IN24).

Role of the mayor in the council

Five additional indicators are used to measure the power of the mayor *within* the council. First, it is an obvious difference if the mayor is a member of the council (IN25), which means that s/he may vote in council decisions. It also makes a difference whether the mayor presides over council meetings (IN26), and whether the mayor is president of the council committees (IN27), or has control over the council agenda (IN28). The last indicator is connected to the formal preparation of council decisions (IN29), which may be used to influence the council.

Relationship between the mayor and the executive officers

All municipal codes stipulate that the municipalities must or may have full-time *beigeordnete*[4] accompanying the mayor. Four codes also prescribe that there is a collective committee consisting of the mayor and *beigeordnete* (and sometimes more members). In most *Länder*, the *beigeordnete* have comparable duties and competences. Typically, they are elected by the council, head a part of the municipal administration and act as deputy mayors. There are eight indicators to measure the relationship between the mayor and *beigeordnete*. First, the municipal code may prescribe an executive committee (IN30) that leads the administration collectively or by taking the 'gap competence'. The second indicator is the length of the *beigeordnetes'* terms (IN31) – if they are longer than the term of office of the elected mayor, they may try to sit an awkward situation out. When electing *beigeordnete*, the council may be obliged to consider the 'order of proportionality' (IN32) which is enshrined in some of the municipal codes. It means that the council should elect them by majority vote, but has to bear in mind the distribution of council seats among the groups. Such a rule strengthens the mayor, because the majority in the council cannot burden the mayor with a large number of 'hostile' *beigeordnete*. Some Länder give their mayors a veto when the council elects executive officers (IN33).

Of at least equal importance is the assignment of competences to *beigeordnete* – which departments of the municipal administration they lead (IN34). Additionally, it is important if the mayor has authority to direct them (IN35). The latter two indicators operationalise the power of the mayor over such executives. However, if mayor and *beigeordnete* disagree in political terms, executive officers may want to deviate from the mayor's standpoint. Some municipal codes empower the mayor to prohibit their *beigeordnete* from expressing dissent. The indicators distinguish between 'standard' *beigeordnete* (IN36) and the treasurer of the municipality (IN37).

Aggregation of indexes according to municipal codes

When combining the 37 indicators to form an aggregate index, it becomes clear that there is remarkable variance between municipal codes (see Table 10.1).

Table 10.1: Institutional powers of mayors

State	Index	Former model of local government system
Baden-Wurttemberg	32.5	southern
Saxony	27.5	quasi-southern
Saxony-Anhalt	26.5	quasi-southern
Bavaria	25.5	southern
Thuringia	25.5	quasi-southern
Rhineland-Palatinate	25.0	mayoral
Saarland	25.0	mayoral
Mecklenburg East Pomerania	22.0	quasi-southern
Lower Saxony	18.0	northern
Schleswig-Holstein	17.5	northern (or magistrate)
Brandenburg	16.0	quasi-northern
North-Rhine Westphalia	15.0	northern
Hesse	11.0	magistrate

It is striking to see that the states' positions on the index reflect well the differences in the literature (Buß, 2002: 107; Holtkamp, 2005: 21).[5] As Table 10.1 depicts, mayors in the states with the traditional southern model score very high on the index (especially Baden-Wurttemberg). The 'mayoral model' states are in the middle of the table. In the states formerly belonging to the northern model, there is still a tendency to curb the power of the mayor, which results in low scores on the index. The same is also true for Brandenburg, which was more oriented towards the northern model from the start. The weakest mayors can be found in Hesse, where the executive board is still the central actor concerning the administration, framing the mayor as first among equals.

Influence on local politics and the power index

Within the frame of two research projects with standardised questionnaires (Bäck et al, 2006; Egner et al, 2013), mayors and municipal councillors in Europe were surveyed, among other things, 'about horizontal power relations' at the local level. Respondents assessed the influence of actors on local politics in their municipality, independently of formal rules. For this purpose, a Likert scale was constructed (from '4'=very high influence to '0'=no influence). The data for Germany can be analysed in three steps:

• First, how mayors and councillors assess the distribution of power in their municipality will be determined. For that purpose, the assessments from both surveys will be used as aggregate data for Germany.
• Second, the aggregate data at the state level will be discussed.
• Third, the extent to which the assessment of actors about influence corresponds to the institutional power index will be examined.

General assessment of influence on local politics

It is obvious that German mayors have a clear idea of who is the one in charge in their municipalities – themselves (see Table 10.2).

Table 10.2: Influence of actors from the mayors' perspective

Actor/group	N	very high	3	2	1	no	mean
		% influence (very high–no influence)					
Mayor	620	83.7	14.7	1.3	0.3	0.0	3.82
Party groups/group leaders in the council	605	26.0	49.3	20.3	4.1	0.3	2.96
Municipal CEO	597	18.1	43.2	27.0	9.4	2.3	2.65
Presidents of council committees	500	9.6	31.6	43.4	13.4	2.0	2.33
Heads of departments	621	5.8	39.8	38.0	14.2	2.3	2.33
President of the council	279	19.4	26.2	28.3	15.1	11.1	2.28
Single councillors	623	2.9	16.5	49.6	28.6	2.4	1.89

Nearly all mayors (98%) see themselves having very high or high influence on local politics. Some way below, party groups and their leaders take the second position. With a further significant gap come the municipal CEO, the president of council committees, the heads of the departments of the local administration and the president of the council,[6] all of whom may be considered similar to each other concerning influence.

Judging influence from the councillors' point of view, a similar picture emerges (see Table 10.3). Councillors also see the mayor as the most influential actor, and they also assess the influence of party groups and their leaders highly. Other actors receive lower scores.

Table 10.3: Influence of actors from the councillors' perspective

Actor/group	N	% influence (very high–no influence)					
		very high	3	2	1	no	mean
Mayor	881	56.0	36.1	6.7	1.0	0.2	3.47
Party groups/group leaders in the council	872	13.0	60.2	23.6	3.0	0.2	2.83
Municipal CEO	715	10.5	42.0	31.5	13.4	2.7	2.44
Presidents of council committees	723	5.0	36.2	42.7	13.0	3.0	2.27
Heads of departments	831	3.9	39.8	39.2	14.3	2.8	2.28
President of the council	598	21.1	33.4	23.4	14.7	7.4	2.46
Single councillors	864	2.0	20.8	46.6	26.6	3.9	1.90

Obviously, mayors and councillors show a similar understanding about who is influential at the local level. These findings fit well to the 'convergence' of municipal codes as explained earlier, which strengthened the office of the mayor (Knemeyer, 1999: 112ff.). Also, by international comparison, German mayors are described as 'strong mayors' (Mouritzen and Svara, 2002: 55) or 'executive leaders' (Heinelt and Hlepas, 2006: 34).

Variances in assessed influence on local politics on the state level

The issue of whether there are variances in the assessment of influence if the data is compared on the state level is now explored. It could be expected that local elites tend to assess their influence differently in different institutional environments. In order to make the analysis clearer, the comparison between the most and the least influential actors as described in the section before, namely the mayor, the party groups in the council and single councillors is now explored (see Table 10.4).

Table 10.4: Perceived influence of actors fi um mayors' view, by state (means)

State	N	mayor	party groups	single councillors.	mayor vs party groups	mayor vs single councillors
Baden-Wurttemberg	104	3.89	3.01	2.26	0.88	0.75
Bavaria	104	3.84	2.74	1.93	1.10	0.81
Brandenburg	17	3.76	2.56	1.76	1.20	0.80
Hesse	69	3.84	2.83	1.81	1.00	1.03
Mecklenburg East Pomerania	8	3.88	2.38	2.25	1.50	0.13
Lower Saxony	78	3.69	3.31	1.70	0.39	1.61
North-Rhine Westphalia	139	3.81	3.14	1.74	0.66	1.40
Rhineland-Palatinate	14	3.86	2.79	2.00	1.07	0.79
Saarland	17	3.81	3.19	2.23	0.63	1.31
Saxony	30	3.86	2.81	1.50	1.05	0.57
Saxony-Anhalt	18	3.72	2.76	1.50	0.96	1.26
Schleswig-Holstein	17	3.81	3.06	1.88	0.75	1.56
Thuringia	14	3.79	2.36	1.79	1.43	0.57
Total	629	3.82	2.96	1.89	0.85	1.07

As Table 10.4 demonstrates, the influence of the mayors from their perspective only varies a little over the states. A greater variance can be seen if one looks at the party groups and party leaders in the council. The order of the states is significant: the highest influence of party groups and party leaders in the council is perceived by mayors in Lower Saxony, the Saarland, North-Rhine Westphalia and Schleswig-Holstein. Three of these states formerly belonged to the 'northern model' and preserved their traditional culture of local politics which was shaped more towards a parliamentary system where party politics is a more important factor than in quasi-presidential systems. This is also true for the Saarland, where the 'mayoral model' was in force before the convergence of the codes, and where the parties are strongly anchored at the local level (Egner, 2007: 118). At the end of the table, four of the five states from the East can be found, together with Bavaria. All of them show much weaker parties at the local level than in the North and a significantly high share of 'free voters associations', local lists and 'local parties' (Egner et al, 2013: 70f; Holtmann, 1999: 222ff). Therefore, party groups in the council and their leaders play a smaller role in those states. A similar spread of states can be observed when analysing the influence of single councillors.

If the same questions are analysed from the view of councillors (Table 10.5), interesting discrepancies can be observed.

Table 10.5: Perceived influence of actors from the councillors' view by states (means)

State	N	mayor	party groups	single councillors	mayor vs party groups	mayor vs single councillors
Baden-Wurttemberg	111	3.50	2.82	2.23	0.68	0.59
Bavaria	106	3.49	2.54	2.11	0.95	0.43
Brandenburg	15	3.40	2.86	2.00	0.54	0.86
Hesse	113	3.51	2.63	1.76	0.88	0.87
Mecklenburg East Pomerania	10	3.80	2.80	1.70	1.00	1.10
Lower Saxony	122	3.42	2.99	1.72	0.43	1.27
North-Rhine Westphalia	236	3.42	2.95	1.83	0.47	1.12
Rhineland-Palatinate	60	3.32	2.90	2.00	0.42	0.90
Saarland	21	3,62	2,71	1,50	0,91	1,21
Saxony	32	3,59	3,06	2,10	0,53	0,96
Saxony-Anhalt	9	3,00	2,33	1,75	0,67	0,58
Schleswig-Holstein	39	3,44	2,89	1,97	0,55	0,92
Thuringia	20	3,90	2,65	1,68	1,25	0,97
Total	894	3.47	2.83	1.90	0.64	0.93

First, councillors also believe that the mayor is most influential actor in town. However, the span between states with very high influence and those with high influence of the mayor is significantly greater than if mayors are asked about their own influence. But the order of the states is somewhat erratic, since councillors from Saxony-Anhalt give their mayors the lowest score, despite the state having an institutionally strong mayor. It is also strange that from the perspective of councillors, one of the states with a strong mayor is Hesse, where the mayor is clearly weak because of the executive board ('magistrate') which was introduced after the war to curb the influence of the mayor. Even more interesting are the assessments of the councillors concerning the influence of party groups and party group leaders in the council, which is deemed especially low in Hesse and Bavaria. This finding is also puzzling, because parties play a major role in Hesse due to coalition government and the executive board. In Bavaria, party groups are extremely important for nominating the mayoral candidates. It is not clear why the councillors' judgements are sometimes counter-intuitive.

Correlations of perceived influence of actors and formal institutions

As found in the previous section, perceptions of mayors and councillors regarding the degree of influence are different in comparison across the Länder. The next question is if there is a statistical connection between institutional rules and perceived influence. For that purpose, correlation coefficients according to Pearson have been calculated (see Table 10.6).

Table 10.6: Pearson correlation of perceived influence of actors and formal institutions

Influence of ...	from the perspective of ...	N	r	p
Mayor	Mayors	13	.31	.31
Mayor	Councillors	13	-.07	.83
Party groups/group leaders in the council	Mayors	13	-.14	.65
Party groups/group leaders in the council	Councillors	13	-.15	.63
Single councillors	Mayors	13	.25	.41
Single councillors	Councillors	13	.50	.08

As Table 10.6 depicts, the perceived influence of mayors, party groups and single councillors is not correlated with mayoral power measured by counting the competences in the municipal codes. This leads to the conclusion that the perceived influence of actors is not dependent on formal power, but may be dependent on personal attributes and the local context. Now those other factors will be included in the analysis.

Individual attributes and local context as determinants for perceived influence

Besides the index of formal mayoral power, additional variables will be included in order to set up statistical models for the individual level. The aim is to find out if institutional rules are important after all, if individual and local circumstances are controlled for statistically.

The following additional variables will be included in the analysis, describing the local context:

- the natural logarithm of the municipality's number of inhabitants which is used as a proxy for the scale of local challenges and also for the importance of the municipality itself (the higher the number of inhabitants, the greater the challenges);
- the effective number of parties within the council calculated by Laakso and Taagepera (1979), which approximates the council capacity to act vis-à-vis the mayor (the higher the number of parties, the more negotiation between groups is needed, which will hamper or enhance the influence of different actors);
- the existence of a single party majority in the council, which may point to a strong position of the council towards the mayor;[7] and
- the degree of party politics, measured by calculating the joint share of council seats occupied by parties with supra-regional significance according to Wehling (1991: 150) which may result in a higher degree of conflict within the council.

In addition, three standard variables for dataset with individual data will be used to control for personal effects, namely age, gender and the education level of the respondents. Also, party membership may be decisive for the assessment of the influence. If the mayor is a party member, s/he may find other party members restricting their own leeway. All potential determinants will be included in multiple linear regression models as displayed in Table 10.7.

The regression analysis shows that institutional arrangements play a smaller role than initially expected. In general, the models – also on the individual level – do not explain the perception of the real horizontal balance of power by the members of the local elite. Nevertheless, some single aspects of the models are worth the discussion.

The most striking finding is that in the model which should illuminate the self-assessment of the mayor's influence (model I), institutional arrangements, political environment and personal attributes of the mayor do not explain the variation. The influence of a mayor as perceived by themselves thus maybe the result of other factors, or simply random.

Also, the influence of the mayor from the eyes of the councillors (model II) is not dependent on the formal rules of power. Contrary to model I, three variables are connected to the perceived influence of the mayor. Surprisingly, councillors rate the mayor's influence higher if there is a one-party majority in the council – contrary to what had been expected. Two other effects are comparatively weak, namely the age and gender of the councillors responding. The older the councillors, the weaker the mayor is perceived to be; women tend

Table 10.7: Regression models for perceived influence

Model number[#]	I	II	III	IV	V	VI
N	578	054	563	845	581	837
R2	.018	.040	.046	.020	.053	.036
adjusted R2	.003	.030	.030	.009	.038	.026
maximum VIF	2.056	1.642	2.052	1.626	2.055	1.649
Durbin-Watson's d	1.947	1.753	1.958	1.826	1.893	1.878
Power of the mayor	.086	.068	-.010	.018	**.204	**.128
Logarithm of inhabitants	-.005	.031	*.094	*.087	-.003	.014
Effective number of council parties	-.092	.013	**-.228	-.080	-.056	.050
Single party majority	.001	**.148	-.042	-.059	-.028	.031
Degree of party politics	-.076	-.059	-.020	.054	-.064	-.057
Age	.006	*-.086	.013	.003	-.033	-.024
Gender	-.003	**-.095	-.018	.014	.002	.060
Education	-.007	.040	-.036	-.022	-.011	.048
Party membership	.072	.056	-.013	.045	.075	.025

Notes: [#] I: self-perception of the mayor; II: influence of mayor according to councillors; III: influence of party groups from the perspective of the mayor; IV: influence of party groups according to the councillors; V: influence of single councillors in the judgment of the mayors; VI: influence of single councillors from the perspective of councillors. Constant included in each model, but not reported. Values in cells represent standardized regression coefficients (β). * = p < .05; ** = p < .01

to rate the mayor's influence higher than men do. Both models show that the perceived influence of the mayor cannot be explained well, at least not using the variables show here.

A similar finding comes from the influence of party groups and party group chairs in the council (models III and IV). Again, institutional settings do not play a role. The size of the municipality is connected with the perceived influence of party groups in both models. This is not surprising, since the size of the municipality determines the size of the council, and the bigger the council, the more important are within-council groups that may organise proceedings and aggregate the councillor's demands and positions. The bigger the city, the more professionalised the council, and the more time councillors spend on party group activities (see Egner et al, 2013: 98). But the models differ in one important point: the fragmentation of the council. As model III depicts, the degree of influence from party groups in the council is perceived higher by the mayor if the fragmentation of the council is low. Interestingly, councillors themselves do not associate council fragmentation with the influence of party groups.

When looking at the influence of single councillors (models V and VI), only one variable can be found significant in both models, and that is the institutional power of the mayor. In both models, the determinant produces a comparably large effect. This means that both mayors and councillors rate the influence of single councillors higher if the mayor has a high degree of formal power. Perhaps the strong position of the mayor towards the council as a collective organ gives single councillors leeway to approach the council with their concerns.

Independently from the interpretations of the models sketched above, all six models have in common that the share of explained variance is very small, even for regression models based on individual data. Additionally, the assumption from the beginning that the perceived influence of actors is correlated with formal power as derived from the municipal codes has to be rejected. Institutional arrangements are only important in two of the six models and show a surprising direction.

Conclusions

This chapter has explored if the degree of influence credited to local politicians depends on the degree of formal competences assigned to them by the municipal code. After empirical analysis, the question can be answered 'no', at least concerning the perceived influence of mayors and party groups in the council. It is clear that the influence of an actor in local politics does not correspond to his formal power position. In general, it is difficult to explain the perceived influence of actors. As the models show, institutional arrangements are mostly without explanatory power, as are specific attributes of the municipalities and of the respondents. On the whole, judgement about the influence of others seems to be highly subjective, and cannot be properly explained by measurable phenomena. These findings are contradictory to the institutionalist perspective on politics – that formal rules shape the individual behaviour (and perspectives) of actors. This is even more interesting if we consider that they were not asked about a policy choice or strategic options concerning their municipality, but about *power relations* between the various groups of actors in local politics. If the formal rules do not shape the actors' perspectives on power, it is not too risky to assume that formal rules are not that important at the local level in Germany. Rather, it seems plausible that the perceived power of mayors may be connected to their individual leadership styles. In most German municipalities, mayors are not only directly elected, but the sole full-time figure in local politics. Thus, they have great leverage in politics and the administrative sphere, where they are the sole politician within the 'administrative world'. The mayor may be characterised as the 'hinge' in local politics, bringing together both worlds and thus exerting strong leadership. Within these circumstances, it seems that formal differences between mayors of different *Länder* are washed out in the wake of the overall strong position of the mayor in local politics. One of the purposes of the institutional reforms was to give more power to the mayor. As it turns out, mayors are perceived as the most powerful figures in German municipalities regardless of their formal competencies. Surely, direct election put the mayors in the midst of public and academic attention. Whether processes of local politics have changed due to changes in the institutional arrangements remains to be discussed.

Notes

[1]   In the large cities of Schleswig-Holstein, however, the 'magistrate model' was introduced, as in Hesse.

[2]   Only one of the five new states adopted a code roughly similar to the former 'northern model' (Brandenburg), while the other four were more oriented towards the southern model.

[3]   Schleswig-Holstein 1990; Brandenburg, Hesse and Rhineland-Palatinate 1993; Mecklenburg-East Pomerania, North-Rhine Westphalia, Saarland, Saxony, Saxony-Anhalt and Thuringia 1994, Lower Saxony 1996. The course of the reforms in each state is described in Schefold and Neumann (1996: 13ff), Haus (2005) and Holtkamp (2005). For North-Rhine Westphalia, see Schulenburg (2000: 49ff).

[4]   *Beigeordnete* are politicians who are elected by the council in order to help the mayor lead the local administration. There may be one *beigeordnete* for social affairs, one for traffic, one for housing etc. They are not members of the council. If they are members of the council when elected as *beigeordnete*, they automatically resign from the council.

[5]   The correlation between the index developed here and the indexes of Buß and Holtkamp are very high (Pearson's r=0.92 for Egner and Buß, Pearson's r=0.92 for Egner and Holtkamp, each with p < 0.001 and N=13).

[6]   The low number of cases for council presidents can be explained by the fact that, in most cases, the mayor presides over the council by law. The question was only to be answered if the mayor is not the president of the council at the same time.

[7]   It is not considered significant whether the party that holds the majority is the party of the mayor or not.

References

Bäck, H., Heinelt, H. and Magnier, A. (eds) (2006) *The European Mayor*, Wiesbaden: VS Verlag.

Banner, G. (1982) 'Zur politisch-administrativen Steuerung in der Kommune', *Archiv für Kommunalwissenschaft*, 21(1), 26–47.

Buß, A. (2002) *Das Machtgefüge in der heutigen Kommunalverfassung*, Baden-Baden: Nomos.

Egner, B. (2007) *Einstellungen deutscher Bürgermeister*, Baden-Baden: Nomos.

Egner, B., Sweeting, D. and Klok, P.-J. (eds) (2013) *Local Councillors in Europe*, Wiesbaden: Springer+VS.

Egner, B., Krapp, M.-C. and Heinelt, H. (2013) *Das deutsche Gemeinderatsmitglied. Problemsichten. Einstellungen. Rollenverständnis*, Wiesbaden: VS Verlag

Haus, M. (2005) 'Lernen im Föderalismus? Die Reform der Kommunalverfassungen in Deutschland' in M. Haus (ed) *Lokale Institutionenpolitik in Deutschland. Zwischen Innovation und Beharrung*, Wiesbaden: VS-Verlag, pp 56–84.

Heinelt, H and Hlepas, N.-K. (2006) 'Typologies of Local Government Systems' in H. Bäck, H. Heinelt and A. Magnier (eds) *The European Mayor*, Wiesbaden: VS Verlag, pp 21–42.

Holtkamp, L. (2005) 'Reform der Kommunalverfassungen in den alten Bundesländern. Eine Ursachenanalyse' in J. Bogumil and H. Heinelt (eds) *Bürgermeister in Deutschland*, Wiesbaden: VS Verlag, pp 13–32.

Holtmann, E. (1999) 'Parteien in der lokalen Politik' in H. Wollmann and R. Roth (eds.) *Kommunalpolitik* (2nd edn), Opladen: Leske + Budrich, pp 208–26.

Knemeyer, F.-L. (1999) 'Gemeindeverfassungen' in H. Wollmann and R. Roth (eds) *Kommunalpolitik* (2nd edn), Opladen: Leske + Budrich, pp 104–122.

Laakso, M. and Taagepera, R. (1979) 'Effective Number of Parties. A Measure with Application to West Europe', *Comparative Political Studies*, 12(1), 3–27.

Mouritzen, P. E. and Svara, J. H. (2002) *Leadership at the Apex*, Pittsburgh: University of Pittsburgh Press.

Schefold, D. and Neumann, M. (1996) *Entwicklungstendenzen der Kommunalverfassungen in Deutschland. Demokratisierung und Dezentralisierung?*, Basel: Birkhäuser.

Schulenburg, K. (2000) 'Die neue Gemeindeordnung in Nordrhein-Westfalen', in R. Kleinfeld, M. Schwanholz, and R. Wortmann (eds) *Kommunale Demokratie im Wandel*, Osnabrück: Hochschule Osnabrück, pp 49–76.

Wehling, H.-G. (1991) 'Parteipolitisierung in lokaler Politik und Verwaltung? Zur Rolle der Parteien in der Kommunalpolitik' in H. Heinelt and H. Wollmann (eds) *Brennpunkt Stadt. Stadtpolitik und lokale Politikforschung in den 80er und 90er Jahren*, Basel/Boston: Birkhäuser Verlag, pp 149–66.

Wollmann, H. (1999) 'Kommunalpolitik – Zu neuen (direkt-) demokratischen Ufern?' in H. Wollmann and R. Roth (eds) *Kommunalpolitik* (2nd edn), Opladen: Leske | Budrich, pp 37–49.

Wollmann, H. (2004) 'The two waves of territorial reforms of local government in Germany' in J. Meligrana (ed) *ReDrawing Local Government Boundaries. An International Study of Politics, Procedures and Decisions*, Vancouver: UBC Press, pp 106–29.

Annex

Table 10.1A: Indicators of mayoral strength

No	Meaning	0	½	1
01	Length of term of office	5–6 years, connected	5–6 years	7–8 years
02	Candidacy	Needs council group nomination		Can stand as independent
03	Council may propose recall	Yes		No
04	Recall proposal council quorum	Simple majority	Two thirds majority	Three quarters majority
05	Recall initiation council quorum	Simple majority	Two thirds majority	Three quarters majority
06	Citizen may propose recall	Yes		No
07	Recall majority	Simple majority	Two thirds majority	Not possible
08	Recall turnout	No minimum turnout necessary	At least one third	At least a half
09	Gap competence: council has	General responsibility	Competence of interception	Neither of the two
10	Restoring competence	Yes		No
11	General information right	Yes		No
12	Minority information right	Yes		No
13	Single councillor information right	Yes		No
14	Substitution decision by mayor	No		Yes
15	Emergency decisions by mayor	No		Yes
16	Public welfare veto	No		Yes
17	Decision over employee	Without mayor	Mayor co-acts	Mayor alone
18	Contract for employees	Without mayor	Mayor co-acts	Mayor alone
19	Day-to-day management for specific tasks from above	No		Yes

No	Meaning	0	½	1
20	Day-to-day management for local tasks in self-government	No		Yes
21	Political representation	No		Yes
22	Binding contracts	Mayor and council president	Mayor and executive officer	Mayor alone
23	Representation in joint associations	Council decides	Association decides	Mayor
24	Representation as share holder	Council decides	Company decides	Mayor
25	Mayor is council member	No		Yes
26	Mayor is council president	No	Council elects	Yes
27	Mayor is president of committees	No	Council elects	Yes
28	Control over council agenda	Council president	Joint decision	Mayor
29	Formal preparation of council decisions	Council president or council committees	Together with executive officers	Mayor
30	Executive committee exists	Yes		No
31	Length of executive officers' term of office long than the mayor's	Yes		No
32	Rule of proportionality	No		Yes
33	Position of mayor for election of executive officers	No veto	Mutual consent	Veto
34	Who decides about assignment of competencies to the executive officers	Council	Mutual consent	Mayor
35	Mayor may direct executive officers	No	Conditional	Yes
36	Mayor may prohibit executive officers from deviating	No		Yes
37	Mayor may prohibit the treasurer from deviating	No		Yes

Breeding grounds for local independents, bonus for incumbents: directly elected mayors in Poland

Adam Gendźwiłł and Paweł Swianiewicz,
University of Warsaw, Poland

Introduction

Poland introduced the direct election of mayors relatively recently, in 2002. Nevertheless, there has already been four elections under that system. To use terminology introduced by Mouritzen and Svara (2002), Polish mayors are closest to the 'strong leader' form of leadership. Following the Heinelt and Hlepas (2006) typology, the Polish case represents a strong executive mayor model. However, as discussed in this chapter, there are some differences between the Polish case and classic features of the strong mayor form.

One of the peculiarities of the Polish case is that directly elected mayors appear at the municipal tier of local government only. They hold executive power in 2,478 municipalities. Both upper tiers of subnational government – 315 counties and 16 regions – have a collective form of leadership with an executive board appointed by county or regional councils respectively. The same collective model of leadership was in place at the municipal level during first three electoral cycles (1990 to 2002) after the restoration of a democratic local government system after the collapse of Communist Party rule in 1989.

Alongside developments in Poland, the introduction of directly elected mayors was a part of a wider, European trend. There are several academic contributions demonstrating that trend (for example, Larsen, 2002; Berg and Rao, 2005; Heinelt and Hlepas, 2006; Magre and Bertrana, 2007). However, it is less known that such a trend was particularly prevalent in post-communist Eastern Europe (see also Koprić, 2009a; Swianiewicz, 2014). The direct election of mayors was introduced almost immediately after the fall of Communism in several countries of the region, including Slovakia, Romania, Bulgaria, Ukraine, Albania, Slovenia, Moldova and Armenia. Hungary followed shortly after in 1994, Macedonia in 1995, Poland in 2002 and Croatia in 2009. Georgia changed its system several times – trying directly elected mayors, then going back to indirect appointment through the council – and recent reforms of 2014 re-introduced the system of direct elections once again. In fact, the indirect election of local executives now exist in a minority of Eastern European countries, including the Czech Republic, Serbia, Estonia, Latvia and Lithuania. Change has been debated in some of these countries (see Jüptner, Chapter Twelve, this volume, for the Czech Republic). Montenegro (in two consequent elections starting from 2003) even experimented with direct mayoral elections, but then returned to the 'old' type of mayors elected by the local councils (Koprić, 2009b).

In this chapter we briefly present the history of the 2002 Polish reforms, which changed not only the method of the mayor's selection, but also the institutional setting of local governments. We then discuss the arguments that were considered in the debate around the direct election of mayors, as well as other factors which influenced the dynamics of the reform. Finally, we try to verify what the main outcomes of the direct election of mayors are. We argue that direct elections strengthened the position of local leaders, and at the same time made local administration more directly dependent on the mayor. Moreover, direct elections have strongly personalised the electoral competition at the local level. Along with strongly personalised elections, independent candidates representing ephemeral local committees (sometimes former party members) became more successful than candidates of nationwide parties. Direct elections preserved the non-partisanship popular in local governments after the transition, and created institutional incentives for new non-party alternatives, but also for more or less evident cases of 'camouflage' used by leaders from nationwide political parties. It also seems that direct elections increased incumbency advantage, which stabilised the leadership in municipalities, but simultaneously limited the competition. We argue that the phenomena described above are dependent on the size of municipality: generally, the 'strong mayor' model is more pronounced in smaller municipalities. Opposite to expectations pronounced by the proponents of the reforms, there is no evidence that the system of direct election has raised citizen participation in local government elections. We conclude this chapter with a discussion of current debates on the model of local leadership in Poland.

How and why were directly elected mayors introduced in Poland?

The idea of strengthening local executives, stabilising them and equipping mayors with stronger legitimacy based on the popular election was discussed several times in the 1990s. Jerzy Regulski, one of the 'founding fathers' of democratic local governments in Poland, noted that in 1990 the reformers had considered the option of direct elections for mayors (Regulski, 2000). However, as they were convinced that the mayor should be a permanent inhabitant of a particular municipality, they were concerned over whether small rural local communities will find good candidates for mayors, if elected directly. They also thought that direct elections made sense if the mayor led the council, but not the local administration (Regulski, 2000: 305). Regulski and others also argued that the collective leadership system introduced in 1990 allowed for the relatively easy removal of the mayor by the council before the end of their term in office, thus making the mayor's position too weak and too unstable.

The suggestion to introduce directly elected mayors returned very soon. In 1992 the change to direct election was suggested by the annual meeting of the Association of Polish Cities. The discussion continued in 1993–94, but eventually it was decided that strengthening of the mayor's position would be achieved by more difficult procedure of his recall during the term, but without the radical change to the system (Piasecki, 2006: 107–18). But the discussion did not stop for long and in 1996 it returned as a formal draft of the law submitted to the parliament by the then President Aleksander Kwaśniewski (a leftist). The suggestion was supported by the national associations of local governments (which are sometimes perceived as almost 'trade unions of local mayors'), but the proposal eventually failed, blocked by opposition parties in the Polish parliament. Michał Kulesza, another prominent expert and one of the architects of local government reforms in Poland, opposed the proposals, arguing that their introduction would be a smokescreen typical of the government to postpone the next stage of decentralisation and the introduction of territorial self-government at the county and regional level (Kulesza, 2008: 218ff). He wrote:

> This solution is promoted in Poland by those who are afraid of the normal political process of democracy, political cooperation, and compromise-seeking. In this proposal one can see a reflex of unitary state power, coming from the times when the local council did not have any significant

prerogatives and the leadership of the local community was held by the mayor (*naczelnik)* [who was appointed by the central government rather than locally elected during the communist period] and the secretary of the local communist party – invisible but permanently present. (Kulesza, 2008: 222)

Kulesza was also wary of conflict between mayor and the council in which a majority of representatives would be elected from political groups opposed to the mayor. Nonetheless, direct election for mayors became important on the political agenda again during the 2001 electoral campaign for the parliamentary elections. Directly elected mayors were also promoted mainly by the newly established right-wing liberal party, Civic Platform (*Platforma Obywatelska*, PO).

Replacing collegial local executives (*Zarządy Gmin*) with the directly elected executive mayors, granted with the new prerogatives, creating the independent corps of civil service in local governments and limiting the number of councillors were presented as ways of enhancing the effectiveness of local governments and improving their responsiveness to citizens. These proposals were also an important element of the PO's anti-party agenda, which presented itself as a 'non-party civic movement'. The direct election of mayors was presented as a way to attribute clearly responsibility for local affairs and to 'de-party' local governments – to limit the influence of nationwide political parties on local politics. Strong independent mayors with managerial skills were frequently juxtaposed against 'party deals' in constantly quarrelling councils.

The direct election of mayors was also supported by the Left Democratic Alliance (*Sojusz Lewicy Demokratycznej*, SLD), a post-communist social democratic party that won the 2001 parliamentary elections, defeating right-wing post-solidarity parties, including the PO. While the SLD generally supported the idea (which it also promoted in the mid-1990s), the legislative proposals of the governing party were rather conservative in comparison to those submitted by the PO. According to the SLD's proposals, mayors would be directly elected only in smaller municipalities (up to 20,000 inhabitants), as an 'experimental stage' before further changes. The SLD's proposal also maintained the collegial character of local executive boards. Both proposals assumed that there would be no popular runoff in mayoral elections: the SLD postulated the use of simple plurality voting rule (first past the post); the PO proposed the majority rule with the runoff in the council, in case it would be necessary. The runoff would take place between the top two candidates if either of them got over 50% of votes.

To sum up, the arguments in favour of directly elected mayors presented during the parliamentary debate can be divided into two broad categories. The first category argues that directly elected mayors would provide a remedy for the deficit of local legitimacy and accountability; the second general that directly elected mayors would enhance the efficiency of local authorities. The former was to be achieved through:

- increasing voter interest, and in turn local election turnout;
- increasing the transparency of local government structures, and clarifying accountability for decision making; and
- reducing the power of political parties in nominating candidates for the mayors – the power was expected to be held by 'regular' citizens and local associations.

The latter would be the result of:

- providing stable leadership, as before the reform the high level of turnover of mayors was seen as problematic; and
- strengthening the position of the mayor, who would be able to implement more coherent policies in a more stable environment.

All of those arguments may be found in the official justifications of the reform proposals prepared by MPs, who submitted the drafts of the new law to the parliament in 2001.

During the legislative process for the reforms, the initial proposals were to some extent radicalised. All the executive power at the local level was granted to the mayor, and collective executives disappeared completely. Parliamentarians agreed to introduce direct elections in all municipalities, including larger cities. They agreed that the mayor need not have a stable majority in the council, but still each candidate for the mayor should be supported by a certain number of candidates for councillors. Thus, it is possible, but rare, that a mayor does not have any councillors from his/her supporters in the municipal council. After many debates, a majority runoff voting system was adopted, despite the concerns about the insufficient turnout in the second round and the additional costs. The first round of mayoral elections take place at the same time as the elections of councillors. If none of the candidates gets more than 50% of valid votes, two top candidates compete in the runoff (second round), which is held two weeks after.

Two of the most recognised architects of the 1990 and 1998 decentralisation reforms – Regulski and Kulesza – and many other experts participating in the public debate were sceptical about the reforms. Kulesza was ready to support the system of directly elected mayors, but in a different shape (Kulesza, 2008: 301, 337, 357). First, he argued that the mayor should also chair the council.[1] Second, he argued that an independent civil service in local administration should be introduced at the same time. Third, he suggested that the candidate for the mayor should at the same time lead a list of their preferred candidates for election to the council (similar to the French system). In the proposed system, the main opposition leader can remain outside the council, which clearly complicates political dynamics of the municipality. Many candidates for mayor also take part in the elections for county councils which are held at the same time as municipal elections. Such an 'insurance policy' is not forbidden by law.

Public opinion was generally favourable towards the immediate introduction of direct elections of mayors, putting additional pressure on political parties debating the new regulations. In three consecutive polls (held by the Centre for Public Opinion Research, CBOS, in January, April and May 2002) between 64% and 68% of respondents said they supported the direct election of the local executive, against only between 7% and 11% for the previous system (CBOS, 2002a: 3). These results correspond with the dominant preference in Polish public opinion towards majoritarian electoral systems (CBOS, 2008). Intriguingly, in 2007, several years after reform, the system of direct election for mayors was also strongly supported by the vast majority of councillors (88%), even when the 2002 reform significantly reduced the power of local councils and councillors themselves (Swianiewicz, 2008).

Finally, the new law on the direct election of mayors, along with the new electoral code, was enacted in July 2002. The first elections under the new system were held in all 2,478 municipalities in October 2002. In contrast to the recent mayoral changes in England, there were no local referendums on the issue in Poland. As the system was changed simultaneously in all municipalities, there was no chance to compare the outcomes between directly elected mayoral municipalities and other municipalities in a quasi-experimental scheme. However, some general patterns of change are visible and could be attributed to the institutional change.

After the 2002 reforms, Polish mayors have become strong figures, relatively independent from councils. Mayors represent the municipality – both local communities and local government institutions. They have also the exclusive right to propose the annual budget or to initiate the amendments to it during the budgetary year. However, once the draft of the budget is submitted to the council, the councillors may not only approve or reject it, they can also introduce the changes in the mayor's draft. Also in other areas, resources necessary for policy formulation (and implementation) are mainly at the mayor's disposal, so s/he dominates the council in the policy process. A mayor serves also as a head of the local administration; s/he is also responsible for the functioning of all municipal institutions (schools, libraries, social services). In many small municipalities a mayor, controlling the appointments in the town hall, schools and municipal units, is the largest employer and a very important investor (local governments are responsible for basic infrastructure and public utilities).

A mayor can be supported in their duties by the deputy mayors (appointed by the mayor). The municipal treasurer has a special position as s/he is appointed by the council at the request of the mayor. A similar arrangement was used in case of the 'municipal secretary', the main executive officer, but since 2008, secretaries are no longer appointed by councils, but by mayors instead. All mayors in Poland are employed full time. For that reason, a mayor cannot be simultaneously a councillor (either in his/her or any other municipality), an MP or a public officer employed in central government administration. Polish mayors do not chair municipal councils, which could lead to conflicts over the 'prestige of function' between the mayor and council's chair.

Directly elected mayors do not always have a stable majority in the councils, and some of them would have never been elected by councillors. A survey of mayors directly elected for the first time, conducted in 2004, demonstrated clearly that the support of the majority in the council was not valued as an important asset of a mayor and scored lower than professional managerial skills (see Table 11.1).

Mayors have considerable discretion in governing municipalities even without majority councillor support. For example, if a council rejects a budget proposed by a mayor, a budget is imposed by the Regional Chamber of Audit. Chambers attempt to balance the budget and can use very tough austerity measures, usually cutting funds for investments. Thus rejecting the local budget is not desirable, either for the mayor or the council. However, the power of a mayor over the budget is not absolute. Councillors can still impose some amendments in the budget proposed by the mayor, provided they do not create demand for additional borrowing or increase the budget deficit.

Table 11.1: The importance of various assets of directly elected mayors

Assets of the mayor	Average score (0–5 scale)
Managerial skills	4.4
Ability to negotiate and manage conflicts	4.2
Ability to manage the employees of the municipal administration	3.5
Legal-administrative skills	3.7
Support of the majority in the council	2.5

Notes: Mayors were asked to rank each asset on a scale ranging from 0 (not important) to 5 (very important); N=650.
Source: Kowalik (2005: 16)

An important element of the Polish model is the ability to recall the mayor. The right to recall elected officials in subnational governments is constitutionally guaranteed. A mayor in Poland can be recalled by popular vote. The recall election, a special type of local referendum, can be initiated either by the council (if it does not grant a 'vote of acceptance' to a mayor after the budgetary year or for other reasons) or by 10% of eligible local voters. The recall election is valid if the turnout is higher than three fifths of the turnout in the previous ordinary election in which a mayor was elected. If the recall election is valid, a mayor can be recalled by a majority of votes. If the council initiates the recall election, and either the referendum is invalid (due to the low turnout) or a majority of voters oppose the recall of the mayor in a valid vote, the municipal council is automatically dissolved. Therefore, the typical strategy of the council (in case it is in conflict with the mayor) is not to initiate the referendum but to stimulate the initiative among voters.

While constitutional impeachment procedures are generally considered extraordinary, it is difficult to claim the same about the local recall referendums in Poland. It is a rare, but not unheard of process – see Table 11.2. For example, during the 2010–14 term, recall elections were held in 111 municipalities (almost 4.5% of mayors in Poland were threatened by recall procedures). However, only 16 were binding and resulted in the recall of a mayor – only 14% of recall referendums were successful. Here lies often the best defence strategy for a threatened mayor: usually he/she tries to demobilise the electorate in order to decrease the turnout below the threshold required by law. Since 2002, there have only been two cases of valid referendums in which a majority voted against the recall of the mayor. Since those referendums were initiated by group of citizens (not by the council), the result did not lead to council dissolution.

Table 11.2: Recall elections of mayors in Poland, 2002–14

Terms	Number of recall elections			% of effective recalls	% turnout (minimum–maximum)
	Held	Binding	Binding and effective		
2002–06	92	12	11	13	2.0–42.0
2006–10	81	13	13	16	3.1–69.1
2010–14	111	16	16	14	3.5–48.8
Total	295	39	40	13	

Sources: Kancelaria Prezydenta RP (2013: 3); Kowalik (2014: 133)

There are also several restrictions on the organisation of a recall referendum. It cannot be organised for 12 months after normal elections, nor less than 6 months before next normal elections. It is also not possible to organise a referendum less than 12 months after a previous (invalid) attempt to recall the mayor.

Outcomes

There is little doubt that directly elected mayors have become firmly rooted in the consciousness of Polish citizens. The majority of Poles supported the model of a directly elected local executive, and it is still widely valued. According to a recent survey (CBOS, 2014; see Figure 11.1), the elections for mayor are generally considered to be the most important among subnational elections.[2] Only in rural municipalities and some medium-sized towns are the elections of local councillors considered most important by more people than mayoral elections. This confirms results of earlier studies (such as Denters et al, 2014) suggesting that perception of local politics is dependent on the size of local government.

Mayoral elections in the largest cities are considered markedly more important than others. The personalised contests for the mayoralities in the largest cities attract the attention of both the local and national media. Polish TV stations that present the results of exit polls after the subnational elections focus on citizens' preferences in the election of regional councils (often a proxy for parliamentary elections), and on the elections of mayors in the largest cities.

Figure 11.1: Public opinion in Poland: which elections do you consider the most important

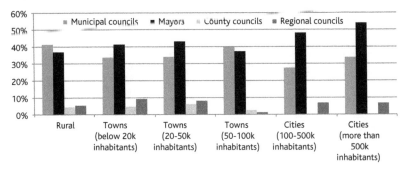

Note: Responses 'all are important' and 'don't know' are omitted.
Source: CBOS (2014)

Mayors are widely recognised in their municipalities. According to a CBOS survey conducted in 2014 (see Figure 11.2), 80% of citizens know at least the last name of the current mayor, higher even than the 74% reported in 2002 (CBOS, 2002b). While in rural municipalities and small towns, mayors are only marginally more well-known than local councillors, the gap is considerably larger in the largest cities. Here, only 20–40% of respondents could mention the name of at least one councillor, while about 90% could name the mayor.

The expectation that the direct election of mayors would visibly increase electoral participation did not materialise (see Table 11.3). In 2002, the first year of direct mayoral elections, the overall turnout was lower than in 1998. It should be also noted that in 1998 elections

Figure 11.2: Respondents able to name elected representatives in different tiers of government

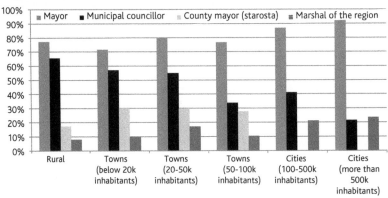

Source: CBOS (2014)

Table 11.3: Turnout in local elections, 1990–2014, %

Year	% turnout
1990	42.3
1994	33.8
1998	45.5
2002	44.2
2006	46.0
2010	47.3
2014	47.4

Source: National Electoral Commission (http://pkw.gov.pl)

voters were for the first time eligible to cast their votes for both the county and regional councillors. It is probable that the system introduced in 2002 created the additional motivation for voters to participate. However, the turnout in local elections seems to be relatively stable over time.

Turnout at the municipal level in Poland differs from about 20% to 70%. Moreover, in smaller municipalities the turnout in local elections is systematically higher that in the parliamentary elections. It means that for many voters the elections of local governments are not considered as less important, subordinated to the dynamics of national politics or 'second order', as mid-term or European Parliament elections are (Reif and Schmitt, 1980; Kjær and Steyvers, 2014).

The direct election of mayors also introduces an additional opportunity for voters to participate. A runoff in mayoral elections (held two weeks after the first ballot) tends to be required in many municipalities (see Table 11.3). In the runoff election the turnout tends to be lower than the first ballot as voters have less motivation to participate – in the first ballot they elect also other subnational authorities. The difference in turnout between the first round and second round of mayoral elections depends also on the margin of victory – the difference between the support for two most popular candidates. The lower the difference between the two leading candidates, the more possible it appears that the runoff will change the initial result, and thus the electoral turnout is higher in the runoff (see Figure 11.3). It is worth noticing that the change of the initial electoral result happens quite frequently – in 25–30% of cases.

The scarcity of data on candidates and mayors elected indirectly before 2002 does not allow us to assess systematically how has the new system changed the composition of local elites, and whether it promoted candidates with managerial experience. Nonetheless, it is clear that the new system initially opened the electoral market and increased the electoral supply of potential local leaders. Simultaneously, the direct election of mayors contributed to the increase of an incumbency advantage for sitting candidates, and growing stability in local authorities – sometimes is considered as a disadvantage for

Figure 11.3: Relationship between the margin of first round victory and run-off turnout, 2014

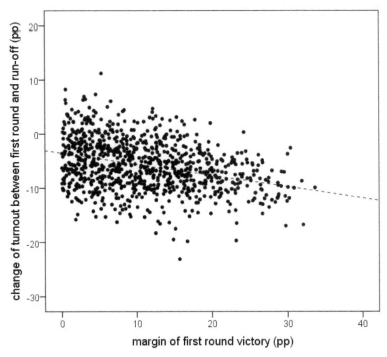

Note: Pearson's r coefficient = 0.332 (p<0.001)
Source: National Electoral Commission (http://pkw.gov.pl)

the local democracy, indicating a lack of real electoral competition. It is interesting to notice that there was an opposite line of criticism popular during the 1990s. The proponents of the reforms argued that the turnover of mayors was too high and that made it often impossible to implement stable, long-term development policies. According their expectations, the system of direct election would help to stabilise local executives. The tune of the present discussions suggests that they were even more right than they had expected. The pendulum moved to another opposite and, while the 1990s were characterised by excessive turnover, the current system is criticised for the over-stability of mayoral positions.

The change has been especially visible in large cities. Figure 11.4 presents incumbency rates in the last indirect election (1998), and the first and the most recent direct elections of mayors (2002 and 2014 respectively). It shows that under the old system the turnover of local mayors was clearly correlated with the size of local government (more stable local elites in small communities, but a high turnover in big

Figure 11.4: Incumbent mayors elected in 1998, 2002 and 2014 elections, %

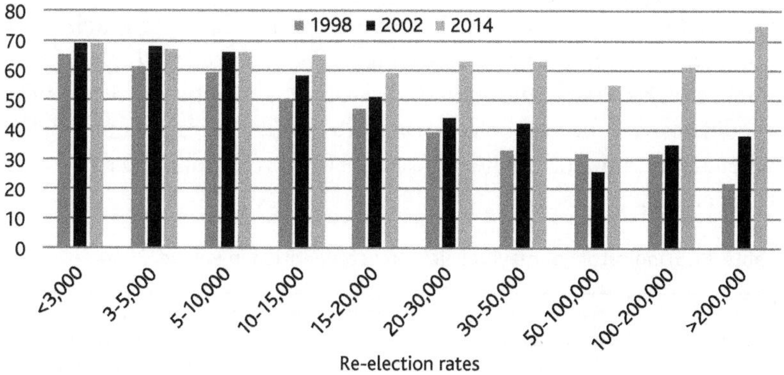

Re-election rates

Sources: 2002, 2014 – electoral results, National Electoral Commission; 1998 – list of mayors holding office

cities), but the system of direct election has gradually strengthened the position of mayors in major cities as well.

There are still some municipalities with only one candidate for mayor, usually the incumbent. In such a situation, the majority of voters should approve the only candidate. If the candidate does not get more than 50% of valid votes, the mayor is elected by the newly elected municipal council. On average, however, three or four candidates compete for the office of mayor (see Table 11.4). In several larger cities the number of candidates has exceeded ten. Generally, mayoral elections are much more competitive in larger municipalities, where local elites are pluralistic, better organised and able to present multiple candidates.

Between 2002 and 2010, we observed the decreasing competitiveness of the mayoral elections in Poland (see Table 11.4). Fewer candidates were registered, fewer run-offs were held and more municipalities experienced non-competitive elections. This trend, however, stopped and reversed in 2014.

Table 11.4: Competitiveness of mayoral elections in Poland, 2002–14

	2002	2006	2010	2014
Average number of candidates	4.19	3.32	3.14	3.24
% of municipalities with one candidate	3.9	11.1	12.2	10.0
% of municipalities in which second round of mayoral election was necessary	49	34	30	36

Source: Gendźwiłł et al (2015)

The competitiveness of mayoral elections is strongly correlated with the size of local government – elections in large cities are much more competitive than in small communities. As indicated in Table 11.5, it is reflected by several important indicators – in big cities there are more candidates, and mayoral elections more often require a second ballot when the number of candidate reaches 50% threshold in the first round of elections.

Table 11.5: Indicators of mayoral electoral competition in Poland, 2014

Size of municipalities	Share of local governments in which second ballot was required	Mean number of candidates for mayorship	Share of municipalities with non-competitive mayor's election
<3,000	25%	2.78	17%
3–5,000	26%	2.77	11%
5–10,000	31%	2.90	13%
10–15,000	39%	3.24	9%
15–20,000	49%	3.76	6%
20–30,000	48%	4.11	4%
30–50,000	61%	4.70	1%
50–100,000	74%	5.72	0%
100–200,000	50%	5.78	4%
>200,000	75%	7.31	0%

Sources: National Electoral Commission; own calculations

One of the durable outcomes of the direct election of mayors is the strengthening of the position of local independent lists, and the corresponding weakening of the penetration of local governments by national political parties. Polish parties were very weak in the first democratic local elections held in 1990, but they gradually gained ground throughout the 1990s. That trend has been stopped by the introduction of directly elected mayors.

Poland is frequently presented as an extreme case characterised by the weak presence of political parties in local governments (Fallend et al, 2006). Polish political parties are organisationally fragile and distrusted; based on a professional party model, they do not develop territorial structures or mass membership. Moreover, in public discourse local politics was successfully separated from national politics, and 'party interests' was displaced by 'local interests', the former being labelled as evil, the latter as noble. For that reason, non-partisans and local independent lists dominate local government in Poland in small peripheral municipalities, and also in many larger cities (Gendźwiłł, 2012; Gendźwiłł and Żółtak, 2014).

Direct elections for mayors visibly enforce this 'anti-party spirit', present in Polish local governments since the establishment of local democracy in 1990. Direct elections, focused on competition between candidates rather than parties, enable victories by charismatic local leaders and political entrepreneurs, even if they are not supported by a strong organisation. Moreover, direct elections give a chance for 'escapers' and 'dissidents' from parties. There are numerous examples of successful mayoral candidates who ran as independents against the will of their former party (Swianiewicz and Klimska, 2003).

Of course, political parties attempt to camouflage their labels by forming coalitions with local associations or presenting their candidates as representatives of local independent groups. Such activity could be interpreted as a sign either of the parties' adaptability to hostile environments, or a sign of their failure caused by unattractive party identity. Nonetheless, the mechanism of camouflage certainly blurs the competition in local arenas; it is difficult to assess how much control political parties have over independent mayors, who visibly or covertly support them.

Swianiewicz and Mielczarek (2005) investigated the position of political parties in Eastern European local governments. They argue that the direct election of mayors generally pushes down party membership among mayors. Based on the comparison of surveys conducted among mayors before and after the introduction of direct elections in Poland, the authors found that after the reforms were introduced, the proportion of mayors that were party members dropped, and that in big cities it is even lower than the proportion of party councillors (Swianiewicz and Mielczarek, 2005: 28).

While survey estimates of party membership among Polish mayors was 46% in 2001, it decreased to 37% in 2003 (Swianiewicz and Mielczarek, 2005: 35). Electoral records allow us to track party affiliations of all elected mayors since 2002, and previous estimations are based on various survey results – see Table 11.6. According to electoral data, in 2002 only 24.5% of mayors were registered as candidates of political parties. The discrepancy between the 2003 Indicators of Local Democratic Governance Project (ILDGP) survey[3] and official data could be attributed to survey bias, but also to the effect of 'independent camouflage'. However, data from consecutive elections demonstrate that until 2010 mayors representing parties were becoming more frequent. The significant decrease of this indicator in the recent

2014 election could be attributed to electoral reform, which replaced the proportional representation system in the elections of municipal councils with the plurality rule in single-member districts (Gendźwiłł and Żółtak, forthcoming). Under the new system, the incentives to use nationwide party labels in local elections were even weaker. Local party organisations, as well as citizens' attachments to party labels, are too weak to become an asset for individual candidates in single-member districts.

Table 11.6: Party affiliations of mayors in Poland, 2002–14

Election	Share of mayors representing party lists (%)
1990	13.3
1994	27.0
1998	46.0
2002	24.5
2006	27.0
2010	30.6
2014	18.6

Sources: 2002–14 electoral data are from National Electoral Commission; 1990–98 figures are survey estimations from Swianiewicz (2003).

Controversies and current debates

How can we summarise the current model of mayoral position in Poland? It very much resembles the 'strong mayor' system, as described in the European typologies of local political leadership (Mouritzen and Svara, 2002; Heinelt and Hlepas, 2006; Magnier, 2006). Mayors are very strong indeed, and some critics suggests that they are too strong. A mayor is directly elected, giving not only a strong formal position, but also direct democratic legitimacy which strengthens him/her in relations with other actors. A mayor may independently decide on many important nominations in local administration (including appointing vice mayors) as well as deciding on important details of the internal structure of local administration. They also have a right to grant individual tax exemptions from local taxes or to defer the payments to be made by individual taxpayers. Finally, it is mayors' exclusive competence to prepare (and present to the council) a draft of the budget as well as to propose amendments to it. Nonetheless, a mayor's control over the budget policy is not complete – the local council not only approves (or disapproves) the draft of the budget, but it may also substantially revise and change the draft submitted by the mayor.

There are also several features which make the Polish system deviate from the typical strong mayor model. First, a mayor in Poland has no guaranteed majority in the council and there are many examples of cohabitation between mayor and council in which the majority of councillors oppose the mayor. As a result, the mayor has to rely on building ad hoc coalitions in order to approve crucial resolutions and make frequent compromises with the majority group.

Second, the mayor can be recalled during their term in office by popular referendum initiated either by the council or a group of citizens. A discussion on tightening or relaxing the conditions to be met by such a referendum to be valid has been one of the main points of the debate on the role and position of the mayor. Initially, the turnout threshold to be passed in order to consider the recall referendum valid was set by the national legislation at 30% (as it is still for any other local referendum). In 2006, however, the threshold was changed to three fifths of the turnout level registered in a regular election in the relevant municipality. It is difficult to say whether the change made a mayor's position more or less stable. If the regular turnout was over 50% (as in most of small local governments) the new threshold is more difficult to be passed than under the previous regulations. But if regular turnout was lower (as in most of large cities), the new regulation makes valid recall referendum more likely. In 2013, the president, supported by many mayors, submitted to Parliament a draft bill raising the threshold to the level registered in the regular election for mayor. It should be added, however, that the proposal has been strongly criticised by several MPs and it is very unlikely to be adopted in the foreseeable future.

Finally, a mayor's control over nominations is not absolute. In particular, the appointment of the city treasurer requires the consent of the local council. Summing up, the position of a mayor is very strong indeed, but not as strong as in some other European systems.

Can we say that expectations of the reform have been confirmed in reality? Only to some extent. There is no proof that the change in 2002 contributed to an increase in citizen participation in local elections. The turnout has been relatively stable in the past five elections, regardless of the mode of election of the mayor. But it is true that a mayor is the most recognised local politician and the responsibility for local affairs is attributed directly to them.

The expectation that direct election would decrease the impact of political parties on local governments seems to be true and it is commonly seen in Poland as a positive development, as it is in accordance with the general anti-party mood rooted both in public opinion and among local elites. However, it is difficult to provide clear arguments why non-partisans are better for local government. There is no evidence that they achieve visibly higher measurable outputs in governing the municipalities than partisan mayors. It is clear, however, that successful local independent lists led by strong local leaders (very frequently incumbents) frequently dominate local political arenas and restrict pluralism in councils. One can also observe that independents cooperate with political parties, which sometimes prefer 'an overt presence' at the local level.

The expectation of a stronger and more stable mayoral position has also proved to be true. Yet, the success measured by those criteria has been so obvious that the pendulum of the debate questions swings the opposite way – whether mayoral power is too strong, too independent from control and too stable. A reversal of the 2002 reform is rarely raised, though it was considered to be one possible option in a recent experts' report (Hausner, 2014: 17). It is more common to call for a legal term limitation for directly elected mayors.

But the fears of the opponents of the direct elections have not materialised either. It is true that there are several cases of cohabitation between a mayor and a council with opposing views and aims. However, they are devastating for local politics only sporadically. Usually, the two parties are able to find compromise solutions and cooperate at least on the most crucial issues (such as adopting the budget). Municipal councils' practical influence on policy making has indeed decreased significantly, and a mayor is currently clearly by far the most powerful actor of the local political scene (see, for example, the illustrations in Swianiewicz et al., 2006; Swianiewicz 2015).

However, the replacement of the directly elected mayor system is not currently on the political agenda and it is very unlikely to appear in the near future. Apart from the discussion on the limitation of a number of years a mayor may spend in office, another much discussed change would strengthen rather than weaken the political importance of the mayor: it is often suggested that mayors should be allowed to stand for the upper chamber of the Polish Parliament (Senate), keeping their local post at the same time. Such a suggestion has bottom-up origin and is often raised by the mayors of some of the larger cities. Interestingly, the controversial experiences of the similar French system to which the proposal refers – *cumul des mandats* – (François, 2006) are not widely discussed in Poland in this context.

The system of directly elected mayors is well rooted and commonly accepted in Poland. It is unlikely to be challenged in the near future.

Notes

1   The mayor acting as council chair was proposed in the first draft of the 1990 Law on Local Governments. The draft was, however, changed by the upper chamber of the parliament, which separated the two positions.

2   Poles elect subnational governments of all tiers simultaneously every four years. Votes typically elect their mayor, municipal councillor, county councillor and regional councillor; voters in Warsaw also elect their district (sub-municipal) representatives.

3   Indicators of the Local Democratic Governance Project (ILDGP) project conducted in 2000–03 in seven countries of Central and Eastern Europe (including Poland). The project was funded by the LGI (Local Government and Public Service Initiative) programme of the Open Society Institute.

References

Berg, R. and Rao, N. (2005) *Transforming Local Political Leadership*, Basingstoke: Palgrave-Macmillan.

CBOS (2002a) *Wybory samorządowe*. Report no. K094.

CBOS (2002b) *Polacy o głosowaniu w wyborach samorządowych*. Report no. K117.

CBOS (2008) *Polacy o proponowanych zmianach w systemie politycznym*. Report no. K056.

CBOS (2014) *Ranga wyborów i zainteresowanie decyzjami władz różnych szczebli*. Report no. K148.

Denters, B., Lander, A., Mouritzen, P.E. and Rose, L. (2014) *Size and Local Democracy*, Cheltenham-Northampton: Edward Elgar.

Fallend, F., Ignits, G. and Swianiewicz, P. (2006) 'Divided loyalties? Mayors beetween party representation and local community interests' in: H Bäck, H Heinelt and A Magnier (eds) *The European Mayor: political leaders in the changing context of local democracy*, Opladen: Verlag fur Sozialwissenschaften, pp. 245-71.

François, A. (2006) 'Testing the 'Baobab Tree' Hypothesis: The Cumul des Mandats as a Way of Obtaining More Political Resources and Limiting Electoral Competition', *French Politics*, 4(3), 269–91.

Gendźwiłł, A. (2012) 'Independent Mayors and Local Lists in Large Polish Cities: Towards a Non-partisan Model of Local Government?', *Local Government Studies*, 38(4), 501–51.

Gendźwiłł, A. and Żółtak, T. (2014) 'Why do non-partisans challenge parties in local politics? The (extreme) case of Poland', *Europe-Asia Studies*, 66(7), 1122–45.

Gendźwiłł, A. and Żółtak T. (forthcoming) 'How single-member districts are reinforcing local independents and strengthening mayors: on the electoral reform in Polish local governments', *Local Government Studies*.

Gendźwiłł, A., Żółtak, T. and Rutkowski, J. (2015) 'Niekonkurencyjne wybory, brakujący kandydaci. Dlaczego niektóre komitety wyborcze nie wystawiają kandydatów na burmistrzów?', *Studia Regionalne i Lokalne*.

Hausner, J. (ed) (2014) *Narastające dysfunkcje, zasadnicze dylematy, konieczne działania*, Kraków: Uniwersytet Ekonomiczny – Małopolska Szkoła Administracji Publicznej.

Heinelt, H. and Hlepas, N. (2006) 'Typologies of Local Government Systems', in H. Bäck, H. Heinelt and A. Magnier (eds) *The European Mayor: Political Leaders in the Changing Context of Local Democracy*, Wiesbaden: Verlag fur Sozialwissenschaften, pp 21–42.

Kancelaria Prezydenta RP (2013) Referenda lokalne. Podstawowe problemy i propozycje zmian przedstawione w projekcie ustawy o współdziałaniu w samorządzie terytorialnym na rzecz rozwoju lokalnego i regionalnego oraz o zmianie niektórych ustaw.

Kjær, U. and Steyvers, K. (2014) 'Second Thoughts on Second-Order: Towards a Second-Tier Model of Local Elections and Voting', paper presented at the ECPR General Conference, Glasgow, 3–6 September.

Koprić, I. (2009a) 'Directly Elected Mayors on the Territory of the Former Yugoslavia: Between Authoritarian Local Political Top Bosses and Citizen-Oriented Managers', in H. Raynaert, K. Stevyers, P. Delwit and J. B. Pilet (eds) *Town Chief, Ciy Boss of Loco President? Comparing a Strengthened Local Political Leadership Across Europe*, Brugge: Vanden Broele and Nomos.

Koprić, I. (2009b) 'Roles and Styles of Local Political Leaders on the Territory of the Former Yugoslavia: Between Authoritarian Local Political Top Bosses and Citizen-Oriented Local Managers', *Croatian and Comparative Public Administration*, 9(1), 79–105.

Kowalik, J. (2005) 'Wybrani w bezpośrednich wyborach', *Samorząd Terytorialny*, No 6/2005, pp 5–30.

Kulesza, M. (2008) *Budowanie samorządu*, Warszawa: Municipium.

Larsen, H. (2002) 'Directly Elected Mayors: Democratic Renewal of Constitutional Confusion', in J. Caufield and H. Larsen (eds) *Local Government at the Millennium*, Opladen: Leske + Budrich.

Magnier, A. (2006) 'Strong mayors? On direct election and political entrepreneurship', in H. Bäck, H. Heinelt and A. Magnier (eds) *The European Mayor: Political Leaders in the Changing Context of Local Democracy*, Wiesbaden: Verlag fur Sozialwissenschaften, pp 353–76.

Magre, J., Bertrana, X. (2007) 'Exploring the limits of institutional change: The direct election of mayors in Western Europe', *Local Government Studies*, 33(2), 181–94.

Mouritzen, P.E. and Svara, J. (2002) *Leadership at the Apex*, Pittsburgh: University of Pittsburgh Press.

Piasecki, A. (2006) *Menadżer i polityk: wójt, burmistrz, prezydent miasta*, Kraków: Profesja.

Regulski, J. (2000) *Samorząd III Rzeczpospolitej*, Warszawa: PWN.Reif, K. and Schmitt, H. (1980) 'Nine Second-Order National Elections – A Conceptual Framework for the Analysis of European Election Results', *European Journal of Political Research*, 8(1), 3–44.

Swianiewicz, P. (2003) 'Partisan Cleavages in Local Governments in Poland After 1990', in T. Zarycki and G. Kolankiewicz (eds) *Regional Issues in Polish Politics*, School of Slavonic and East European Studies, University College London, Occasional Papers No. 60, pp 179–201.

Swianiewicz, P. (2008) 'Portret radnego 2007', *Samorząd Terytorialny*, 4/2008, 5–16.

Swianiewicz, P. (2014) 'An Empirical Typology of Local Government systems in Eastern Europe', *Local Government Studies*, 40(2), 292–311.

Swianiewicz, P. (2015) 'The Politics of Local Tax Policy Making in Poland', paper presented at Annual NISPAcee Conference, Tbilisi, 20–23 May.

Swianiewicz, P., Klimska, U. and Mielczarek, A. (2006) Uneven Partnerships: Polish City Leaders in Search of Local Governance, In: H. Heinelt, D. Sweeting, P. Getimis (eds.) *Legitimacy and Urban Governance*, London-New York: Routledge, pp 114–130.

Swianiewicz, P. and Klimska, U. (2003) 'Czy wielkie miasta są sterowalne? Wpływ sytuacji politycznej na warunki zarządzania największymi miastami Polski', *Samorząd Terytorialny*, No. 3/2003, 12–28.

Swianiewicz, P. and Mielczarek, A. (2005) 'Parties and Political Culture in Central and Eastern European Local Governments', in G. Soos and V. Zentai (eds) *Faces of Local Democracy: Comparative Papers from Central and Eastern Europe*, Budapest: Open Society Institute, pp 13–78.

TWELVE

Debating directly elected mayors in the Czech Republic: political games and missing expertise?[1]

Petr Jüptner, Charles University,
Prague, Czech Republic

Introduction

The Czech Republic, unlike its near neighbours, does not currently have any directly elected mayors. Recently, the Petr Nečas government of 2010–13 attempted to implement the direct election of mayors in small municipalities in the country in time for the municipal elections in 2014 (Jüptner, 2013: 109–11). However, the reform failed, and the Czech Republic thus remains a Central European outlier, having indirectly elected local political leaders, surrounded by countries that have implemented fully the direct election of mayors (Slovakia, Poland), expanded it (Germany) or facilitated it (Austria) (Jüptner, 2013: 102–4). So, as it is not possible to examine the impacts of the direct election of mayors in the Czech Republic, the aims of this chapter are:

1. to characterise the nature of debates on directly elected mayors in the Czech Republic, define their actors and their roles;
2. to locate the Czech debate on directly elected mayors in a broader European context;to outline the model of direct election proposed, and to present its advantages and disadvantages.

Owing to the lack of a wide range of material on this subject in the Czech Republic this text is somewhat contextual in nature. For European comparison the chapter draws on sources such as a foreign literature and articles, monographs, working papers and – exceptionally – seminar group theses.[2] The analysis of the Czech model utilises in particular two analyses by the Ministry of Interior, rulings of the government, legislative proposals and information from seminars attended by academics and policy, departmental and political officials.

Delimitating the discussion: what it is and – primarily – what it is not

Since the 19th century Czech local government executive structures have been based on executive committees and collective decision making, where groups of elected councillors would make decisions. The roots of the model are based in the Austrian Empire, particularly Austria-Hungary, and an executive model of Czech municipal self-governments largely conforms to an Austrian model in which some federal states implemented the direct elections of mayors (Trauner, 2001). Following the founding of the Czechoslovak Republic in 1918, the collective executive was preserved (Balík, 2009: 46–52; Čopík, 2014: 73–4). When municipal self-government was restored in 1990 after the fall of communism, the same collective executive model was also reinstated. The council became the main body of the municipal self-government and it elected from its ranks the municipal board as an executive collegium. The mayor was one of its members and represented the municipality externally (Kruntorádová and Jüptner, 2015: 29–30).[3] Higher levels of the Czech political system also correspond to the tradition of executive committees. The Czech regions are headed by councils with indirectly elected governors; moreover, until 2012 the Czech president was also indirectly elected. In the absence of much experience with the model of direct election, political debate can become more emotional and extreme, with parallels to the debate in the UK (for example, Copus, 2004: 247), and rather less pragmatic. Of course, the implementation of the direct election of the president may alter this; however, such an election has so far been perceived with controversy in connection with the election of President Miloš Zeman. Zeman used the legitimacy of a direct election to shift an interpretation of the constitution governing his position. He became the target of criticism for appointing a government of officials in 2013 without prior consultation with the leading political parties; he was criticised for appropriating the position typical of a semi-presidential or even presidential system (Jüptner et al, 2015: 287–8).

First, it is crucial to demarcate a municipal level and emphasise the role of its specificities – vis-à-vis the higher levels of political system or municipal systems in other countries. The constitution defines a two-level self-government which consists of regions and municipalities. A mixed model of public administration is applied within which larger municipalities execute public administration through their delegated powers for an administration district, involving smaller municipalities in the neighbourhood. Development towards decentralisation has been continuous since a renewal of self-government after 1989; Swianiewicz ranks the Czech Republic among the cluster of 'relatively decentralized' municipal systems along with Latvia and Estonia (Swianiewicz, 2013: 14). If anything undermines local self-government, it is the limited resources connected with high fragmentation of municipalities – see Table 12.1. The Czech municipal structure, along with Slovak and French structures, is among the most fragmented in Europe (Illner, 2010a: 219–25; 2010b: 214–15; Ryšavý and Bernard, 2013: 833–5).

Table 12.1: Size structure of municipalities in the Czech Republic, 2007

Population size	Municipalities		Population	
	Number	%	Number	%
<199	1,591	25.5	194,563	1.9
200–499	2,019	32.3	656,020	6.4
500–999	1,307	20.9	913,985	8.9
1,000–1,999	685	11.0	950,291	9.2
2,000–4,999	375	6.0	1,135,272	11.0
5,000–9,999	140	2.2	947,225	9.2
10,000–19,999	69	1.1	962,930	9.4
20,000–49,999	42	0.7	1,242,789	12.1
50,000–99,999	16	0.3	1,156,650	11.2
>100,000	5	0.1	2,127,464	20.7
Total	6,249	100.0	10,287,189	100.0

Source: Illner (2010a: 224)

While in Nordic countries experiments with executive models tend to follow the consolidation of a municipal system, there is no such reform potential in the Czech environment. Almost 80% of municipalities have fewer than 1,000 inhabitants (Illner 2010a: 219–25; 2010b, 214–15), and a considerable proportion of mayors are not released from employment to perform their municipal role.

The fragmentation of the municipal structure therefore makes it difficult to consider managerial reforms (for example, Larsen, 2005: 207–10; Vetter and Kersting, 2003: 14–17; Reynaert et al, 2009), as the administrative capacity of municipalities is very low and some of them even do not have any employees (Kruntorádová, 2013). Nevertheless, and despite weak executive competences of municipalities in which mayors operate, mayors maintain a strong informal position in local communities. Therefore, it has been argued that the introduction of direct elections is unlikely to impact greatly on executive leadership of these self-governments (Larsen, 2005: 196–200; Wollmann, 2008: 80–8, 300). This difference in relation to other systems determines a significantly distinct discussion about direct elections. Within this discussion the direct election of mayors would only be a formal confirmation of their already strong executive leadership, which regardless of the type of election may be also evident in other countries with small municipalities, such as France or Slovakia.

The strategy of Czech political parties in relation to the direct election of mayors is influenced by the constitution, which defines a city council as the main institution of local self-government, as in Austria (Trauner, 2001). Political actors assume that an eventual implementation of direct elections combined with a strong mayor form (Heinelt and Hlepas, 2006: 31–2) would require the adoption of a constitutional amendment which would have to gain a three fifths majority of deputies and senators in the national parliament. Legal aspects of the discussion bring into question the value of analytical documents as well. They were procured for the Czech government by the Ministry of Interior (Ministry of Interior, 2008; 2011). However, the analyses related to European comparisons were superficial and exhibited numerous flaws (Jüptner, 2009: 326–8).

In consequence of all the aforementioned circumstances, a new space has been opened for political discussions regarding directly elected mayors, which reflect the programmes and above all the pragmatic interests of political parties. This direction of this discussion is also shaped by the nature of the Czech party system, where mayoral, local and regional parties are represented in both chambers of the national parliament. These parties express a specifically Czech motivation of political actors to implement directly elected mayors. In addition to the strong position of mayors, municipal politics is perceived more as a matter of individuals and personalities rather than about candidates' lists or parties (Jüptner, 2005). This works against the party list system combined with hard conditions for entry of independent candidates into a political race. An eventual direct election thus hypothetically bridges a gap between a natural functioning of municipal politics on one hand and an adjustment of the electoral system (including distribution of key competences to executive bodies) on the other. Emphasising individuals as actors of politics, a direct election thus forms an inherent part of the programmes endorsed by mayors' initiatives and parties primarily anchored at a local level.

The political character of discussions around the direct election of mayors is linked to the questions of their general popularity. In

2011 a Czech Ministry of Interior survey of municipalities found that approximately two thirds of mayors who responded favoured the direct election of mayors (Šaradín, 2010: 309). Independent polls have shown that the direct election of mayors is supported by roughly three quarters of municipal councillors (Šaradín, 2010: 310). According to a poll by the mayors' association STAN (*Starostové a nezávislí*; Mayors and Independents) from 2011, up to 86% of the population would welcome a direct elected mayor, and the number of citizens willing to participate in elections would rise. However, regular surveys into the satisfaction of voters with the political system do not imply that a continuation of the system of indirect election would pose any significant problem, and implementing direct mayoral elections may not be regarded by voters as a priority.

Current position of mayors within municipalities

The institutions of local government in the Czech Republic comprise the mayor, a municipal council and a municipal board (Jüptner, 2008: 22–3). The municipal council is an elected body; the Czech constitution defines it as an institution executing self-government of a municipality. An electoral period of the municipal council is four years. The size of the council is determined by the council itself, in compliance with the boundaries stipulated by the law (see Table 12.2). In reality, the council determines the basic parameters for the running of local self-government. In particular, it approves the budget, municipally

Table 12.2: Range of the number of municipal council members

Number of municipality inhabitants	Number of council members
Up to 500	5–15
More than 500 up to 3,000	7–15
More than 3,000 up to 10,000	11–25
More than 10,000 up to 50,000	15–35
More than 50,000 up to 150,000	25–45
More than 150,000	35–55
City of Prague	55–70

Source: Kruntorádová and Jüptner (2015)

binding ordinances and sales of property, and it establishes the organs of the municipality. Furthermore, it elects a mayor from within its ranks, his or her deputies, and other members of the municipal board to comprise a collective executive. A municipal board exists in municipalities with at least 15 councillors; the number of its members accounts for one third of the number of council members at the maximum (however, not more than 11). In practice, the municipal board exercises all the executive powers and secures the everyday functioning of municipality – it pursues economic management in line with an approved budget, concludes lease agreements and oversees the functioning of the municipal administration. Even though a mayor outwardly represents a municipality, as a member of the municipal board he or she does not hold direct executive competences; only in staff matters do mayors appoint or dismiss a head secretary of municipal office (Jüptner, 2008: 23). In this regard an executive model corresponds to a collective model in the typology of Mouritzen and Svara (Heinelt and Hlepas, 2006: 31–3). A formally stronger position is held by mayors in the municipalities numbering fewer than 15 councillors, as there is no municipal board, and competences are shared by both a mayor and the council.

Nevertheless, the real position of mayors – except for perhaps in the largest cities – is for a number of reasons quite strong (Jüptner, 2008: 23). A mayor chairs the sessions of the council as well as the municipal board and may thus affect the outcomes of negotiations of both bodies. Unlike councillors, and most board members, mayors are more frequently (than other councillors) full time, and present at the town hall on a daily basis. In the smallest municipalities the mayor may often be the only paid official in a municipality, and has considerably greater access to information compared to others. Owing to the prevailing consensual nature of councils and a very weak party system, mayors often encounter little electoral or party opposition. Moreover, and in a manner similar to South European systems, mayors frequently fulfil the role of local patron who defends the interests of municipality in the regional assembly or the upper chamber of the Czech Parliament (Jüptner, 2011: 113–14). For this reason, and also due to the personalised nature of municipal politics and small local communities, mayors generally enjoy popularity with their voters. It can be argued that even when only partially enhancing the competences of mayors, an eventual implementation of their direct election might result in the unwanted introduction of an ultra-strong mayor form (Jüptner, 2013: 116–18).

Periodisation of the Czech discussion

I suggest it is helpful to divide the Czech experience regarding the direct election of mayors into four broad stages: the debate-free stage; the stage of discussion, the implementation stage and the stage of the restart of a political game – see Table 12.3.

Table 12.3: Stages of the Czech debate about the direct election of mayors

Stage	Period
Debate-free stage	up to 2006
Stage of debate	2006–10
Implementation stage	2010–13
Back to discussion – restart of political game?	2014– ?

Source: Author's compilation, based on Jüptner (2013); Jüptner et al (2014)

In the first stage, the debate-free stage, the issue of the direct election appeared only at the margins of local government reform discussions, and only then from fringe actors. These actors included smaller non-parliamentarian centre-right parties and mayors' political movements (Jüptner, 2009: 307); relevant parliamentary parties were not active in these debates.

The second debate stage coincided in particular with the period of the Topolánek government of 2006–09 which, drawing especially on the programme of the coalition Green Party, proposed the launch of a discussion regarding the implementation of direct mayoral elections. This was to be supported by the compilation of a comparative study of other European Union countries discussing the legal powers, responsibilities and electoral arrangements concerning the possibility of the introduction of that sort of executive (Jüptner, 2009). The resulting publication was drafted by the Ministry of Interior (2008) and provided the main foundation material for the discussion. Numerous flaws in the analysis demonstrated that the issue of the direct election of mayors did not present a priority. Conclusions of the 'analysis' were also negative, accentuating a variety of risks stemming from the reforms. According to the analysis, negative aspects of the direct election lie particularly in the collision of a traditional model of collective decision making of self-government and a mixed model of public administration within which the municipalities also exercise public administration in delegated powers. Last but not least, the analysis voiced concerns regarding an increase in financial costs for the elections as well as for mayors' salaries (Ministry of Interior, 2008). The prevailing negative attitudes to directly elected mayors were also evident in the contributions presented at a conference entitled 'Reforming aspects of public administration' held by the Ministry of Interior in June 2008; the conference preceded the presentation of the above mentioned analysis. Contributions by the Ministry of Interior and the Union of Towns and Municipalities came out as negative. Only a representative of the then newly established Local Government Association, representing primarily small municipalities, was in favour of direct election (Jüptner, 2009: 307–13). This second stage can be characterised by discussions themselves being the main priority, not the implementation of the direct election itself.

The third stage coincides with the period of the Nečas government. Its governmental programme reflected coalition compromise, offering 'thorough analysis aiming to provide conditions for the direct election in small municipalities in the elections of the year 2014' (Government of the Czech Republic, 2010). A new updated version of the analysis – Ministry of Interior (2011) – however did not differ much from the original analysis. Most passages from the original analysis were incorporated into the new document, including the analysis of the Slovak model, an out-of-date analysis of the German model, and factual mistakes in the survey of European countries. Descriptions of the Polish system direct election and of indirectly elected French mayors were incorporated, as well as the analysis of possibilities of the implementation of the direct mayoral election in municipal constitutions. However, the conclusions of the document are quite different. While the original analysis (Ministry of Interior, 2008) preferred to maintain and improve the existing model of local political leadership, the updated document is more open to direct election, and states 'should it be decided by politicians that the direct election of mayors is desirable, this updated draft contains a proposal for its incorporation into the Czech legal system' (Ministry of Interior, 2011). The second version of the analysis thus explicitly yields the decision around the introduction of direct elections to politicians. This reflects the declaration by the government which approved the legislative proposals for the constitutional amendment to provide for direct mayoral elections. However, the coalition collapsed, and the amendment was not enacted.

The onset of the fourth stage is linked with the elections of 2013 and the resulting centrist Sobotka government. It contrasts sharply with the second and third stages of discussion. New governmental parties have not prioritised direct elections, thus such discussion is essentially over.

Yet, the issue of direct elections continues to be promoted by STAN and populist party Úsvit, which revisited the foundation materials of the Nečas government and attempted to promote the topic prior to the 2014 municipal elections. Karel Janeček, via a project Democracy 2.1,[4] also offered an electoral system based on the possibility to cast a negative preferential vote. What also characterises the fourth stage is new parties joining in the discussion. However, while Úsvit strove to strengthen its position via support for direct elections, governmental party ANO2011, led by billionaire Andrej Babiš, refrained from voicing any opinions regarding the direct elections. The elimination of direct elections from the governmental programme took the direct election of mayors off the agenda and the issue reverted back to the second discussion stage.

The proposed model of direct election

The only concrete proposal for the implementation of direct elections for mayors in the Czech Republic came from the Nečas government in the period 2010–13 (Jüptner, 2013: 108–11). The main restriction was that it only applied to small municipalities. The government offered two alternatives. The first was that the mayor would be elected directly in municipalities with up to 1,500 inhabitants according to the register of inhabitants. The other alternative, the preferred option that was incorporated into the corresponding legislative proposals was that the mayor be could directly elected in municipalities with fewer than 15 councillors (Ministry of Interior, 2011). Such an alternative could lead to the implementation of the direct election of the mayor in municipalities with up to 10,000 inhabitants. If opting for such an alternative, even the smallest municipality in the Czech Republic could retain an indirectly elected mayor; and towns with the number of inhabitants amounting to 10,000 could, through the stipulation of the minimum number of councillors (fewer than 15), select direct election.

Even though such an alternative appeared to be the preferred option in the later Ministry of Interior report, a seminar at the Institute of Public Administration entitled 'The direct mayor election and elements of direct democracy in the Czech Republic' held in 2012 indicated that the discussion included restricting the reform to small municipalities only – although coalition parties had not yet agreed on the exact number of inhabitants. The political character of the discussion, and its rather arbitrary nature, was demonstrated by the deputy of TOP09/STAN Stanislav Polčák.[6] He stated that during heated coalition negotiations, when attempting to agree on the size of small municipalities to be included, Prime Minister Petr Nečas asked the chairman of the parliamentary party TOP09/STAN Petr Gazdík how many inhabitants the municipality Suchá Loz had (Gazdík used to be the mayor of this municipality). Gazdík replied around 1,100 and the prime minister is said to have concluded that therefore mayors would be elected directly in municipalities with up to 1,200 inhabitants.[7]

The alternative between the models with and without direct mayoral election demonstrates that the proposed directly elected mayor implies a powerful figure who assumes the competences of the council as the executive centre of local government, or acquires his/her own and powerful executive competences. This evidently relates to the genesis of the government documents (e.g. Ministry of Interior, 2008, 2011) where the alternative of preserving existing executive model never appeared. On the contrary, the very first version of the analytical document from the period of the Topolánek government (Ministry of Interior, 2008) already implied enhancement of competences of mayors inspired by a Slovak model. Therefore, in alignment with the government proposals (e.g. Ministry of Interior, 2011: 24, 28), the powers of directly elected mayors would aggregate their existing powers and the powers of the council.

There is a noticeable distinction regarding the relations between the mayor and the council; according to the proposals (Ministry of Interior, 2011: 23-9), the functions of the mayor are separate from the functions of a member of the local council. The mayor would appoint his/her deputies from the ranks of councillors and would not be required to gain council approval. Thus the contact areas between the two institutions are firmly separated, which could be eliminated if the mayor chaired the meetings of the council. As the government documents (Ministry of Interior, 2008, 2011) mention no changes involving the establishment of an institution of the so-called 'second peak' (or chair of the local council, the 'main councillor') we can assume that the mayor would henceforth chair the meetings of the council.

The proposals (Ministry of Interior, 2011) also suggested holding mayoral elections and council elections simultaneously. The discussion regarding the choice of a suitable electoral system emphasised the high costs incurred by municipal elections. Therefore, the 'Slovak' one-round majority system was incorporated into the discussion from the beginning. The Local Government Association originally proposed a cheaper 'Slovak' model in small municipalities, and a two-round majority system requiring an absolute majority in larger municipalities (Jüptner, 2009: 308). However, the analysis from the Nečas government specifies that 'in terms of the costs, organisational simplicity and citizen understanding the one-round system involving a relative majority seems to be the most suitable solution' (Ministry of Interior, 2011: 29).

Key variables: political games?

In attempting to highlight the features that seem to be significant in the outcomes of this decision making process, the standpoints and interests of political parties come to the fore. Like in north German states (Holtkamp, 2005: 23–26), parties emerge which seek to exploit the question of the direct election of mayors owing to their general popularity in direct elections. In doing so they put an issue on the agenda that hardly any governmental or any other party show opposition to. This creates a political 'game' in which some actors – political parties – tend to mask their rather negative attitudes towards a direct election, the implementation of which would restrain their own power. Attitudes of individual parties can be more accurately accessed on the basis of case studies which stem from monitoring of media, materials of political parties, contents of specialised seminars, semi-structured interviews or questionnaire surveys (see Table 12.4).

None of the main political parties openly opposes direct election (Šaradín, 2010: 83). Nevertheless, in each of the scrutinised election periods only one or two relevant political parties actively advocated them. Such parties may be divided into two groups. The first group

Table 12.4: Positions of political parties on direct election of mayors, by election periods

Position	Party	2006–10	2010–13	2014– ?
Supporters	Green Party		Not in parliament	Not in parliament
	TOP09/STAN	Not in parliament		
Shallow support	Věci veřejné	Not in parliament		Not in parliament
	Úsvit	Not in parliament	Not in parliament	
Ambiguous	Christian Democrats		Not in parliament	
	Civic Democrats			
	Social Democrats			
	Communists			
	ANO2011	Not in parliament	Not in parliament	

might be labelled as supporters and included the Green Party (Strana Zelených), and later STAN, acting in alliance with TOP09. When we examine the priorities of other actors supporting direct election we may summarise that this group primarily involves smaller centrist liberal parties and mayors' political movements (Jüptner, 2009: 306–7). This other group comprises the parties with the elements of direct democracy incorporated into their strategy. Even though such subjects initiate and embrace the topic of direct elections, they are willing to give it up in case any problems arise, or they are ready to 'swap' it for political agreements for other objectives. This group includes Věci Veřejné. Coincidentally, their dissolution under the Nečas government might have been one of the main reasons for moving away from the implementation of direct elections. In the following election period the group included a populist party, Úsvit, which timed its support for the topic of direct elections for the 2014 municipal elections. These populist parties differ from the group of 'supporters' not only with the shallow nature of their preference for direct election, but also with their willingness to drop it. They often enjoy representation in the parliament for one election period only, during which they can dissolve or disintegrate into two fractions or subjects.

By contrast, most parliamentary parties do not hold any clear standpoints towards the direct election of mayors. Very often these subjects offer general support for, for example, 'extending the elements of direct democracy' which is not, however, clearly defined, and the parties in question in reality resist the implementation of the reforms. Such latent aversion, or passive resistance, by these parties may be motivated by their establishment within a Czech political system. With the exception of ANO2011, all parties have been part of the system for a long time and they are well established at a municipal level, holding numerous positions of mayors and chief magistrates. Yet, as these parties are simultaneously reluctant to oppose direct election, they often seek spurious excuses in the form of objections to concrete proposals. Accordingly, the Social Democrats argued that the proposals of the Nečas government were insufficiently prepared, while the Civic Democrats in the same period seemed to overemphasise the issues connected with the demarcation of small municipalities where direct election was supposed to be implemented. They saw insurmountable problems in an 'inability' to define small municipalities. A common explanation for the resistance to the direct election of mayors is the fear of a potential deadlock between a mayor and a council of differing political persuasions.

We may thus summarise that the implementation of directly elected mayors has apparently many supporters; however, only some of them demonstrate a strong interest in its implementation and are also able to keep their positions in Parliament for more than one election period. Most actors approach the issue of a direct election as a political game and support it only until its implementation is actually pending. The success of a proposal to implement the reforms rests on the number and strength of supporters, and their relation to the government. But there is also an element of randomness in a cyclical political game which may reach the point where there is no way of return for its actors, and momentum may carry the proposals to the statute book. The implementation of a direct election of mayors this way would not be utterly unexpected as a similar political game was played in the Czech Republic in 2012 and led to the direct election of the country's president.

Conclusion

Owing to the tradition of collective models of decision making, and inexperience with direct elections, the Czech Republic does not yet provide suitable conditions for the implementation of the direct election of mayors. A debate of a cyclical nature around its implementation has been ongoing since 2006 where a proposal is discussed, debated and then dropped, and the debate goes back to the beginning. The narrow political context of the discussion has been dominated by the pragmatism of political parties which results in a political game, involving a restricted and heterogeneous group of initiators; however, the role of most actors in the game is somewhat opaque. Although this pragmatism corresponds to the experience of other countries, there is a Czech specificity embodied in the initiatory role of a mayor's coalition, STAN, with an entirely unique motivation in a European context. The significance and relevance of mayoral roles and functions are connected with a fragmented municipal structure in combination with difficult conditions for the candidacy of nonpartisan associations in local elections. Consequently, mayors and local independent groups across municipalities cooperate in broader platforms. Their original intention was to facilitate their standing for municipal election, but such political parties and movements have gradually penetrated regional councils and national parliament and have become a way – among others – of enforcing the interests of municipalities at higher levels of a political system. The mayors of smaller municipalities regard individuals as the actors of local policy, and not the parties risen from the list electoral system; accordingly, they regard direct elections as natural. At the same time, due to their popularity they do not fear the implementation of direct elections.

Should we assess specific proposals for the implementation of directly elected mayors, we must refer to the proposal of the Nečas government (2010–13). As this proposal drew on the older analyses by the Ministry of Interior, and subsequent proposals by Úsvit allude to it, we may assume that any eventual future proposals for the implementation of direct elections may build on it as well. There are two aspects of this concrete proposed model of direct election worth noting. Primarily, it has been framed without any up-to-date European comparison or processing of relevant experience across other European countries; estimated impacts of direct elections are often rather groundless hypotheses. The other aspect lies in the inspiration by the Slovak model of the direct election and the position mayor. The inspiration by the Slovak model has been evident since the beginnings of the debate. Officials from the Ministry of Interior (who originally opposed direct election) and the local government associations were among the main initiators of direct elections which, in common with the Slovak model, advocate the model of a strong mayor. The foreign comparisons found in the analyses by the Topolánek and Nečas governments show a significant overrepresentation of the Slovak model and supposed impacts and experience generally relate to it. The proposed model in government documents is actually identical to the Slovak model. In keeping with Slovak experience, the proposal mentions a one-round majority electoral system, the incompatibility of the functions of mayor and councillor, and in particular the concentration of the crucial executive competencies in the hands of a mayor. It also, absurdly, refers to the significance of the tradition regarding the system of local government in the Czech lands up to 1864 while their authors ignore the fact that the Slovak model is in particular in its electoral aspects quite unique and does not correspond to the Czech model.

Now we can proceed to the insufficient foreign comparison within the governmental analysis; for example, it disregarded the Austrian model and thus made it impossible to design a system which would correspond to the Czech traditions up to the 19th century. In Austria, direct election was partly implemented in the 1990s, not necessitating the removal of a collective executive as part of this traditional model. Furthermore, we may suppose that better awareness of an Austrian model and afterwards its eventual implementation would be politically and technically easier and would also present fewer risks in regards to the impacts on the relations between individual institutions of local self-government.

Czech mayors already now hold quite strong positions, due to the size of municipal administrations, frequent releases from their jobs in order to perform mayoral duties, chairing the meetings of local government and council as well as the uncompetitive political system in smaller municipalities. They would undoubtedly be even stronger after the transfer of the main executive competences. It is a great paradox that copying the Slovak model was not consistent in areas where it would have been suitable. The resulting proposals rather deepened the risks connected with the cohabitation of mayor and 'antagonistic' council, despite efforts by the government to eliminate them. In their inspiration by the Slovak model, the Czech government did not take into account the institution of the council which in Slovakia can serve as the committee of the local government or an advisory board of the mayor. Furthermore, unlike the Slovak model, the nomination of the deputy mayor in the Czech proposals will not be subject to the approval by local councillors (Jüptner and Ezechiášová, 2009: 207). Such parameters – along with the separation of the mayor and the local council and a one-round majority system – can expand the risks connected with such cohabitation.

We may only speculate about the inspiration by the Slovak model and whether it is rooted in good personal relations between the officials at both Ministries of Interior, insufficient knowledge of English and German on the part of authors of the government analyses or the birthplaces of the deputies Stanislav Polčák and Petr Gazdík in Zlín region constituting a 'Slovak frontier'. However, it is an interesting part of the knowledge regarding individual implementations of direct mayor elections in Europe –direct election of mayors in the northern German Federal states was introduced within the dismantling process of the Anglo-Saxon 'occupational' model (Holtkamp, 2005) and the concrete shape of the Croatian implementation was influenced by US advisers (Podolnjak, 2010: 127–8). If we relate the terminology of the concept of policy transfer to the inspiration by Slovakia, we might in the Czech case speak of a potentially inappropriate transfer in the degree of emulation of primarily civil servants (Dollowitz and Marsh, 2000: 9–20). The transfer was established on bounded rationality and a number of its parameters may best be explained as 'happy accidents'.

The Czech Republic represents an exceptional case, not only with regard to the countries treated within the framework of this book from the perspective of directly elected mayors, but also regarding general specifics of the municipal level of its political system. From a comparative perspective, the Czech case shows that the debates about directly elected mayors or their implementation may not only be an effort to reform an executive model, establish leadership or increase an interest in politics, but primarily a pragmatic game of political actors. Such a game may become a decisive trigger for the implementation of direct elections even where a reform aspect is being discussed, as for instance in some German federal states (Holtkamp, 2005: 23–6). The second comparative finding is confirmation of the importance of inspiration from abroad in the implementation of direct elections, especially when a language barrier is absent. Bureaucratic, academic and media interactions affecting the setup of local government may occur in contexts broader than the successor states of the ceased federations, such as Czechoslovakia or Yugoslavia.

Notes

[1] This chapter was prepared within the project of the Project PRVOUK P17 – 'Sciences in society, politics and the media in contemporary challenge', at the Institute of Political Studies, Charles University, Prague.[2] The seminar series 'New approaches to the local government and direct mayoral elections', offered in the academic years of 2013–14 and 2014–15 at Charles University in Prague served as inspiration for some of the material in this chapter.

[3] However, prior to the split-up of Czechoslovakia in 1993, a Slovak part of the federation implemented a different model conforming to the Transleithanian traditions of territorial administration, which comprised direct elections of mayors (Klimovský, 2014).

[4] www.democracy21.com[5] The system is based on a one-round majority electoral system with the possibility to cast two positive and one negative preferential votes. Janeček initiated the simulation of an application of his system via questioning the voters during municipal elections of 2014; he cooperated with the STAN association on this simulation.

[6] The Mayor's association STAN formed an alliance with the party TOP09 in 2009, which came to an end in December 2016.

[7] There is no collection of speeches from the seminar; the author noted down this part of Polčák's speech.

References

Balík, S. (2009) *Komunální politika: Obce, aktéři a cíle místní politiky*, Praha: Grada Publishing.

Čopík, J. (2014) *Proměny a kontinuita české komunální politiky. Územní samospráva v nové době (1850–2010). Díl I – do roku 1945*, Praha: Scriptorium.

Copus, C. (2004) *Party Politics and Local Government*, Manchester: Manchester University Press.

Dollowitz D. and Marsh, D. (2000) 'Learning from Abroad: The Role of Policy Transfer in Contemporary Policy-Making', *Governance: An International Journal of Policy and Administration*, 5(1), 5–24.

Government of the Czech Republic (2010) *Programme declaration*. Available at www.vlada.cz/assets/media-centrum/dulezite-dokumenty/Programove_prohlaseni_vlady.pdf

Heinelt, H. and Hlepas, N. (2006) 'Typologies of Local Government Systems', In H. Bäck, H. Heinelt and A. Magnier (eds) *The European Mayor. Political Leaders in the Changing Context of Local Democracy*, Wiesbaden: VS Verlag für Sozialwissenschaften, pp 21–42.

Holtkamp, L. (2005) 'Reform der Kommunalverfassungen in den alten Bundesländern – eine Ursachenanalyse', in J. Bogumil and H. Heinelt (eds) *Bürgermeister in Deutschland. Politikwissenschaftliche Studien zu direkt gewählten Bürgermeistern*, Wiesbaden: VS, pp 13–32.

Illner, M. (2010a) 'The Voluntary Union of Municipalities: Voluntary Bottom-up Territorial Consolidation in Czech Republic?', in P. Swianiewicz (ed) *Territorial Consolidation Reforms in Europe*, Budapest: Open Society Institute, pp 219–36.

Illner, M. (2010b) 'Top-Down or Bottom-Up? Living with Territorial Fragmentation in the Czech Republic', in R. Baldersheim and L. E. Rose (eds) *Territorial Choice. The Politics of Boundaries and Borders.* London: Palgrave Macmillan, pp 214–33.

Jüptner, P: (2005) 'Europeizace a komunální politické myšlení', in B. Dančák, P. Fiala and V. Hloušek (eds) *Evropeizace: nové téma politologického výzkumu*, Brno: Mezinárodní politologický ústav, pp 125–33.

Jüptner, P. (2008) 'Local lists in the Czech Republic', in M. Reiser and E. Holtmann (eds) *Farewell to the Party Model? Independent Local Lists in East and West European Countries.* Wiesbaden: Springer VS, pp 21-37.

Jüptner, P. (2009) 'Ministerská diskuse k případnému zavedení přímé volby starostů: velmi nízká priorita?', *Acta Politologica*, 1(3), 305–31.

Jüptner, P. (2011) 'Le système local Tchèque: un modèle a l'écart des tendances européennes?', *Revue de Institut du Monde et du Developpement*, 1(2), 103–18.

Jüptner, P. (2013) 'Direct Election of Mayors in the Czech Political Debate and Within the European Context', in U. Pinterič and L. Prijon (eds) *Selected issues of administrative reality.* Novo Mesto: Fakulteta za organizacijske študije, pp 100–18.

Jüptner, P. and Ezechiášová, M. (2009) 'Slovensko', in P. Jüptner and M. Polinec (eds) *Evropská lokální politika 2*, Praha: IPS FSV UK, pp 393–405.

Jüptner, P.; Valušová, P. and Kruntorádová, I. (2015) 'Participation and Elements of Direct Democracy in the Czech Republic: Part II', *Public Policy and Administration*, 14(2), 279–90.

Klimovský, D. (2014) *Základy verejnej správy*, Bratislava: Wolters Kluwer.

Kruntorádová, I. (2013) 'Political Aspects of Financing of Municipalities in the Czech Republic', *Politické vedy*, 16(2), 31–57.

Kruntorádová, I. and Jüptner, P. (2015) *Local Government in the Czech Republic*, Paris: IMODEV.

Ministry of Interior (2008) 'Analysis of the possibilities of the implementation of the direct mayor election', http://www.mvcr. cz/clanek/informace-opriprave-analyzy-moznosti-zavedeni-prime-volby-starostu-v-cr-a-vyzva-k-zasilanipodnetu-a-pripominek-k-teto-problematice.aspx

Ministry of Interior (2011) 'Analysis of the implementation of the direct mayor election', http://www.mvcr.cz/odk2/clanek/informace-o-moznosti-zavedeni-prime-volby-starostu-v-cr.aspx

Larsen, H.O. (2005) 'Transforming Political Leadership: Models, Trends and Reforms', in R. Berg and N. Rao (eds) *Transforming Local Political Leadership*, London: Palgrave Macmillan, pp 195–211.

Podolnjak, R. (2010) 'Institutional Reform of the Croatian Local Government: from cabinets to directly elected mayors and county governors', *Politička misao*, 47(5), 117–43.

Reynaert, H., Steyvers, K., Delwit, P. and Pilet, J. B. (eds) (2009) *Local Political Leadership in Europe. Town Chief, City Boss or Loco President?*, Brugge: Vanden Broele.

Ryšavý, D. and Bernard, J. (2013) 'Size and Local Democracy: the Case of Czech Municipal Representatives', *Local Government Studies*, 39(6), 833–52.

Swianiewicz, P. (2013) 'An Empirical Typology of Local Government Systems in Eastern Europe', *Local Government Studies*, 39(4), 1–20.

Šaradín, P. (2010) 'Direct elections of mayors in Czech Republic? Data from research and political support', *Contemporary European Studies*, 2010(2), 77–85.

Trauner, G. (2001) *Der direkt gewählte Bürgermeister*, Linz: IKW.

Vetter, A. and Kersting, N. (eds) (2003) *Reforming Local Government in Europe. Closing the Gap between Democracy and Efficiency*, Opladen: Leske + Budrich.

Wollmann, H. (2008) *Reformen in Kommunalpolitik und -verwaltung*, Wiesbaden: VS Verlag.

Part III
Comparative perspectives

New and established mayoralties: lessons for local governance in constructing new political institutions – the English and Polish cases

Colin Copus, De Montfort University, Leicester, UK, Alasdair Blair, De Montfort University, Leicester, UK, Katarzyna Szmigiel-Rawska, University of Warsaw, Poland, and Michael Dadd, De Montfort University, Leicester, UK

Introduction

Central–local government relations are a common point of discussion across Europe and have spawned considerable literature often viewed through the lens of 'territorial politics' as a means of understanding the distribution of power relations (see Jeffery, 2008; Swianiewicz, 2010; Loughlin et al, 2011). The chapter examines one dimension of these relations by analysing the shift in power towards directly elected mayors that has taken place in England and Poland. In both cases, directly elected mayors have been viewed by central (and local) government as a means of rebalancing and redesigning the political landscape. While reaction to the introduction of elected mayors has ranged from lukewarm to outright hostility among local political elites (particularly in England – Copus, 2006) – as established political elites see a transfer of power from themselves towards the citizen through direct election – such antipathy is not surprising as elected mayors have changed the power balance within local government.

In the case of England, the arrival of directly elected mayors through the Local Government Act of 2000 provided for some local citizens choice over the system of local leadership, as a 'yes' vote was required from a referendum before a mayor could be introduced. The 2007 Local Government and Public Involvement in Health Act, however, enabled councils to resolve to adopt an elected mayor without a referendum. Although this meant that councils – rather than citizens – were in the driving seat of change, the legislative change did not lead to a widespread adoption of directly elected mayors. Indeed, by 2015 only two city councils – Liverpool and Leicester – had chosen this route. Such a limited uptake ran counter to the rhetoric of the Conservative government (and the previous Conservative–Liberal Democrat coalition) elected in 2015 with a localism agenda that included greater devolution to urban areas and a preference for elected metro-mayors heading newly formed combined authorities (collaborative working arrangements between several urban local authorities). But, at the time of writing in 2016 there were only 16 elected mayors (excluding the Mayor of London) in England from a total of 352 councils. All of this begs the question as to whether elected mayors are a significant development or a failed experiment in the long history of central–local relations.

In exploring these issues in detail it is apparent that the English experience contrasts with that of Poland on a number of fronts; one of the most obvious is the backdrop of the fall of Communism in 1990 and shift towards democratic government in Poland which led to the introduction in 2002 of directly elected mayors to all of the country's 2,478 municipalities. As Gendźwiłł and Swianiewicz show in Chapter Eleven of this book, elected mayors were seen by reformers as a remedy for the deficit of local legitimacy and accountability and as a way of enhancing the efficiency of local authorities, which also reflects the arguments put forward in England (see DETR, 1998a; 1998b; 1999; DTLR, 2001; DCLG, 2010a; 2010b; 2011). Yet, the office of mayor in Poland faces pressure for redesign by central government and there is an ongoing debate about changing the nature of this institution by, for example, limiting the period of office that any one individual can hold a mayoralty, to two consecutive terms. The office has similarly faced changes in England, most notably in 2007 when, as an indication of central government's leverage over local politics, the mayor and council manager model was abolished in the same Act that allowed councils to resolve to adopt an elected mayor without a referendum. Other substantive central government changes and debates about elected mayors are discussed in the chapter.

It is apparent from current debates in England and Poland that the implications of the shift towards directly elected mayors is viewed through different lenses depending on whether the issue is examined from the vantage point of central or local politics. On the one hand, direct election enables the centre to redesign local leadership to meet shifting and changing political circumstances and address new and emerging democratic values and challenges (Borraz and John, 2004), which makes the redesign of local political institutions by the centre all the more likely (Olsen, 1997). Direct elections, however, bring to the fore the manner by which local politicians are able to adapt newly emerging political structures to suit their political objectives (Stone, 1995; Kotter and Lawrence, 1974; Svara, 1987; Leach and Wilson, 2000; Lowndes and Wilson, 2001; Rhodes and 't Hart, 2014) which can often lead to local political leaders taking action to cement their control over newly created power structures. Thus, mayoral government means that holders of that office must ask themselves a series of redesign questions (Copus, 2011): how can maximum political resources be designed into the system? How, can new mayors provide themselves with the institutional support and resources they require? How can established patterns of political and managerial behaviour be reshaped to align with a mayor's policy agenda? There are also wider questions about the office of mayor that national designers will consider: how democratic and accountable is the office of elected mayor? Has the national design met the original intentions of reformers?

In taking these questions as our guide, the chapter analyses how mayors in England and Poland have managed to redesign their own institutional setting to enhance their political resources and to realign the political, organisational and managerial dynamics within which they operate. It also explores the continued concern for a national redesign of the office that exists among central policymakers in Poland. The two countries were selected because of their different approaches to the mayoral office: the complete restructuring of local government with elected mayors in Poland and the voluntary approach in England. In the latter case, the acceptance by councils seeking devolution deals in England, by agreeing with other neighbouring councils to form a combined authority, has provided the government with opportunities to insist that these new combined authorities are headed by elected mayors.

The chapter takes our two distinct national settings to examine what institutional design can tell us about the macro and micro restructuring of local politics by central government and what mayors themselves can then do to successfully re-engineer the office to suit their own local requirements. While not claiming to be a comparative study, the chapter seeks to draw lessons about the design of local political institutions, from two separate national experiences, of how local political structures are reshaped to meet two sets of requirements – the policy objectives of the centre and the political and practical needs of local political leaders. The chapter also explores, from our two different national and local contexts, whether central design and local redesign of political institutions have different objectives or whether the centre constrains what can be achieved locally. Having provided the overall context of the discussion, the next section sets out the theoretical model of institutional design which provides a framework for our analysis of the English and Polish case studies, before highlighting in the concluding section the lessons that can be drawn from the selected case studies.

Designing local politics

As Lowndes and Roberts (2013) note, institutions matter when attempting to understand political behaviour and the outcomes of political decisions. Institutions in this context provide not just a reference point that can be used to explain past events, but shape our understanding of continuing and future political projects. The study of institutions has generated material which have often been divided between 'old' and 'new' institutionalism and, while such rudimentary divisions do not fully reflect the breadth of writing within this field, a fuller analysis of the literature is beyond the scope of this chapter. Rather, our focus here is to address the change in central–local relations through the broad lens of institutional theory as this provides a framework to explore the origins of institutions as well as to address how they became institutions (Pierson, 2000). Generally, four broad responses are given, by: accident (Arthur, 1994; David, 1985), intention (Pierson, 2000; Skelcher et al, 2005), evolution (Shirley, 2005), or some combination of the three. It is often the case, however, that emphasis is placed on one specific approach to institutional design from these possibilities (Goodin, 1996). To provide a framework for our discussion we adopt three assumptions from the literature:

1. Effective institutional design in the political realm is vital to provide an architecture within which political decision making is conducted (Lowndes, 2001).
2. The process of designing an institution and an institutional design, which is the effect of this process, can differ to a large extent across settings (North et al, 2000; Pierson, 2000).
3. A political institution can be constructed to accomplish any set of political objectives but the efficiency of any institution towards those goals is not guaranteed (Pierson, 2000).

The first assumption is derived from the functions institutions have in social and political life as a tool for solving problems arising from bounded rationality where effective design can speed up the decision making process – often seen as positive in local politics (Douglas, 1986). But, how political institutions are designed can, and often does, reflect the experiences as well as the objectives of the designer. As a result, an institution can be designed with an inbuilt bounded rationality. Understanding the bounded nature of institutional design throws light on the effectiveness of designers because institutions are sometimes referred to as a system of rules for putting order into political life (Klijn and Koppenjan, 2006). The rules encompassing a political society define the limits of power and politics. The rules might be formal and informal; are addressed as a routine, norm, and/or incentive; can have written form as well as having unwritten customs and conventions (Lowndes and Wilson, 2001).

The second assumption results from the acceptance of the basic features of institutions as an effect of non-linear, stochastic, self-reinforcing mechanisms. Arthur (1994: 5) shows how path dependency processes can be generated by numerous 'individual transactions' which serve to provide positive feedback to designers of the actions they take but that arises from a dynamic and almost random series of events implying a loss of control by designers. In constructing a political organisation, a politician will set out to create a norm congruent with their goals but the effect of design activity is often difficult to manage once the process has begun. Designing a political institution is intentional, but the design is often the effect of contingency (Goodin, 1996). As Lowndes suggests, institutions 'evolve in unpredictable ways as actors seek to make sense of new or ambiguous situations, ignore or even contravene existing rules, or try to adapt them to favour their own interests' (2001: 1960).

The third assumption is the result of the first two. Since institutions are an effect of self-reinforcing mechanisms which are difficult to manage and can be driven by accident, the efficiency of the institution when it comes to supporting the achievement of political goals can also be a matter of contingency. Central to understanding the design of institutions is the tacit assumption that commonly repeated behaviour is the result of a rational decision-selection process taken at the beginning of the path. In our case this is when a choice or decision is made by a government or a mayor seeking to restructure the local political architecture, which then leads to the decision being reproduced by the other actors in a similar situation and as a result taken as a model. The creators of the concept argue that the first choice does not have to be, and sometimes is not, rational and rather is the result of contingency (David, 1985; Arthur, 1994). Any accidental inefficiency – or deviation from the intention of the designer – designed into a system is commonly derived from the importance of transaction costs for social exchange and barriers in access to information for key designers (Arthur, 1994; David, 1985; North, 1990). More detailed reasons for that effect are described as: inefficient perception of reality; the mismatch between the institution and reality; insufficient control of policy makers over institutions (North et al, 2000); a non-instrumental design (actors can be motivated by appropriateness logic rather than effectiveness logic); short-term thinking versus long time horizon consequences of institutions; and errors made in the design which makes the effects difficult or impossible to foresee (Pierson, 2000).

Whereas inefficiency can, in evaluations of institutions, refer to some general morality (Hardin, 1996), in evaluations of democratic institutions it can refer to the democratic rules of the game that distort the efficient design of a political institution. Thus, the efficiency of democratic institutions can refer to the intention of the designer – central government – and the outcomes of that design locally. Local political institutions are created in general designs crafted by central government but the final shape might differ between councils, as well as being influenced by different sets of designer intentions at different levels of input. These factors are important for the local political community, but nonetheless are difficult to identify for the 'central designer'. Moreover, they also cause self-reinforcing mechanisms for the institution building processes (lock-in) in their local manifestation. In addition, local political actors will want to be designers themselves. The enactment of the general scheme set by the centre, and its reshaping by local politicians (in our case directly elected mayors), constitutes institutional micro-design.

In examining the effectiveness of institutional design, analysis needs to focus on factors that will improve the efficiency of institutions: how well they are adapted to specific environments, how they respond to changes in circumstances, how they react to competition from other models, and how designers themselves learn (Cusack, 1999; Pierson 2000; Engerman and Sokoloff, 2005). Differentiation between local institutions of the same type – the options of micro-design – stems from a greater adaptive capacity and flexibility resting with local politicians. As such, we need to explore two sets of intentions: the centre and the locality. We can conduct this exploration by looking at directly elected mayors in England and Poland and analysing the rules created by central government, the manner of the redesign that has been performed at a local level, and the extent to which individual mayors have managed to reshape their political setting to enhance their capacity to take action.

The power of the centre

The debate across Europe about the move to directly elected mayors has been based on central demands for greater transparency and accountability in local decision making and for flexible structures to enable responses to complex and interlinked problems faced by local political leaders (Wollmann, 2008). The pressures exerted on local government by Europeanisation, globalisation, urbanisation, increasing public demand and economic downturn have resulted in the institutional restructuring of local politics (Kersting and Vetter, 2003; Berg and Rao, 2005; Denters and Rose, 2005; Magre and Betrana, 2007; Elcock, 2008; Wollmann, 2008). In post-communist countries, such as Poland, the direct election of the mayor resulted from the need to respond to the collapse of an established political regime and its replacement by a democratic alternative (Gendźwiłł and Swianiewicz, Chapter Eleven in this volume).Borraz and John (2004) identified European-wide trends that have shaped the context of local political leadership: new and complex governing networks; emerging and changing political values (citing Clark and Hoffmann-Martinot, 1998; also see Szucs and Stromberg, 2009); the need for stronger, executive local leadership; and borrowing institutional leadership arrangements from other nations. These trends reflect the need for local leaders to operate in two leadership dimensions: the organisational (the council as a managerial and administrative machine) and political (the council as a representative body). The elected mayor's role is as a corporate leader of the council as an organisation and as a political leader to the councillors. Copus (2011) has displayed these roles as shown in Table 13.1.

Thus, the design of local political structures by the central authorities must not only take into account the broad nationwide and global factors and trends energising change, but also the specific dimensions within which mayors operate. Yet, mayors in their localities will attempt to micro-redesign the governing arrangements given to them by the centre and it is to this we turn in detail.

Table 13.1: Leadership roles

Corporate Leadership

Mayor constructs and sets the direction, policy and priorities of the council as a public service machine

Mayor controls, directs and holds to account the council bureaucracy (council also has a role in the latter)

Mayor must operate to ensure that the chief executive plays a subordinate organisational leadership role to that of the mayor

Mayors focus on only that administrative detail that is necessary to implement key priorities through the council bureaucracy, but maintains a strategic view

Political Leadership

External political leadership

Mayor:
- constructs a shared political vision
- sets out policy priorities and objectives
- develops and maintains a clearly identifiable political platform and trajectory
- constructs alliances and coalitions: single issues + broad policy platform

Internal political leadership

Mayor provides:
- political leadership to councillors through clear political priorities and direction
- a focus for political decision making, responsibility and accountability
- an identifiable governing administration
- the perception or reality of leading the party locally and if not actual party leadership then influence within the party

Source: Copus (2011: 340–1)

Designer intention: institutional micro-design – the English experience

In this section we take two English mayoral councils – Newham and Leicester – to explore how the first mayors that were elected to the new office set about redesigning the council as a political and managerial organisation. We do this to examine how micro-institutional design can augment political resources available to the mayor and to improve on the central design to overcome its inefficiencies. Following a local referendum, the London Borough of Newham was an early adopter of the elected mayor model, with the current incumbent, Sir Robin Wales, becoming the first directly elected mayor for the borough in 2002 and then achieving re-election in 2006, 2010 and 2014. In contrast to Newham's early adoption, Leicester City Council resolved in 2010 to adopt an elected mayor, with Sir Peter Soulsby being elected in 2011 and re-elected in 2015.

Organisational redesign

Given that politics is about the exercise of power, it was not surprising that the redesign of the council as an organisational and political construct loomed large in the thinking of our two directly elected mayors. In particular, they sought early on to rebalance the relationship between the political leader and the organisational leader – the chief executive. The redesign was to establish the mayor as not just a politician who was dislocated from the administrative and managerial team, but rather as the recognised leader of the employee side of the council. Although the two mayors took different strategies towards this aim, a common thread which underpinned their approach was a desire (and need) to cement their leadership and control over the council. To limit the discussion because of space we take single, but powerful, exempla of mayoral organisational control in the case of Newham and Leicester. In Newham the elected mayor had previously held the position of council leader and so had already exercised considerable influence on staffing positions. The existence of a 'legacy effect' meant that the mayor did not feel an automatic need to reshape the managerial leadership of the council and as such maintained key posts, including the position of chief executive, whom the mayor had appointed, and which by virtue meant that the mayor had already politically shaped the council's staffing. But, the question of a visible power balance, in favour of the mayor, within the organisation, remained and through institution redesign, the mayor used his direct political mandate to cement his leadership over senior management.

The desire and need to demonstrate and exercise his own personal leadership led the mayor in 2010 to concentrate the council offices that had been dispersed across 26 sites into one new building at a cost of £111 million. The action was both a politically symbolic and real move as well as one the mayor considered would produce costs saving of around £50 million. The benefit of centralising in a single site was that it reflected and made real the mayor's desire to exercise personal organisational control. Sir Robin commented: "everyone knows who I am and that they work for me as mayor. I talk to who I need to when I need to; I don't have to go through any senior managers as I am the senior manager" (interview with the Mayor).

The Mayor of Leicester was not at the time of his election a sitting councillor, although he had served as a councillor from 1974–2003 and as council leader from 1981–99, as well as being a city MP from 2005 to 2011. He stood down from Parliament to seek what he called a 'proper job': the office of elected mayor (see Copus and Dadd, 2014).

The journey to the mayoralty meant that the mayor's re-engineering of the council management took a different turn to that of the Mayor of Newham. Yet, Sir Peter took highly visible, very powerful and in some cases symbolic actions of redesign as a means of publically demonstrating that not only was he the political leader but also the organisational leader. For example, on the day after his election he not only located his office in the building which housed the council managerial leadership (the previous council leader's office had been located in a different building), but commandeered three offices from senior managers and had them extended into a single office to serve as the mayor's base.

With this simple but powerful move the mayor stamped authority over the council's organisational leadership. Indeed, he had made it publically known prior to his election that post of chief executive would be abolished and most of its responsibilities transferred to the mayor (which would have been permitted by a clause in the 2011 Localism Act had it not been removed in the House of Lords during the passage of the Bill). The mayor was, however, clear that his office was to be that of chief executive. Yet, as he was legally unable to merge the two offices, it was only after a bruising and protracted legal battle that Sir Peter was able to delete the post of chief executive from the management structure. For Sir Peter, this meant that he was the de facto chief executive and as such responsible for reviews of senior management and its re-organisation which was then reshaped to meet his political goals. Thus, just like his Newham counterpart, the Mayor of Leicester ensured that senior managers supported his political objectives. In both cases the critical issue was that of ensuring that the mayors had command of the managerial machine. But what about the political structure of the council?

Political redesign

The desire of central government to shape and control the structures of the office of elected mayor was evidenced in the 2000 Local Government Act and subsequent regulations. There was a highly prescriptive approach which sought to create a standardised, almost nationalised, model of the office of mayor and as such make it difficult for mayors to shape the political processes of their council to meet their own priorities. In practical terms this meant that the mayors operated in a policymaking environment that was constricted by central government stipulation. Examples of such strictures are found in the rules that a mayoral cabinet cannot exceed a membership of ten, that a mayor can only appoint one adviser, and that certain parameters had to be followed in relation to how responsibilities could be allocated between the mayor, cabinet, full council and scrutiny committees as well as what could and could not be delegated and to whom (TSO, 2002). The case study highlights how our mayors worked within these constraints to shape political institutions that support their need to take political action (Svara, 1987; 1994; Stone, 1995; Mouritzen and Svara, 2002). In Newham and Leicester, the mayors sought to enhance their political power by a careful construction of their cabinet and its portfolios, as will be shown.In his first cabinet in 2002 the Mayor of Newham filled all ten cabinet seats and used his ability to select cabinet members to bolster his own support within the ruling group. The ability to shape a cabinet in the manner of his own thinking was something that Sir Robin relished given that in his previous capacity as council leader it had been the ruling group which elected the cabinet and decided the portfolio allocation for councillors. More than anything else, mayoral cabinet making saw, in this case, a private sector 'hire and fire' mentality, whereby the mayor was able to ensure – in contrast to the previous council model – that all members were able to undertake the requirements of the job. The shift of power was exemplified on the Friday after Sir Robin's first election as mayor in 2002, by the sacking of a councillor the Labour Group had continually elected to his cabinet while he was council leader. As Sir Robin commented, 'I can't have people in the cabinet that are not up to it'. In this way the mayor was able to design the political structure to provide maximum patronage and support within the ruling group, while making it clear to those outside the mayoral orbit that career progression was dependent on him. In practical terms this represented a shift away from collectivist decision making to an individualised system where the mayor had the capacity to overrule cabinet members' decisions. Newham highlights the manner by which Sir Robin was able to re-engineer the politics of the council to cement his own power base, despite the constraints of a centrally designed system. As he reflected, not only did this enhance his political position, but it also marginalised opposition within his own group.

In Leicester the mayor faced a similar need to establish political authority over the council and cabinet. For Sir Peter Soulsby this was achieved through a more public display of his influence by taking control of the key portfolios of economic development, transport and regeneration, constitution and governance, emergency planning and resilience. The remaining executive responsibilities (not portfolios in the first cabinet) were spread around a six-member cabinet that was formed after his first election (now expanded to nine) that met three times a week. One notable change has been that Sir Peter instructed that cabinet members would be referred to as 'assistant mayors' to indicate that their role is to do just that: assist the mayor. But not only has this institutional structure reinforced the mayor's own authority, the creation of a deputy mayor position also ensured that there was a clear link back to the ruling Labour Group as well as being a mayoral enforcer in the group.

To achieve control, Sir Peter showed little reticence in sacking cabinet members whose performance failed to reach his own standards. Indeed, by 2015 four cabinet members had been summarily removed from office after inadequate performance; the most recent after a poor government inspection of the children and young people's service which resulted in the immediate dismissal of an assistant mayor and the mayor taking on the portfolio, as well as the transfer of a senior council officer to other duties. While these actions indicate a level of control more often seen in the highest offices of state, it is also the case that the mayor's authority is equally dependent on the support of cabinet colleagues, the party group and the electorate. As such the mayor's power can be tested when there are alignments of interests that challenge his decisions. A notable example was when Sir Peter sought to replace a female Asian councillor from his assistant team. The councillor, with the support of the ruling Labour Group and wider Asian community, fought a successful campaign using ethnic and gender issues as leverage which resulted in her retaining the position of assistant mayor.

These two admittedly brief examples of mayors redesigning their political institution are presented to exemplify the findings of the research that elected mayors both need and are able to reshape the office as it is structured by the centre and to do so to augment their organisational and political standing. To examine how the centre creates imperfect local political organisations in the first place – even if that was not the aim – we turn our attention to Poland.

Poland: the logic of non-electoral politics

Sat against the background of the micro-design of the two mayoral case studies above, the picture in Poland is one shaped by developments at the macro level where a widespread concern exists that elected mayors have largely failed to deliver on the principles of the reforms of 1990. Particularly concerning policymakers in Poland is the longevity in office of incumbent mayors some of whom assumed the role when the office was first introduced. Indeed, by 2014 some 262 mayors had held office for five terms since 1990 (pre-dating direct elections). The power of incumbency is a trend replicated in urban and rural areas with the city of Gliwice having the notable position of the longest-serving mayor who was re-elected in 2014 with 55.7% of the vote, having been first elected in 1993. In Poland questions of accountability and democracy loom large particularly as some mayors have held office since communist rule when the position was dependent on central government largess rather than the electorate. The Mayor of Żarnowiec, Eugeniusz Kapuśniak, for example, has held office since 1981. His grip on power was evidenced by being the only candidate at the 2014 election, which inevitably led him to being elected in the first round with 84.4% of the votes on a turnout of 60% (the national average was 47.4%). While such longevity is unusual, the norm is for incumbent mayors to be re-elected with the average figure for re-election for at least two terms (over 2002–14) being 68%, for three terms 45% and for four terms 28%; indeed 5% of all mayors have held office for seven terms (Miros, 2015). It is with these figures in mind that reformers at the centre have sought term limits because of the argument that a lack of a change in local government can lead to corruption, cronyism and a negative lock-in in which the democratic institutions, participation in power or political opposition, do not function effectively. Yet the stability of the Polish mayoral office – which has now become to be seen as a problem – is linked to another issue that central designers are re-considering: the lack of effective electoral competition.

Lack of local competition versus national parties' competition

The lack of effective electoral competition for the office of mayor in Poland is exemplified by arguments about the power of incumbency. As former mayoral candidate in 2014 for Krakow, Tomasz Leśniak, said: 'the mayor runs an election campaign for the whole term of his office and he has greater access to local media and non-governmental organisations than anyone opposing him'. Indeed, in almost 10% of mayoral elections there was only one candidate, who nonetheless had to gain more than 50% of the votes cast (Trutkowski and Kurniewicz, 2015). Given the often lack of local electoral choice, reformers seeking to redesign the mayoral office, argue that the continued re-election of the same individual decreases citizen engagement in politics and hinders effective mayoral governance. But despite such an argument, turnout in local elections has steadily increased over the past five years and is comparable to general and presidential elections (Państwowa et al, 2014).

The possible decrease of mayors' mobilisation, understood as the effectiveness of the mayor, is more difficult to measure and this is particularly true in policy areas such as socioeconomic development about which many citizens have little knowledge or interest. As with many political offices, newly elected mayors tend to focus on political learning and how to manage problems, whereas with mayors that have won successive elections we can identify successes in socioeconomic development policy (Jarczewski, 2007).

A further argument for term limits is to generate improvements in the quality of policy; there are examples where candidates have resigned from senior political or administrative posts to be elected mayor and by limiting the number of times a mayor could stand, fresh experiences and new thinking would be injected into the office. The opponents of term limits argue that such a move is an attempt by political parties to gain power in those big cities in which independent mayors are continually re-elected. As Mayor Majchrowski of Krakow commented:

> Leading a city or municipality for many terms strengthens the position of the mayor and frees him or her from the policy of the particular political party. Hence the plans to limit the legal terms – political parties suffer from that. (Gość Krakowski, 2015)

The comment above reflects the position of the Association of Polish Cities, one of the most influential Polish local government associations. It claims term limits are incompatible with the designers' first conception of elected mayors which was to give the decision about who will have local power to the voters. The reasons for nationally redesigning the system are not to improve local democracy, it argues; rather, it is to improve the chances of national political party candidates winning mayoral office so weakening strong, independent local leaders (Porawski, 2014).

Overlapping generations model

The question remains: will national redesign of the mayoral office achieve what reformers intend and that if there is negative lock-in of mayors, will changing the general design create the desired change? The so-called Putin-Medvedev model (Flis, 2009) explains the likely failure of a change as observed in Katowice – one of Poland's largest cities – when the incumbent mayor of 16 years, Piotr Uszok, decided not to seek re-election in 2014 and supported and campaigned for his deputy mayor, Marcin Krupa, as successor. Krupa polled more than 40% of the votes in the first round and more than 70% in the second. Yet, Uszok did not give up local politics and in the 2014 local elections, his list won 12 of the 28 city council seats; he later resigned as a councillor to become the new mayor's investment adviser.

There is also second argument based on the observation of national policy inefficiencies which may be called the Schröder model or 'lost second legal term' (Flis, 2009). Here behaviour in the last possible legal term of office is used by the incumbent to secure private interest even against the public interest. The idea develops from the appointment of former German Chancellor Schroeder to a position with a Russian energy company (*Washington Post*, 2005).

There is a complex redesign question here with term limits, which those at the national level view as a solution to an original inefficiency in the system, but which mayors see as unnecessary because they are linked and accountable to local citizens. Moreover, Polish mayors can be dismissed by local referendum or by the prime minister if they are persistently found to be violating legal rules, so alternatives to term limits do exist.

General social context

There is a national redesign argument based on the general institutional context that has been present in Poland for some 20 years in that the arrival of elected mayors in 2002 came just before Polish accession to the European Union (2004). The contemporary stability of local power and the strong position of mayors is to large extent built on EU structural funds, sometimes colloquially referred to as 'crude oil' and Polish mayors compared to Arab sheikhs, building their local communities on petrodollars (euros) (Danielewski, 2014). Thus, local political stability could be temporary and in danger when external funds run dry.

In this discussion of the design by the centre of the office of Polish mayor the important aspect has been the scale of inefficiency in the original design. Even though the general effectiveness of local government is well recognised and receives strong citizen endorsement (CBOS, 2015), there are nevertheless locally manifested inefficiencies such as excessive periods of office for incumbent mayors. Somewhat perversely, the democratic transition that was necessary for Poland to join the EU may have created a situation whereby external EU funding has provided stability at the local level and limited the capacity for a competitive democratic model to develop in local politics. The question is, however, whether such inefficiencies require national redesign or whether they can be eradicated by mayors redesigning at the micro level – as we saw with the English case studies. If inefficiencies have emerged from central design and the office is now strongly rooted and vastly popular locally, who can redesign it most effectively: the centre or the localities?

Conclusions

The chapter has explored the design and redesign of the directly elected mayoral office from a macro and micro level. It also examined how centrally imposed models have required re-engineering by both the centre as the original instigator of change in local political structures and by the localities as those needing to make changes work in practical local politics. Redesign, whether locally or centrally, emerges from perceived inefficiencies in the original model and we saw with our two English case studies how both mayors acted to construct a managerial and political team designed to overcome the restrictions placed on their office by the macro-designers at the centre. Micro level redesign by our mayors enabled them to enhance the resources available to them to act locally by strengthening the organisational and political support they received from the council and councillors. In the observations from Poland we saw that inefficiencies in a nationally designed system had produced a result which the centre felt had damaged democracy – the lock-in of mayors and low turnover in office. We also saw that the willingness of local citizens to re-elect incumbents was not design inefficiency, rather something which reflected the popularity of the office of mayor and certain incumbents. The arguments of supporters of terms limits were based on generating political competition so as to improve efficiency in a belief that the strong position of mayors distorts competition. Thus, in both our countries inefficiencies existed in the original central design of the mayoral office which mayors had either capitalised on or had to re-engineer to meet local political needs.

Reflecting on the theoretical assumptions on which this chapter was based, drawn from the literature, we can make a few conclusions. First, the central redesign of the institutions of local political decision making in England and Poland demonstrates that past experiences of the designer, can, but do not always, influence the choice of models. In Poland, the existence of a directly elected president, as part of the governing national machine, found reflection in the introduction of the direct election of the mayor. Yet, in England, no such directly elected national executive office exists, but still institutional designers at the centre, offered local government the opportunity of a local directly elected executive leader. The lack of such national experience partly explains why mayors have not been compulsorily introduced across local government – resistance from councillors being another major part of the lack of compulsion (Kukovic et al, 2015). Rationality may well be bonded in institutional design, but it is not bounded by direct experience, rather by the unwillingness to experiment anew in the structuring of the mechanisms of local political decision making, beyond existing models – wherever they may exist.

The second conclusion about our assumptions is that while there is an often random and unpredictable outcome to institutional design, which can be the result of unintended consequences, such consequences could, had they been sufficiently thought through, be dealt with at the initial design stage. Had Polish reformers considered the nature of Polish local politics, particularly given the countries communist past, then the inefficiencies we identified – incumbency and lack of effective political choice and opposition – may have seen term limits, a different power balance between councillors and mayors and alternative electoral systems to alter the architecture of local politics, introduced at the outset.

While in England the balance of power was tipped in favour of the mayor over the council, reflecting the power balance in favour of the national executive over Parliament, mayors were constrained in the powers and resources that the centre decided to make available for the new office. Our case studies show, however, that mayors are able, even given institutional and legal constraints, to find sufficient room for local manoeuvre to conduct a micro level redesign of the structure within which they operate. In addition, both our mayors overcame the collectivist rules of the local political game to produce a highly individualised leadership dynamic. We can draw from this that path dependency in restructuring local politics is not restricted to a single path, but that it is more a multi-lane highway, heading in the same direction but with different junctions and turn-off points.

The third assumption, that institutional efficiency is a matter of contingency and therefore often dependent on an initial first design which may not be rational, must be refined to account for the political objectives of the designer, the processes of political interaction and the negotiation and compromise needed when developing new local political decision making structures. While objectives, interactions and negotiation could be seen as contingent factors themselves – that is the outcome of events or circumstances – they are not entirely unpredictable or unreflective of specific choices, all be it choices that are the result of compromise. Indeed, we could conclude that inefficiencies are highly predictable but may be acceptable outcomes of a given political negotiation over decision making systems, which were always intended to be redesigned when circumstances permit.

Equally, inefficiencies may be designed out of a system at the local level either by skilful political action by local leaders, or by central government providing local leaders with a sufficient range of freedom and choices when it comes to institutional redesign. Indeed, the English case studies and Polish examples suggest that the rules of the game, custom and informal arrangements can also be challenged and altered by mayors seeking to shift the political culture from one embedded in collectivism, to an acceptance of a more individualised approach to decision making.

What we can draw from our English case studies and the overarching exploration of the Polish experience is that the macro-design of the institutions and arrangements for local political decision making must provide for the micro-redesign of the system to ensure the local differentiation needed to make centrally designed institutions operate effectively. As skilful local leaders will attempt to carve out additional political resources and increase their room for manoeuvre they will identify system inefficiencies – disappointed national reformers will also point to problems from their original design as desired improvements fail to emerge or unintended consequences become apparent. The lesson here is that the centre needs to operate at the level of the broad strategic framework for models of local political office and that local office holders should be left to get on with making the institutions work – but it was ever thus with central and local relationships.

References

Arthur, W. B. (1994) *Increasing Returns and Path Dependence in the Economy*, Ann Arbor, MI: University of Michigan Press.

Berg, R. and Rao, N. (eds) (2005) *Transforming Local Political Leadership*, Palgrave.

Borraz, O. and John, P. (2004) 'The transformation of urban political leadership in Western Europe', *International Journal of Urban and Regional Research*, 28(1), 107-20.

Clark, T.N. and Hoffmann-Martinot, V. (eds) (1998) *The new political culture*. Westview Press, Boulder.

Copus, C. (2006) *Leading the Localities: Executive Mayors in English Local Governance*, Manchester University Press.

Copus, C. (2011) 'Elected mayors in English local government: Mayoral leadership and creating a new political dynamic', *Lex Localis: The Journal of Local Self-Government*, 9(4), 335–51.

Copus, C. and Dadd, M. (2014) 'It's a Proper Job: Process, People and Power in an English City', *Public Money and Management*, 34(5), 323–30.

Cusack, T.R. (1999) 'Social capital, institutional structures, and democratic performance: A comparative study of German local governments', *European Journal of Political Research*, 35(1), 1–34.

Danielewski, M. (2014) *Jak zmienić polski samorząd: Najpierw musimy obalić monarchię*, www.wyborcza.plDavid, P.A. (1985) 'Clio and the Economics of QWERTY', *The American Economic Review*, 75(2), 332–7.

Denters, B., and Rose, L. (2005) *Comparing Local Governance: Trends and Developments*, Palgrave MacMillan.

Department for Communities and Local Government (DCLG) (2010a) *Structural Reform Plan*, London.

DCLG (2010b) *Business Plan 2011–15*, London.

DCLG (2011) *A Plain English Guide to the Localism Bill*, London.

Department of the Environment, Transport and the Regions (DETR) (1998a) *Modernising Local Government: Local Democracy and Community Leadership*, London.

DETR (1998b) *Modern Local Government: In Touch with the People*, London.

DETR (1999) *Local Leadership: Local Choice*, London.Department of Transport, Local Government and the Regions (DTLR) (2001) *Strong Leadership: Quality Public Services*, London.

Douglas, M. (1986) *How Institutions Think*, Syracuse: Syracuse University Press.

Elcock, H. (2008) 'Elected mayors: Lesson drawing from four countries', *Public Administration*, 86(3), 795-811.

Engerman, S. L. and Sokoloff, K. L. (2005) 'Institutional and non-institutional explanations of economic differences', in C. Ménard and M. M. Shirley (eds) *Handbook of New Institutional Economics*, Berlin: Springer-Verlag, pp 639–65.

Flis, J. (2009) 'Ograniczenie kadencji w samorządach', *Salon24 Blog*, http://jaroslawflis.salon24.pl

Goodin, R. E. (1996) 'Institutions and Their Design', in R. E. Goodin (ed) *The Theory of Institutional Design*, Cambridge: Cambridge University Press, pp 1–53.

Gość Krakowski (2015) 'Samorząd to podstawa', www.krakow.gosc.pl

Hardin, R. (1996) 'Institutional Morality', in R. E. Goodin (ed) *The Theory of Institutional Design*, Cambridge: Cambridge University Press, pp 126–53.

Jarczewski, W. (2007) Duch przedsiębiorczości w proinwestycyjnych działaniach władz lokalnych, *Przedsiębiorczość-Edukacja*, 3, 72–80.

Jeffery, C (2008) The challenge of territorial politics, *Policy and Politics*, 36(4), 545–57.

Kersting, N., and Vetter, A. (eds) (2003) *Reforming Local Government in Europe: Closing the gap between Democracy and Efficiency*, Opladen.

Klijn, E.H. and Koppenjan, J. F. (2006) 'Institutional design: changing institutional features of networks', *Public Management Review*, 8(1), 141–60.

Kotter, J.P., Lawrence, P. (1974) *Mayors in Action: Five Approaches to Urban Governance*, London: John Wiley.

Kukovic, S., Copus, C., Hacek, M. and Blair, A. (2015) 'Direct Mayoral Elections in Slovenia and England: Traditions and Trends compared', *Lex Localis*, 13(3), 697–718.

Leach, S., and Wilson, D. (2000) *Local Political Leadership*, Bristol: The Policy Press.

Leśniak, T. (2014) *Debata samorządowa "Rzeczpospolitej"*, www. rp.plLoughlin, J., Hendricks, F. and Lindstrom, A. (2011) *The Oxford Handbook of Regional Democracy in Europe*, Oxford, Oxford University Press.

Lowndes, V. (2001) 'Rescuing Aunt Sally: taking institutional theory seriously in urban politics', *Urban Studies*, 38(11), 1953–71.

Lowndes, V. and Wilson, D. (2001) 'Social capital and local governance: exploring the institutional design variable', *Political Studies*, 49(4), 629–47.

Lowndes, V. and Roberts, M. (2013) *Why Institutions Matter: The New Institutionalism in Political Science*, Houndmills: Palgrave Macmillan.

Magre, J. and Bertrana, X. (2007) 'Exploring the limits of institutional change: The direct election of mayors in Western Europe', *Local Government Studies*, 33(2), 181–94.

Miros, M. (2015) Samorządowy samoregulator. *Wspólnota. Pismo samorządu terytorialnego*, May, vol 10, www.wspolnota.org.pl

Mouritzen, P. E. and Svara, J. H. (2002) *Leadership at the Apex, Politicians and Administrators in Western Local Governments*, Pittsburgh: University of Pittsburgh Press.

North, D. C. (1990) *Institutions, Institutional Change and Economic Performance*, Cambridge: Cambridge University Press.

North, D. C., Summerhill, W. and Weingast, B. R. (2000) 'Order, Disorder and Economic Change: Latin America vs. North America', in B. B. de Mesquita and H. Roots (eds) *Governing for Prosperity*, New Haven: Yale University Press, p 19.

Olsen, J. (1997) 'European Challenges to the Nation State, Political Institutions and Public Policy', in Steunenberg, B. and van Vught, F. (eds), *Perspectives on European Decision Making*, Springer, pp 157-88.

Pierson, P. (2000) 'The limits of design: Explaining institutional origins and change', *Governance*, 13(4), 475–99.

Porawski, A. (2014) 'Związek po wyborach', *Samorząd miejski*, 11(213), 9.

Rhodes, R. and t'Hart, P. (2014) *The Oxford Handbook of Political Leadership*, Oxford: Oxford University Press.

Shirley, M. M. (2005) 'Institutions and development', in C. Ménard and M. M. Shirley (eds) *Handbook of New Institutional Economics*, Berlin: Springer-Verlag, pp 611–38.

Skelcher, C., Mathur, N. and Smith, M. (2005) 'The public governance of collaborative spaces: Discourse, design and democracy', *Public Administration*, 83(3), 573–96.

Stone, C. N. (1995) 'Political Leadership in Urban Politics', in D. Judge, G. Stoker, and H. Wolman (eds) *Theories of Urban Politics*, London: Sage, pp 96–116.

Svara, J. H. (1987) 'Mayoral Leadership in Council Manager Cities: Preconditions versus Preconceptions', *Journal of Politics*, 49(1), 207–27.

Svara, J. H. (ed) (1994) *Facilitative Leadership in Local Government: Lessons from Successful Mayors and Chairpersons*, San Francisco: Jossey-Bass.

Swianiewicz, P. (2010) (ed) *Territorial Consolidation Reforms in Europe*, Local Government and Public Service Reform Initiative, Open Society Institute-Budapest.

Szucs, S. and Stromberg, L. (2009) 'The more things change, the more they stay the same: the Swedish local government elite between 1985 and 2005', *Local Government Studies*, 35(2), 251–70.

Trutkowski, C. and Kurniewicz, A. (2015) Bilans Kadencji 2010–2014. Wyniki badania CAWI, Fundacja Rozwoju Demokracji Lokalnej, www.frdl.org.pl

TSO (The Stationery Office) (2002) *The Local Authorities (Elected Mayor and Mayor's Assistant) (England) Regulations*, London: TSO.

Wollmann, H. (2008) 'Reforming Local Leadership and Local Democracy: The Cases of England, Sweden, Germany and France in Comparative Perspective', *Local Government Studies*, 34(2), 279–98.

FOURTEEN

Directly elected mayors: a route to progressive urban leadership?

Robin Hambleton, University of the West of England, Bristol, UK

Introduction

It is incontestable that place-less power has grown significantly in the past 30 years or so. By place-less power I mean the exercise of power by decision makers who are unconcerned about the impact of their decisions on communities living in particular places. Some writers take the view that the forces of globalisation have now completely undermined local democracy. They believe that the growth of multinational companies operating on a global basis is now so well developed that localities are best viewed as helpless victims in a global flow of events. Distant, unelected decision makers now determine city futures, not urban residents. This chapter questions this view and offers a fresh way of thinking about the future of urban leadership. The presentation draws on arguments that are set out at greater length elsewhere (Hambleton, 2015).

How does the fairly specific debate about the strengths and weaknesses of the directly elected mayor model of governance relate to this broader debate about place-based versus place-less power? On the one hand, some critics of the directly elected mayor model of urban governance fear that it gives an unwelcome boost to the influence of place-less decision makers. They argue that the model can make local government institutions vulnerable to international business pressures, certainly more vulnerable than collective models of civic leadership. This is because, they claim, too much power is concentrated in the hands of one individual, and these individuals may find it very difficult to resist the demands of powerful economic actors. On the other hand, enthusiasts for the directly elected mayor model claim that the opposite is true. They argue that, by granting significant political legitimacy to a single person, via a process of direct election, the model bolsters the place-based power of the locality. A progressive directly elected mayor, so the argument goes, is well placed to take on place-less power and advance the causes of social and environmental justice in the city.

In this chapter I offer a contribution to this debate. In particular, I explore whether the directly elected mayor model of governance can contribute to progressive policy making. In this context I am using the word 'progressive' to mean the active implementation of policies and practices designed to move away from exploitation of people and the planet. In contrast to neo-liberal politicians, progressive civic leaders strive for just results while caring for the natural environment on which we all depend.

First, I outline a way of conceptualising the political space available to place-based leaders in any given context. The discussion then considers the way place-based power is exercised and the notion of realms of place-based leadership is introduced. Three examples of mayoral leadership in different countries are then presented.[1] These are chosen to show how directly elected mayors in very different countries and contexts have been able to develop and implement policies that promote progressive objectives. They are also chosen to show how mayoral governance can have a progressive impact at very different geographical scales: Greater London, UK (population 8.6 million); Portland, Oregon, USA (610,000); and Freiburg, Germany (230,000). The chapter closes with a comparative discussion of the progressive potential of mayoral leadership.

Framing the power of place

Place-based leaders are not free agents able to do exactly as they choose. On the contrary, various powerful forces shape the context within which civic leaders operate. These forces do not disable local leadership. Rather they place limits on what urban leaders may be able to accomplish in particular places and at particular moments in time. Figure 14.1 provides a simplified picture of the four sets of forces that shape the world of place-based governance in any given locality. At the bottom of the diagram are the non-negotiable environmental limits. Ignoring the fact that cities are part of the natural ecosystem is irresponsible, and failure to pay attention to environmental limits will store up unmanageable problems for future generations (Girardet, 2008; Jackson, 2009). This side of the square is drawn with a solid line because, unlike the other sides of the square, these environmental limits are non-negotiable. On the left hand side of the diagram are socio-cultural forces – these comprise a mix of people (as actors) and cultural

Figure 14.1: Framing the political space for place-based governance

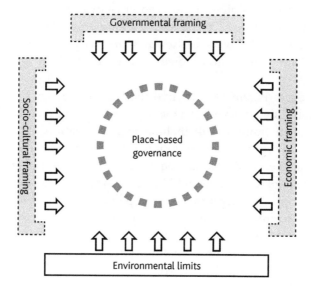

Source: Hambleton (2015: 114).

values (that people may hold). Here we find the rich variety of voices found in any city – including the claims of activists, businesses, artists, entrepreneurs, trade unionists, religious organisations, community-based groups, citizens who vote, citizens who do not vote, children, newly arrived immigrants, anarchists and so on. The people of the city will have different views about the kind of city they wish to live in, and they will have differential capacity to make these views known. Some, maybe many, will claim a right to the city (Brenner et al, 2012). We can assume that, in democratic societies at least, elected leaders who pay little or no attention to these political pressures should not expect to stay in office for too long. Expression of citizen voice, to use Hirschman's term (1970), will see them dismissed at the ballot box. On the right hand side of the diagram are the horizontal economic forces that arise from the need for localities to compete, to some degree at least, in the wider marketplace – for inward investment and to attract talented people. Various studies have shown that, contrary to neo-liberal dogma, it is possible for civic leaders to bargain with business (Savitch and Kantor, 2002). Recognising the power of economic forces, including the growth in global competition between localities, does not require civic leaders to become mere servants of private capital. For example, a detailed study of the governance of London, New York, Paris and Tokyo concluded that:

> Global forces are not making the politics of place less
> important. Globalism and local governance are not mutually
> exclusive but are deeply entwined ... important differences
> remain in the ways particular world city-regions are
> mediating international forces. (Kantor et al, 2012: 241)

On the top of Figure 14.1 we find the legal and policy framework
imposed by higher levels of government. In some countries this
governmental framing will include legal obligations decreed by
supranational organisations. For example, local authorities in countries
that are members of the EU are required to comply with EU laws and
regulations, and to take note of EU policy guidance. Individual nation
states determine the legal status, fiscal power and functions of local
authorities within their boundaries. These relationships are subject to
negotiation and renegotiation over time.

It is clear that Figure 14.1 simplifies a much more complex reality.
This is what conceptual frameworks do. In reality the four sets of
forces framing local action do not necessarily carry equal weight, and
the situation in any given city is, to some extent, fluid and changing.
For example, Richard Flanagan in his analysis of American mayoral
leadership stresses the importance of timing (Flanagan, 2004: 13–16).
The space available for local agency is always shifting, and a key task
of local leaders is to be alert to the opportunities for advancing the
power of their place within the context of the framing forces prevailing
on their area at the time.

Figure 14.1 indicates that place-based governance, shown at the
centre, is porous. Successful civic leaders are constantly learning from
the environment in which they find themselves in order to discover new
insights, co-create new solutions and advance their political objectives.
Note that the four forces are not joined up at the corners to create a
rigid prison within which civic leadership has to be exercised. On the
contrary the boundaries of the overall arena are, themselves, malleable.
Depending on the culture and context, imaginative civic leaders may
be able to disrupt the pre-existing governmental frame and bring about
an expansion in place-based power.

The realms of place-based leadership

In the 1980s New Public Management (NPM), which involves the
use of private sector management practices in the public sector,
gained popularity in many countries (Christensen and Laegried,
2001; Hoggett, 1991; Hood, 1991). In essence, the approach stems

from the belief that government should be run like a private business. In my recent book I argue that the introduction of NPM techniques has often done great damage to the public service ethos, and that treating citizens as self-interested consumers is a peculiarly narrow way of thinking about public service reform (Hambleton, 2015: 61–3). I suggest that those interested in progressive public policymaking might find a notion that I describe as New Civic Leadership (NCL) to be more relevant and useful. NCL involves strong, place-based leadership acting to co-create new solutions to public problems by drawing on the complementary strengths of civil society, the market and the state. If we are to understand effective, place-based leadership, we need a conceptual framework that highlights the role of local leaders in facilitating public service innovation. Here I provide a sketch of a possible framework.

Figure 14.2 suggests that in any given locality there are likely to be five realms of place-based leadership reflecting different sources of legitimacy:

- *Political leadership* – referring to the work of those people elected to leadership positions by the citizenry
- *Public managerial/professional leadership* – referring to the work of public servants, including planners, appointed by local authorities, governments and third sector organisations to plan and manage public services, and promote community wellbeing
- *Community leadership* – referring to the many civic-minded people who give their time and energy to local leadership activities in a wide variety of ways
- *Business leadership* – referring to the contribution made by local business leaders and social entrepreneurs, who have a clear stake in the long-term prosperity of the locality
- *Trade union leadership* – referring to the efforts of trade union leaders striving to improve the pay and working conditions of employees

These roles are all important in cultivating and encouraging public service innovation and, crucially, they overlap. I describe the areas of overlap as innovation zones – areas providing many opportunities for inventive behaviour. This is because different perspectives are brought together in these zones and this can enable active questioning of established approaches. It is fair to say that the areas of overlap in Figure 14.2 are often experienced as conflict zones, rather than innovation zones. These spaces do, of course, provide settings for power struggles between competing interests and values. Moreover,

Figure 14.2: The realms of place-based leadership

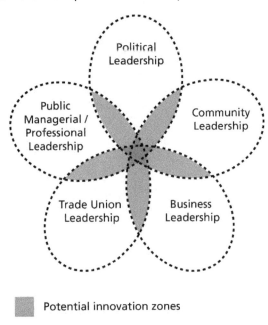

Potential innovation zones

Source: Hambleton (2015: 127)

power is unequally distributed within these settings. This is precisely why place-based leadership matters. The evidence from my research on urban governance is that civic leadership is critical in ensuring that the innovation zones – sometimes referred to as the 'soft spaces' of planning (Illsley et al, 2010) or 'space for dialogue' (Oliver and Pitt, 2013: 198–9) – are orchestrated in a way that promotes a culture of listening that can, in turn, lead to innovation. Civic leaders are, of course, not just 'those at the top'. All kinds of people can exercise civic leadership and they may be inside or outside the state.

The role of directly elected mayors in place-based leadership

We now turn to consider how this discussion of place-based power and realms of place-based leadership bears on the debate about directly elected mayors. But first we should sound a warning note. It is far too simplistic to claim that directly elected mayors are 'good' or 'bad' for local democracy and place-based leadership in general. For a start there are many different forms of mayoral governance. There is no one model. Other chapters in this volume throw light on the diversity of these arrangements. We should also note that political cultures vary significantly and institutional design ideas that might be seen as attractive in one country, or locality, may be seen as unhelpful in another. It follows that we should guard against generalising too freely about the 'mayoral form of governance'. Notwithstanding this caveat we can, perhaps, make three general points about the mayoral model.

First, there is, usually but not always, a 'separation of powers' between the directly elected mayor (let's call this person the executive) and the other politicians elected to serve the city (let's call them the assembly). The balance of power between the executive and the assembly can vary dramatically. For example, Clarence Stone notes that, in the US, the strong mayor form of governance '... is in some ways a miniature presidency' (Stone, 1995: 110). In the strong mayor form the executive is enormously powerful. By contrast, in cities where the assembly remains strong, the executive will have much less administrative power and budgetary control. In US cities the balance of power between the executive and the assembly is constantly up for reconsideration – cities are free to modify or transform their governance structures and they do (Svara and Watson, 2010). Moreover, some US cities, and we will encounter this later in the chapter when we consider governance arrangements in Portland, Oregon, have a directly elected mayor working alongside directly elected commissioners.[2]

Second, the process of direct election appears to give mayors a level of personal legitimacy that they would not otherwise have. In the UK context there are a number of directly elected mayors who, in an earlier period, served as council leader. These individuals are well placed to know, from their own direct, personal experience, how the process of direct election influences their effectiveness as leaders.[3] When asked about the difference between being council leader and being directly elected mayor Sir Steve Bullock, Mayor of Lewisham, said:

> Local residents hold me directly accountable as executive mayor in a way they never did as council leader. It gives my decisions legitimacy but also places a responsibility on me to clearly explain how and why I have made them – and to listen before I decide.[4]

When asked the same question Sir Peter Soulsby, Mayor of Leicester, said:

> A directly elected mayor gives the executive a clear democratic mandate from those they represent, and makes the office-holder accountable to the public and not just

to members of the council. A council leader has to be constantly responding to the political dynamic of their party group to ensure re-election each year, and is much less able to make longer-term decisions unencumbered by looking over their shoulder and by the necessity to appease their group members.[5]

Another insight is provided George Ferguson, Mayor of Bristol from 2012–16. While he never served as a council leader in the past, he is forthright about the value of being directly elected:

> Being elected by the whole electorate creates a huge difference to my authority to do things. It also gives me the courage to make changes that, otherwise, would be very difficult to make. (Hambleton, 2015: 135)

A third general point about the mayoral model is that directly elected mayors usually see themselves as 'leader of the place', rather than 'leader of the council'. In most models of mayoral governance, the mayor is elected for a term of three or more years. This enables them, in theory, to be more outward looking than a leader who is answerable, often on a month-by-month basis, to her or his party group.

In terms of the realms of place-based leadership shown in Figure 14.2 the directly elected mayor is clearly in the political realm. In practice, effective city mayors often locate themselves at the heart of the realms of leadership, that is, at the centre of this figure. They put great value in positioning themselves at the hub of leadership networks, and put considerable energy and effort into working closely with leaders from the other four realms of place-based leadership.

Two other important general points about mayoral governance should be highlighted. First, the context within which mayoral leadership is exercised is critical. Effective leaders tune their efforts to the environment both within and outside their organisation. The forces shaping local political space – see Figure 14.1 – need to be understood. Knowing what steps to take, and at what point, to advance the cause of place-based power requires political judgement. This, in turn, requires an understanding of civic capacity and civic drive in the local population. By this I mean '... the desire and motivation to be involved in social issues and to see new social opportunities' (Sun and Anderson, 2012: 317).

Clarence Stone understands this well enough and notes that leadership goes to the heart of politics, that is, to the capacity of citizens to act together on their shared concerns. He draws on Hanna Arendt's ideas to suggest that leadership involves contributing to a creative process that calls something into being that did not exist before: '... leadership alters events, not as an individual act of heroism, but through interaction with followers' (Stone, 1995: 98).

Second, and it is a closely related point, the personal qualities of the leader matter. Qualities like vision, resilience, persistence, energy, inventiveness, passion, humility and judgement are associated with successful leadership in the public and the private sectors. This personal element is a critical factor for our discussion. It is clear that the individuals involved in local leadership can shape the performance of an urban governance system. It follows that the directly elected mayor model of governance creates possibilities for the exercise of progressive leadership. Institutional design cannot, in and of itself, guarantee improved civic leadership – the qualities and wisdom of the people in leadership positions matter.

Progressive mayoral leadership: three inspirational examples

In this section, we consider three examples of mayoral leadership.[6] These have been selected to illustrate how directly elected mayors can exercise progressive civic leadership at different geographical scales and in very different countries. These cameos cover experiences in three countries at three very different geographical scales: (1) metropolitan leadership in Greater London, UK (in the period 2000–08); (2) city leadership in Portland, Oregon, USA; and (3) city leadership in Freiburg, Germany.

Progressive metropolitan leadership: the London congestion charge

In May 2000 Ken Livingstone, when he was elected Mayor of London, became the first directly elected, political leader in UK history (Sweeting 2002). He became the leader of the Greater London Authority that, it should be noted, is a strategic metropolitan authority, with a population of around 8.6 million people. Livingstone, a very experienced left-leaning politician, had a reputation for daring initiatives and his approach to mayoral leadership in London in the period 2000–08 reflected his willingness to push at the boundaries of what might be possible. In his autobiography, *You Can't Say That*, Livingstone provides his own account of a remarkable environmental initiative – the introduction of the London congestion charge

(Livingstone, 2011: 469–78). He notes that it was very challenging – even his own political advisers told him not to do it.

A congestion charge is a fee imposed on most motor vehicles operating within a designated zone within a city. Singapore deserves credit for being the first major city to introduce such a scheme in 1998, where the approach is known as electronic road pricing. But the London scheme introduced by Livingstone is far larger, and his decision to take such a radical step has attracted interest from city leaders from across the world. The aims of the charge were to reduce traffic congestion, enhance the environmental quality of central London and raise funds to invest in major improvements to London's public transport system.

In the period before the introduction of the charge, particularly during 2002, there was massive opposition to the idea. The *London Evening Standard*, the capital's newspaper, orchestrated a vitriolic campaign against Livingstone in general, and the charge in particular. Opposition also came from the Conservative Party, car users, petrol companies, motoring correspondents, theatre 'luvvies', various residents' groups and numerous business interests, including Smithfield meat traders. As the pressures mounted Livingstone's advisers concluded that it would be a foolish move to introduce the charge. They advised him that he would be finished politically if he went ahead because the media would portray him as 'the mayor who introduced a new tax'. They begged him to delay the idea until after he had won a second four-year term in 2004. To his lasting credit Livingstone ignored all of them.

Mayor Livingstone introduced the London congestion charge in February 2003. On the first day of operation, traffic in the congestion charge zone declined by 25%, a figure that shifted to around 15% to 20% of pre-charge levels in subsequent weeks. Livingstone pumped the income generated by the charge into public transport improvements. An independent evaluation of the policy concluded 'it is clear that the scheme has been a great success in its primary target of reducing traffic congestion within central London, and contributing to improving access by bus' (Richards, 2006: 216).

Additional new buses were introduced and there were big improvements in bus reliability. The roads were made more attractive to cyclists, whose numbers increased significantly, and there was a 20% reduction in carbon emissions. Within ten days Livingstone's opinion poll ratings were up 10%. The following year, in the May 2004 Greater London elections, Mayor Livingstone was rewarded for showing vision and courage in leadership. He was elected mayor for the period 2004–08. Moreover, more people voted for him in 2004 than in his previous victory in 2000. He had imposed a new tax and become more popular than ever. This is because he used the funds generated to advance the public good, and voters appreciated the benefits.

We can note that Boris Johnson, the 2008 incoming Conservative Mayor of Greater London, did not discard the congestion charge. Indeed, no serious politicians are now advocating its abolition. It seems clear that the main reason why London was able to make this major step towards a more sustainable city was the exercise of bold civic leadership by a powerful directly mayor in the capital.

Progressive city leadership in Portland, Oregon

Portland, Oregon has acquired an international reputation for progressive city planning (Ozawa, 2004; Irazabal, 2005). A city of 610,000 in a metropolitan area of 2.3 million, Portland has a long established commitment to sustainable urban development. Over a long period, the political leadership has secured an integrated approach to land use and transportation planning, and the city is regularly praised for its leadership in increasing public transportation and bicycling, energy efficiency and recycling. For example, the city's first bicycle master plan was completed in 1996, and the city now has a higher percentage of workers commuting by bike than any other city in the US (Fitzgerald, 2010: 160). It was the first US city to adopt a firm position on climate change – it set ambitious targets for the reduction of greenhouse gas emissions in 1993.

Support for a progressive approach to local policymaking comes from an active network of neighbourhood associations. Campbell (2012: 114) notes that an important driver of change is '… a system of internal networks of trust formed by mainstream civic-minded persons who care about the city and devote professional and personal time to community deliberation, discussion and planning'. In 2012 the city council adopted a new plan for the city – the Portland Plan. Sam Adams, Mayor of Portland from 2008–12, deserves credit for pushing equity up the local political agenda, and making it a central feature of the Portland Plan. This is innovative as it puts advancing equity at the heart of the strategy. The city is attempting to build on its successful approach to sustainable development by building in a stronger commitment to social justice in the period through to 2035. For example, in 2011 a city-level Office of Equity and Human Rights was created. This office is working to elevate considerations of fairness in the city to a central position within political debates, and these efforts have influenced decision making in relation to, for example, the climate action plan for the city (Schrock et al, 2015).

The governance arrangements for the city are, in fact, rather unusual. As explained with great clarity by Morgan et al (2010), the city has gained its own distinct, international reputation for being different, if not 'weird'. The city is odd in that it is the only major US city to retain a commission system of government. And, on closer examination, Portland's commission system is, in itself, weird when compared to the traditional commission model. The original commission form involves the election of officials who run to be commissioner of, for example, police, roads, fire and so on. In Portland, commissioners run for office without portfolios; the directly elected mayor assigns portfolios after their election. The city has six directly elected officials: the mayor, four commissioners and the auditor. The appointment power of the mayor is supplemented by the power to prepare and present the annual budget to the commission for adoption. In theory this arrangement grants significant powers to the directly elected mayor but, in practice, the mayor needs to maintain at least three votes to support her or his agenda.

In the period since he took office in January 2013 Mayor Charlie Hales has focused his efforts on four priorities: (1) creating liveable neighbourhoods with fair access to services and jobs; (2) growing the number of jobs in the city and improving access to employment; (3) police reform; and 4) improving governance. His report on priorities and accomplishments offers an assessment of progress (Hales, 2015). The theme of enhancing fairness in the city is a key feature of his administration and, as mentioned earlier, this commitment to advancing equity is the central plank of the Portland Plan.

Several factors explain the continuing commitment of the elected city council to a progressive agenda for Portland. Three stand out. First, there is a long established civic culture at both neighbourhood and city levels: 'There is a rich web of professional, political, grassroots, formal, and informal relationships across organisational and jurisdictional boundaries that has accounted for Portland's success' (Morgan et al, 2010: 297).

Second, the political will shown, not just by a succession of mayors but also by commissioners, has maintained a strong commitment to sustainable development and, more recently, to equitable development. Third, the professional leadership of appointed officers, across numerous departments and agencies, has ensured good quality work on topics like transportation, energy conservation and access to services. The role of the directly elected mayor, and Sam Adams and Charlie Hales provide good examples, is to set a tone for local leadership. By working in a collaborative way with the commissioners and other civic leaders, the directly elected mayor is able to orchestrate a variety of progressive initiatives. At the same time the commission form diffuses leadership and responsibilities, and provides an effective mechanism for holding the mayor to account.

Green leadership in Freiburg, Germany

Freiburg, Germany's southernmost city, has established itself as a world leader in relation to sustainable development. The city, which has a population of 230,000, has been successful in promoting a civic culture that combines a very strong commitment to green values and respect for nature, with a buoyant economy built around, among other things, renewable energy. The UK-based Academy of Urbanism was so impressed with the achievements of the city that it published *The Freiburg Charter for Sustainable Urbanism* to promote imaginative city planning and sound urban design (Academy of Urbanism and Stadt Freiburg, 2012).

Visitors from across the world flock to the city to learn about the many green innovations the city is now famous for – in public transport, renewable energy and city planning. Many head for the Vauban district on the south side of the city. Here they find a newly created, family-friendly neighbourhood full of green spaces and attractively designed homes. The energy to power this neighbourhood is 95% from renewable resources. Joan Fitzgerald, a US sustainable development expert, was astonished by what she found when she visited the area, saying 'Vauban goes beyond anything we are thinking of in the United States under the banners of smart growth, transit-oriented development, or new urbanism' (Fitzgerald, 2010: 2).

The origins of the community activism that underpins current innovations in Freiburg can be traced to the late 1970s. A successful, local and regional campaign against a proposal to locate a nuclear power station in nearby Wyhl provided the original impetus. A colourful coalition of anti-nuclear activists was born and, from small beginnings, this new green movement became increasingly successful.[7] As early as 1986, the year of the Chernobyl disaster, the city council declared Freiburg to be a nuclear power free zone. Many articles have now been published on Freiburg's high quality approach to city planning and urban design, and Peter Hall (2014) provides a good overview in a chapter in his recent book headed 'Freiburg: The city that did it all'. In trying to explain the success of Freiburg Hall highlights the importance of civic leadership '... what stands out in Freiburg is the role that visionary leadership can play in changing a city's direction' (Hall, 2014: 248).

Freiburg is located within the state of Baden-Württemberg and the local authority has two political institutions: the city council (*Gemeinderat*) with 48 members who are elected on an 'at large' basis for a term of five years; and the mayor, who is directly elected for a fixed term of eight years. The mayor is the chief executive officer of the city administration and is supported by four deputy mayors. Local authorities in Germany are relatively strong – they have a constitutional right to local self-government and they have the legal power to levy their own taxes to finance activities as they think fit.

The leadership provided by successive directly elected mayors has had a significant impact on the quality of life in the city. Special praise should go to Dr Rolph Böhme, a Social Democrat mayor. Elected in 1982 he was to remain in office until 2002 and, during this period, he was very active in bringing about many of the innovations that now make Freiburg famous. He worked closely with appointed officers, and special mention should be made of his close working relationship with Wulf Daseking, Director of Planning and Building in Freiburg for many years, before retiring in 2012. Mayor Dr Dieter Salomon, a member of the Green Party, who was elected in 2002 and re-elected in 2010, is deeply committed to the green agenda for the city.

Successive directly elected mayors and elected councillors have promoted ambitious thinking in Freiburg. Their consistent commitment to green values, coupled with an enthusiasm for trying out new approaches, has set the tone for the pursuit of a forward looking progressive agenda for the city.

Progressive mayoral leadership: themes and possibilities

Having examined experience on the ground in three progressive cities, we can now address the question posed in the title of this chapter: can directly elected mayors provide a route to progressive urban leadership? The examples of mayoral leadership presented in this chapter suggest that the answer is 'yes'. We have seen how directly elected mayors in rather different countries – in this instance, the UK, the US and Germany – have been able to develop and implement world-leading policies designed to create more inclusive and more sustainable cities.

It is important to emphasise that the progressive achievements of these cities are substantial. These cities have gained international recognition for breaking new ground and independent researchers have praised their efforts. In addition, it is clear that the directly elected mayors in these cities have played a key role in bringing about progressive change. Moreover, our examples show that progressive mayors have been successful at very different geographical scales: London is a vast metropolis with a population of 8.3 million; Portland is a sizeable city with 610,000 residents; and Freiburg is a relatively small city of 230,000. The evidence presented here suggests, then, that the argument that directly elected mayors will inevitably serve powerful economic interests at the expense of progressive possibilities is disproved. Contrary to the dominant neo-liberal discourse, these case studies show that place-based power can be mobilised to erode the impact of place-less forces and, at times, make significant steps away from exploitation of people and the planet.

In making these points I am not advocating the virtues of a particular model of urban governance. Rather I am trying to stimulate a more sophisticated debate about ways of advancing the progressive potential of urban – or place-based – governance. For too much of the time the arguments for and against the directly elected mayor form of urban governance have been needlessly polarised. Simplistic claims and counter claims proliferate. This is particularly noticeable in the British public policy discourse, but gut feelings for and against the model run high in other countries as well, for example Australia. In the discussion that follows I seek to open up a more thoughtful conversation about the strengths and weaknesses of mayoral governance. Our starting point is that directly elected mayors can contribute to progressive urban leadership – the case studies demonstrate this. But, and this is equally important, introducing a directly elected mayor form of governance will not, in and of itself, advance the cause of progressive politics. The discussion below is structured around three inter-related themes.

The role of mayors in expanding place-based power

Earlier in the chapter I explained how various powerful forces shape the context within which place-based leaders operate. Figure 14.1 provides a simplified picture of the way these forces bear on any locality. The examples of mayoral leadership presented in this chapter show that directly elected mayors – in these three cities at least – have been able to articulate the importance of environmental issues (bottom side of the diagram), listen to community-based pressures (left side of the diagram) and push back against narrow economic interests (right side of the diagram). The directly elected mayors in the three cities presented here have, by exercising proactive leadership, taken advantage of the political space available to them to pursue progressive policies.

The governmental framing (top side of the diagram) has, in all three examples, been relatively supportive to local, democratic decision making. For example, the Greater London Authority Act 1999 contains powers enabling the authority to establish and operate schemes for imposing charges on road users. Without this power Mayor Livingstone would not have been able to introduce the London congestion charge. The cities of Portland and Freiburg operate within federal government systems and, in both cases, the elected local authorities have considerable freedom to act in ways that elected members think fit. The higher levels of government, at state and federal levels, do not exercise detailed control of local policymaking. There is a clear lesson here for central and state governments. It is important for higher levels of government to trust elected local authorities to get on with the job of local governance.

The examples presented in this chapter suggest that the directly elected mayors in each city have exercised sound judgement in the way they have promoted radical measures. They have assessed the political prospects for reform, taken risks by pursuing untried policies and practices and, in a subtle way, they have expanded the place-based power of their cities. However, it would be misleading to suggest that only cities with directly elected mayors can expand the amount of political space available to local communities. Copenhagen, for example, provides a world-class example of place-based leadership, and the city has pursued socially and environmentally progressive policies for decades. It does not have a directly elected mayor – the approach to urban leadership is more collective. However, the evidence presented in this chapter suggests that directly elected mayors can use the political legitimacy granted to them by the process of direct election to advance progressive policies.

Connecting the realms of place-based leadership

The directly elected mayors in our three case studies have been effective in working with other leaders in their locality. In Figure 14.2 I suggested that, in any locality, there are likely to be several overlapping realms of place-based leadership. Effective mayors facilitate collaboration across the realms of place-based leadership. For example, while Mayor Livingstone was pretty much forced to adopt a public strategy of 'go it alone' leadership in driving forward the introduction of the congestion charge, it is also the case that he worked very closely indeed with his officers to ensure that the scheme was workable.

The Mayor of Portland, partly because of the distinctive commission form of governance, is required to operate in a collegial way with the four commissioners. The mayor needs votes from commissioners to deliver change. However, the mayor is not rooted in City Hall – he works closely with leaders in all the realms of civic leadership shown in Figure 14.2. In this context it is important to highlight the care and attention the mayor gives to the neighbourhood associations within the city. As mentioned earlier, there is a very active network of neighbourhood organisations in Portland. The city has an Office of Neighbourhood Involvement (ONI) to support the work of these bodies and to promote the civic life of the city. Mayor Hales spends a lot of time out in the neighbourhoods and his first priority is to create liveable neighbourhoods.

The Mayor of Freiburg also works closely with leaders in all the realms of civic leadership shown in Figure 14.2. As with Portland, neighbourhood activism is vibrant in Freiburg, and civic leaders ignore grassroots pressures at their peril. In practice, under Mayor Rolph Böhme, Freiburg developed sophisticated arrangements for ensuring that local communities have an important say in the design and management decisions affecting their neighbourhoods. Mayor Böhme was also aware that the officers and professionals appointed by the city have an important role in pushing at the boundaries of good practice. His partnership with Wulf Daseking, Director of Planning and Building, was particularly effective. Directly elected mayors in Freiburg, as in Portland, have also worked closely with place-based business interests to enhance the economic performance of their city. Freiburg is experiencing rapid economic growth, and it is significant that the local university and the city meet very regularly to discuss common issues.

Bringing progressive values back into city politics

Benjamin Barber, in his largely favourable account of mayoral leadership in a variety of countries, argues that successful mayors exhibit 'a preference for pragmatism' (Barber, 2013: 90). In his view a virtue of mayoral leadership is that it can focus on getting things done. Barber notes that, in a world that seems to be growing increasingly cynical about politics, mayors remain astonishingly popular, and this is, he believes, because they focus, not on ideology, but on problem solving. A number of other scholars have also noted this trend towards pragmatism in the public policy discourse. However, they are troubled by it. They note that shifting the focus of political attention to 'what works' runs the risk of removing important political choices from the public discourse. There is now a substantial body of literature on this process of 'depoliticisation', and a variety of terms have emerged in an effort to characterise aspects of this shift – for example, terms like 'post-political', 'post-democratic' and 'post-politics' all have their adherents (Crouch, 2004; Mouffe, 2005).

What are the implications of this discourse for city politics? A central point made by many critics of neo-liberalism is that it subordinates the political to the economic. Despite the unprecedented breakdown of the so-called 'free market' system in 2008–09 we are told that there is still no alternative:

> As banks are bailed out with public money and the welfare state is dismantled in the name of austerity, electorates are told that "We're all in this together", and are called upon to unite in support of the expert managers of the global economy. (Wilson and Swyngedouw, 2014: 8)

A fundamental flaw in neo-liberal thinking is that moral judgement is edged out of the picture. State and business actors work to construct a political 'mainstream' – one that emasculates fundamental value conflicts. In my view it is misguided to suggest that we have entered a 'post-political' era. Political dividing lines may well be in a process of being redrawn, but this does not mean that fundamental political conflicts about who gains and who loses in the modern city have disappeared. A more accurate phrase to describe current developments would be to suggest that, in many public policy settings, and in urban governance in particular, we are at risk of experiencing a managerialisation of politics. Political clashes are hidden from view if public attention is focused on 'what works' – on how to manage change – and such an approach is bound to foster unadventurous thinking and cautious behaviour.

The examples of mayoral leadership presented in this chapter challenge the view that urban political leadership is becoming a 'post-political' arena, one in which ideology has been replaced by a focus on the practicalities of getting things done. By standing up for specific social and environmental values and, to some extent, taking risks, these directly elected mayors have raised the bar for civic leadership. For example, many transport and technical experts regarded Mayor Ken Livingstone's proposal to introduce a congestion charge in London as impractical – at best, a very risky idea. The fact that, over a decade after the scheme was introduced in 2003, very few other cities in the world have been able to introduce a congestion charge scheme on anything like this scale, despite its manifest benefits, suggests that such a policy continues to be regarded as politically impractical in most cities. Mayor Livingstone was, then, not pragmatic – he made a political judgement, took a bold step and it came off. Mayoral leaders in Freiburg and Portland have also demonstrated a high level of willingness to try out new kinds of progressive policies and practices.

The successful directly elected mayors discussed in this chapter are all, to be sure, competent city leaders – competent in the sense of being able to plan and manage major public services and work in a collaborative way with other civic leaders. They know how to 'to do things that work'. But the main reason why they have acquired international recognition for their achievements is not because they were pragmatic and they were good at 'getting things done'. These mayors have gone beyond pragmatism and made significant improvements to the quality of life in their cities by exercising bold, forward looking progressive city leadership.

Notes

[1] In this chapter, when I refer to mayoral governance I am referring to arrangements in which the mayor – the executive leader of the city – is directly elected by the citizens. There are, of course, many examples of mayoral governance around the world in which the mayor (or leader) is indirectly elected by, for example, the elected councillors.

[2] Portland's commission form of government is almost certainly unique. In the US context it is unusual for a sizeable city to have not just a directly elected mayor, but also four directly elected commissioners and a directly elected auditor.

[3] Sir Steve Bullock, Mayor of the London Borough of Lewisham, and Sir Peter Soulsby, Mayor of Leicester, are both directly elected mayors who previously served as council leader in their local authority.

[4] Personal communication with the author, 1 July 2015.

[5] Personal communication with the author 1 July 2015.

[6] The three examples are discussed at greater length in Hambleton (2015).

[7] This local activism was to lead, with inputs from many others, to the creation of a new political party – the Green Party.

References

Academy of Urbanism and Stadt Freiburg (2012) *The Freiburg Charter for Sustainable Urbanism* (2nd edn), London: Academy of Urbanism.

Barber, B. (2013) *If Mayors Ruled the World. Why They Should and Why They Already Do*, New Haven, CT: Yale University Press.

Brenner, N., Marcuse, P. and Mayer, M. (eds) (2012) *Cities for People, not for Profit. Critical Urban Theory and the Right to the City*, Abingdon: Routledge.

Campbell, T. (2012) *Beyond Smart Cities. How Cities Network, Learn and Innovate*, London: Earthscan.

Christensen, T. and Laegried, P. (eds) (2001) *New Public Management*, Aldershot: Ashgate.

Crouch, C. (2004) *Post-Democracy*, Cambridge: Polity Press.

Fitzgerald, J. (2010) *Emerald Cities. Urban Sustainability and Economic Development*, Oxford: Oxford University Press.

Flanagan, R. M. (2004) *Mayors and the Challenges of Urban Leadership*, Lanham MD: University Press of America.

Girardet, H. (2008) *Cities, People, Planet. Urban Development and Climate Change* (2nd edn), Chichester: John Wiley.

Hales, C. (2015) *Priorities and Accomplishments*, Portland: City of Portland.

Hall, P. (2014) *Good Cities, Better Lives. How Europe Discovered the Lost Art of Urbanism*, Abingdon: Routledge.

Hambleton, R. (2015) *Leading the Inclusive City. Place-based Innovation for a Bounded Planet*, Bristol: Policy Press.

Hirschman, A. O. (1970) *Exit, Voice and Loyalty*, Cambridge, MA: Harvard University Press.

Hoggett, P. (1991) 'A new management in the public sector?' *Policy and Politics,* 19(4), 243–56.

Hood, C. (1991) 'A public management for all seasons?' *Public Administration,* 69, Spring, 3–19.

Illsley, B., Jackson, T., Curry, J. and Rapaport, E. (2010) 'Community involvement in the soft spaces of planning', *International Planning Studies,* 15(4), 303–19.

Irazabal, C. (2005) *City Making and Urban Governance in the Americas*, Aldershot: Ashgate Publishing.

Jackson, T. (2009) *Prosperity without Growth. Economics for a Finite Planet*, London: Earthscan.

Kantor, P., Lefevre, C., Saito, A., Savitch, H. V. and Thornley, A. (2012) *Struggling Giants. City-region governance in London, New York, Paris and Tokyo*, Minneapolis: University of Minnesota Press.

Livingstone, K. (2011) *You Can't Say That. Memoirs*, London: Faber and Faber.

Morgan, D., Nishishiba, M. and Vizzini, D. (2010) 'Portland. "Keep Portland Weird". Retaining the commission form of government' in J. Svara and D. J. Watson (eds) *More than Mayor or Manager. Campaigns to Change Form of Government in America's Large Cities*, Washington DC: Georgetown University Press, pp 279–301.

Mouffe, C. (2005) *On the Political*, London: Routledge.

Oliver, B. and Pitt, B. (2013) *Engaging Communities and Service Users. Context, themes and methods*, Basingstoke: Palgrave.

Ozawa, C. P. (ed) (2004) *The Portland Edge: Challenges and Successes in Growing Communities*, Washington DC: Island Press.

Richards, M. G. (2006) *Congestion Charging in London. The Policy and the Politics*, Basingstoke: Palgrave.

Savitch, H. V. and Kantor, P. (2002) *Cities in the International Marketplace. The Political Economy of Urban Development in North America and Western Europe*, Princeton NJ: Princeton University Press.

Schrock, G., Bassett, E. M. and Green, J. (2015) 'Pursuing equity and justice in a changing climate: Assessing equity in local climate and sustainability plans in U.S. cities', *Journal of Planning Education and Research*, 35(3), 282–95.

Stone, C. N. (1995) 'Political leadership in urban politics', in D. Judge, G. Stoker and H. Wollman (eds) *Theories of Urban Politics*, London: Sage, pp 96–116.

Sun, P. Y. T. and Anderson, M. H. (2012) 'Civic capacity: Building on transformational leadership to explain successful integrative public leadership', *The Leadership Quarterly*, 23, 309–23.

Svara, J. H. and Watson, D. J. (eds) (2010) *More than a Mayor or Manager. Campaigns to Change Form of Government in America's Large Cities*, Washington DC: Georgetown University Press.

Sweeting, D. (2002) 'Leadership in urban governance: the Mayor of London', *Local Government Studies*, 31(4), 465–78.

Wilson, J. and Swyngedouw, E. (eds) (2014) *The Post-Political and Its Discontents. Spaces of Depoliticisation, Spectres of Radical Politics*, Edinburgh: Edinburgh University Press.

FIFTEEN

Conclusions and reflections

David Sweeting, University of Bristol, UK

This book has brought together contributions from seven countries on the topic of directly elected mayors. Drawing on the inter-related themes set out in the opening chapter of mayors as institutional and political figures who operate in a context of urban governance, that itself is set in the context of a collaborative and competitive globalised environment, and the material offered in the substantive chapters, I now offer some concluding thoughts that emerge from the works presented here.

One of the key debates to emerge in several chapters is one that cuts across the institutional and political context within which mayoral leadership takes place; that of mayoral power and powers. The dimensions of the debate here surround the extent and importance of formal powers that are endowed on them by the institution within which they operate, the ability of mayors to extend their powers informally, through parties or relationships with other actors in governance, and the checks and limits on mayoral power.

Typically, mayoral governance involves concentrating powers in the figure of the directly elected mayor. However, such concentration is not necessarily the case; as the discussion on US mayors by Svara indicates, there are systems of mayoral governance that do not endow the mayor with considerable formal powers. Rather, they are shared with other figures, such as councillors, and perhaps a council manager. There is variability around mayoral power, both in relation to the formal powers that they have at their disposal, and their ability to extend their powers beyond and outside the confines of the office. The trend presented by the cases in this volume appears to be towards strengthening urban political leadership in terms of formal institutional powers; this appears to be the case in England, New Zealand, Germany and Poland. This is accentuated by the process of direct election, giving greater influence and legitimacy to a political leader.

Nevertheless, there are important caveats to be made around the interplay and intersection of formal and informal powers, and the ability of mayors to take advantage of them. Egner's contribution about directly elected mayors in Germany suggests that formal powers are not especially important in perceptions of mayoral strength, suggesting that informal powers may be more significant to other actors. Burton notes that in Australia skilful mayors can extend their limited formal powers, and in New Zealand Cheyne notes that even where mayoral powers are modest, individual factors around personality and coalition building are important in exercising political leadership. Moreover, in context where the mayor has no formal powers, for example in dealing with other authorities or sectors, or other levels of government, then the only powers that a mayor has are informal.

On that basis it is tempting, but I would argue misleading, to conclude that therefore the informal powers exercised by mayors, generated through factors such as direct election and personal charisma, are of greater importance than their formal powers. Formal powers are of critical importance in certain contexts, particularly for relationships inside the institution of the municipal government. For example, Copus, Blair, Szmigiel-Rawska and Dadd's description of the use of hiring and firing by the Mayor of Leicester offer a vivid account of how using these powers cemented his authority in the party and municipality in a way he would not have been able to without those specific competences. It is surely the perception of someone being formally 'in charge' that lays the foundation for the exercise of influence and persuasion by the mayor in contexts external to the city hall or council chamber; informal powers rest on the existence of formal powers, and the interaction of them, coupled with the resources available to the mayor, enable the exercise of political leadership. Even where formal powers are limited, such as in weak mayor, facilitative or council manager systems, the mayor is still granted a formal, specific and leading institutional position.

The mayor as political figure raises issues in relation to the exercise of and limits to mayoral power. The relationships that mayors have with political parties and other locally elected actors, including local councillors, are relevant here. There is evidence of ambivalence on the part of councillors towards directly elected mayors. The Czech case shows councillors supporting the idea of direct election of mayors, right up to the point at which the idea might become a reality, when support dissipates. In Poland, the introduction of mayors was seen as a way to rise above quarrelsome parties that were holding councils back, and the reforms there were supported by a majority of councillors. Yet in England, many councillors object to the introduction of the mayoral system, partly as it takes powers away from them, and partly as the system enables the election of a mayor who is not a party candidate.

There are clearly tensions in the relationships between mayors, parties, and councillors. These tensions can be exacerbated when the mayor is independent, or where the majority party on the council is from a different party to the mayor. Oliver's analysis of Bristol suggests that, initially at least, the independent mayor was hampered by the absence of informal channels of support that a sympathetic party might have opened. Nevertheless, as Burton points out, even when mayor and council are formally in opposition, productive relationships can and do occur across political divides, perhaps supporting Barber's (2013) argument about the ability of mayors to simply get on with the job of serving their communities.

From the perspective of mayors themselves, there is clearly something of a sense that mayors can position themselves above the party political fray; Elcock's study of English mayors reveals mayors as leaders of place as much as leaders of councils and, while they might be party politicians, they also aim to represent the city as a whole. That is not to say that mayors are detached – there is a symbiotic relationship between mayors and other actors in governance. Even though mayoral governance does provide a focus for strong political leadership, mayors, as Svara notes, are unlikely to get very far in implementing their own vision without support from within and beyond the council.

This raises issues around the ways that mayors relate to and operate in urban governance, and how influential they might be over urban affairs more generally, and how open to influence they are beyond city hall. Several chapters indicate how active mayors are beyond their town halls – Ismail and Elcock particularly in the English case. The Bristol case also indicates how mayoral governance can underpin more outgoing leadership on the international stage; the Mayor of Liverpool appears more active in terms of city representation than was previously the case under the old system; and the thrust of Hambleton's place-based leadership is that mayoral leadership is well placed to go beyond the formal sectors of politics into realms of communities and businesses.

One of the issues in modern governance is around the vexed question of responsiveness to business. Mayors are in part driven to a position of being expected to attract business, and be open to business views; yet they are not to be beholden to business interests to the detriment of representation of the interests of the city. One of the arguments used against mayoral systems in the US is that mayors might become too closely associated with campaign funders from business. There is a blurred line, as a consequence of the nature of modern urban governance and as a result of the nature of neo-liberal capitalism, around the roles and interactions of city decision makers and business interests, and whether there are business links to be cultivated, and others to be avoided. The Bristol case indicates that different interests respond in varying ways to the introduction of a mayor – with business interests much more positive about mayoral governance than the previous system of decision making. Oliver's chapter indicates that the new mayor was able to use his influence over local transport, something which previous (non-mayoral) administrations had been unable to achieve. Hambleton's contribution puts forward the argument that it may be possible for progressive politics to be underpinned by mayoral leadership, sometimes acting against the 'place-less power' of corporations.

The multi-level governmental context for mayoral governance emerges as a theme in several chapters. It is clear that in some systems, especially in more centralised states, that mayoral governance is shaped and constrained by legislative frames from national governments. This is clearly the case in the UK and New Zealand, and to a lesser extent Poland. Directly elected mayors can serve central governments' interests as much as local governments' interests. For example, the Liverpool case explored by Headlam and Hepburn reveals that the institution of the mayor is part of a much broader, longer term and intricate process of central–local relations between the national government in London and various interests in and around the city of Liverpool. This in some ways benefits the city – such as the greater access to central government – but also allows central government to assert and insert its influence in the city. One of the interesting variables is how local actors are able to reshape centrally led governance arrangements towards their own interests, as shown in the comparison of English and Polish cases.

In relation to the activities of mayors acting in the context of a more globalised world, there are some examples of leadership that invest time and resources in placing their cities 'on the map' and attempting to generate economic development and inter-city collaborations by interacting with interests well beyond their boundaries, especially such as in the examples of Bristol and Liverpool in England. It is difficult to conclude, though, that the institution of the directly elected mayor alone is necessarily potent enough in itself to generate the sort of economic development that it is charged with, as suggested by the quotation at the very start of this volume on page 2. It is easier though to make the case that directly elected mayors, in external relations at least, are very well placed to take on the role of representing the city as a whole in a way that other actors are unable to, perhaps in terms of making or remaking the image of the city, or elaborating on the niche position of their urban area on the broader stage.

From the perspective of mayoral office holders, the chapters in this volume paint a broadly positive picture of mayoral governance, one where, while there are frustrations around the functioning of the system, there are gains to be had around the exercise of local political leadership, especially in terms of profile and legitimacy. Nevertheless, the move towards more individualised leadership that the office necessitates is likely to be a better fit in some contexts rather than others. For example, to speculate on countries that have not been included in this book, the Spanish system of local political leadership is already individualised, in contrast to Scandinavian systems where more collective forms of leadership remain dominant, and it is therefore easier to imagine directly elected mayors taking hold in the former rather than the latter.

In introducing and reforming a directly elected mayor form of government, there are many considerations around the functioning of the institution. Some of these concern the detail and design of the institution itself, and are probably of most concern to other actors in the municipality. Appointment and decision making powers, for example, are likely to impact keenly on councillors and officers, as they find their roles constrained or changed with the introduction of a mayor. Loyalties might shift for example, if the mayor is able to appoint cabinet members or senior administrative and managerial positions. Some considerations seep into broader debates about the powers and roles for municipalities within the broader system of local government. If stronger leadership is introduced, it seems very likely that there will be times when this power is directed towards restructuring the external relationships that municipality has, the powers it uses, the taxes it raises, and functions it is responsible for, with a view to strengthening the power of the organisation over which the directly elected mayor presides. Hence the impacts of mayoral governance can be a factor in matters such as the development of central and local relationships, taxation policy and the extent of discretion of particular policy areas.

One variable which, however, makes the impacts of the office particularly difficult to predict is the election is for an individual person, with their own personal characteristics, preferences and capabilities. While the style of leadership is one which might be influenced by form of leadership – mayors with few formal powers can flourish using a facilitative style, for example – it is, however, clear that the directly elected mayoral model leaves considerable space for human agency, both in relation to the policy choices that mayors are able to make, and in relation to the way that the office is exercised.

One aspect of the debate that needs further attention is around representation and directly elected mayors. This reveals itself in several ways. The most obvious is the small number of women in urban leadership positions. It is encouraging to see women mayors in office some major cities, such as Washington DC, Rome, Prague, Madrid and Paris. However, these examples are exceptional, and many major cities have never elected a female mayor (directly or indirectly). The lack of gender diversity also has parallels in the number of black and minority ethnic mayors. Again there are exceptions – the current incumbents of London and Bristol are Muslim and mixed race respectively, yet there can be similar concerns over the racial profile of mayors not reflecting their populations. This is of particular concern when power is centralised in a mayoral system. Unlike a council, which may be comprised of people of different genders, religions and races, and from different socioeconomic backgrounds, a mayor is an individual, and can only have one set of socioeconomic characteristics. This is problematic if descriptive representation is important – that is, that decision makers resemble those people they are representing (Rao, 2000). Moreover, mayors often claim to represent the whole city, or the broader interests of the area. The representational aspects of governing become further problematised when diversity is a common feature of modern cities, more so if the interests of different communities are obviously in conflict.

There are no easy answers in this representational debate, but one (perhaps too easy) way out is to argue that descriptive representation, as well as being unattainable for mayors, is somewhat overemphasised. Mayors will not be the only elected representatives in a governing system, and councillors can ensure descriptive representation. Also, it can be argued that it does not necessarily follow that the interests of a certain group are best represented by members of that group, and that substantive representation of a section of society is not necessarily furthered by having key decision makers from that group.

In any case, from an academic standpoint it can also be argued that theories of representation have moved on. A fruitful avenue for further research around representation and directly elected mayors is around their activities in making 'representative claims' (Saward, 2006). The essence of Saward's approach is that politicians aim to garner support by making claims about what they represent, and are successful if those claims have resonance with voters or constituents. They are able to align their own goals with the interests of voters, crystallising issues in a way that audiences are receptive to. The relationship between represented and representative is dynamic and is subject to reframing on both sides. This approach chimes well with the direct relationship that directly elected mayors have with voters, who may or may not stand on party labels, and make various claims around their understanding of local issues, their identity as citizen of the city and their abilities to represent the interests of the city as a whole. It enables a rounded view of the activities of political representatives to be offered.

In a more far-reaching context, there is the direction that cities are heading as actors that respond to matters such as climate change and migration, and the role of mayors generally, and directly elected mayors within them. Barber's (2013) account sees cities becoming even more active as the nation state declines in importance, prompting greater inter-city and cross national collaboration. Directly elected mayors would seem to be very well placed within these developments in order to galvanise the support of their populations in pursuit of goals which might require considerable coalitions of support in order to achieve. Quite how such a role would be won, which powers would be ceded from which other levels of government and how remain open questions. An alternative scenario may see the current possibilities for urban areas pass, with cities unable to fulfil their perceived potential, and their leaders left frustrated as the capacity for change that they are able to effect becomes limited by forces beyond their control.

Clearly the debates around the merits or otherwise of the directly elected mayor form of governance will continue, and will be tested by future developments in urban politics and governance. It is clear that directly elected mayors do provide a vehicle for the exercise of urban political leadership that is widely recognised and is attractive to policymakers at different levels of government in many countries, including local political leaders themselves. The way that the institution has spread to different national systems of government, and has become embedded and associated with matters such as economic development and democratisation, and as a response to global trends – as well as the profile of particular mayors – would indicate that the institution will continue to be one of the ways in which policymakers concerned with urban governance seek to respond to a variety of pressures.

References

Barber, B. (2013) *If Mayors Ruled the World. Dysfunctional Nations, Rising Cities*, New Haven and London: Yale University Press.

Rao, N. (2000) 'The changing context of representation', in N. Rao (ed) *Representation and Community in Western Democracies*, Basingstoke: Macmillan.

Saward, M. (2006) 'The representative claim', *Contemporary Political Theory*, 2006(5), 297–318).

Index

Page numbers in *italics* refer to figures or tables.